THE RISING SIGN PROBLEM

A SERIES OF ESSAYS ON THE PHYSICAL CHARACTERISTICS AND PERSONALITY TRAITS OF INDIVIDUALS FOR THE TWELVE ASTROLOGICAL SIGNS ON THE ASCENDANT

by John Willner

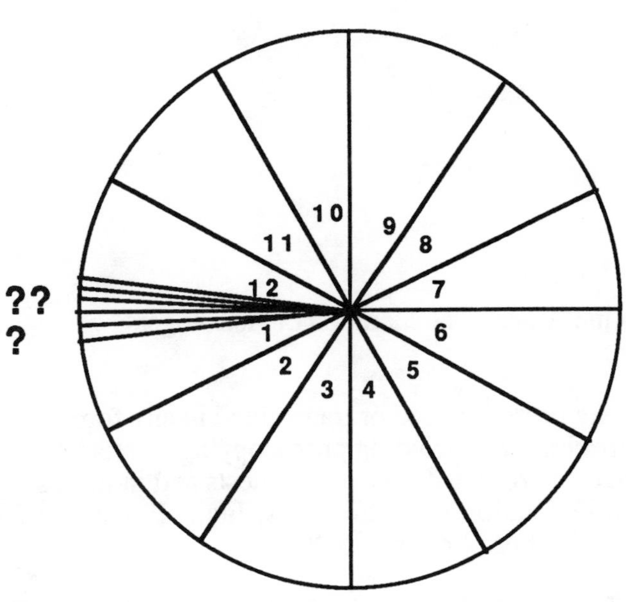

Published by
American Federation of Astrologers, Inc.
P. O. Box 22040, 6535 South Rural Road
Tempe, Arizona 85282

First Printing 1992
ISBN: 0-86690-409-3
Library of Congress: 91-77416

Cover Design: John Willner

Published by:
American Federation of Astrologers, Inc.
P. O. Box 22040, 6535 South Rural Road
Tempe, Arizona 85282

Printed in the United States of America

The Rising Sign Problem

by John Willner

COMMENCING A SERIES OF ESSAYS ON THE PHYSICAL CHARACTERISTICS AND PERSONALITY TRAITS OF INDIVIDUALS FOR THE TWELVE ASTROLOGICAL SIGNS ON THE ASCENDANT

TABLE OF CONTENTS

OVERVIEW

A Statement of the Problem

The single most often heard doubt expressed by people who possess their own horoscopes, whether calculated by themselves, someone else or with the aid of a computer program, is an uncertainty about the rising sign. "My horoscope shows Scorpio rising, but the description of Libra seems to fit in some ways," is an often heard lament, or one like it. "I was born on the cusp, so it seems that some characteristics of both signs apply to me," is another. Or, someone you are talking to makes a statement like, "I have a Taurus Sun and Virgo on the Ascendant." But what you see in front of you is a person with a large nose, not thin-bridged, straight or down pointing, no triangular features in the shape of the head, but one that is much more rectangular in shape and no Virgo characteristics of constantly trying to be exact, but instead a person who is large of frame, chesty and who likes attention. This is only a small sampling of frequently overheard chit chat, and you have probably heard many similar remarks yourself. Depending upon your experience in astrology, you have probably made similar mental notes.

It is possible to quantify this problem, although that has not been seriously undertaken except in a casual way. At most astrological conventions, for example, attendees wear badges that show the Rising sign, Sun sign and Moon sign in addition to their names. Now all of these professionals and amateurs have an interest in astrology, and all represent the astrological community as we know it today. There is no question about their sincerity in entering signs on their badges. Yet, at one recent conference a conclusion was reached from looking at these badges that something was amiss. Using experience that comes from calculating and verifying thousands of horoscopes, over a period of greater than half a century, approximately 60 percent of the Ascendant signs seemed correct. This means roughly 40 percent could have been in error. No proofs exist at this point, but they did appear to be wrong. The Sun Signs and Moon signs were not the problem. Most of them fit the person, as would be expected from the widespread availability of modern ephemerides, but the Ascendant signs were in question. So, the basis for a more accurate determination was present, and will probably be present again, if anyone would care to take the time. Yet the exact percentage of errors is not really so important as the bigger picture it represents. If the 40 percent approximation is even close to being correct, that represents a devastatingly huge proportion of the astrological community. This uncertainty suggests one reason why astrology is not as well accepted as it could be, and why this series of essays might be needed. Besides, in private discussions more than one person has requested this book be written.

In the past certain other astrologers have recognized the same problem resulting from inaccurate timing, although perhaps not in the same way. Back in the 1940's an astrologer by the name of Cedric Lamont wrote many articles in *American Astrology* dealing with inaccuracies and what might be done to correct them. Howard Duff, a past president of the American Federation of Astrologers, wrote a booklet on the subject of recognizing signs entitled, *Astrological Types*. He hedged his bet somewhat, by specifically defining types to be, "all the known characteristics associated with the signs which assemble in one face as a mixture showing Sun, Meridian, Ascendant, Moon and angular dominance." That is not necessarily an incorrect statement. However, these named components are without equal weight, and Ascendant plus angular dominance represent a duplication of sorts having increased importance. But the primary reason for listing this reference is because it made an attempt to reinforce the description of physical attributes with drawings.

Many text books on natal astrology have provided the physical and mental descriptions of zodiacal signs on the Ascendant. E. Parker of Amersfoort, Holland, in 1927 wrote a good text book on natal astrology called *Astrology and Its Practical Applications* that included a Section VIII entitled, The Twelve Signs Ascending. It described personality traits more extensively than physical traits, but contained excellent insights. Isabelle Pagan, in an older book now out of print called *From Pioneer to Poet,* described the signs generally. In a later section she stated, "....the sign ascending affects the outward man, his expression and action, and is therefore the most easily recognized....." Llewelyn George, in his *A to Z Horoscope Maker and Delineator,* included a better than average description of the signs on the

Ascendant, addressing each one in three parts under the headings Personality, Physical Appearance and Mental Tendencies. Incidentally, most authors of older books on natal astrology included sections on physical appearance versus zodiacal signs on the Ascendant. But this important subject seems to be diminished or omitted in books of more recent vintage. What a pity. It is no wonder that many current astrologers seem to ignore this important influence in their rectification of horoscopes and in their delineations.

One Cause of the Problem

It would not be proper to identify an astrological problem, and to be critical of these apparent errors, without offering reasons and proofs wherever possible. In doing so, however, it is only fair to state in advance that certain popular ideas must be targeted. That will be upsetting to some and could result in negative emotional reactions. Be that as it may, the truth needs to be told when it is essential to the well being of an entire body of knowledge. The truth is, if the Ascendant sign is wrong, the horoscope is wrong. Therefore, we can start by asking a simple question. When should a natal horoscope be judged correct? Logic tells us that if the correct time was used in casting the horoscope the Ascendant sign will be correct also--do you not agree? By reverse logic we may use a knowledge of Ascendant signs to help arrive at the proper time for a horoscope. Also, positive agreements between factors in an individual's life and indicators in the natal horoscope support one another, they interrelate. We may be on the right track to solving the problem of incorrect rising signs, if astrologers in general reached an agreement as to what constitutes a correct horoscope. At the moment there is no standard, unless one accepts the idea that everyone has their own. It follows that a standard is needed. Accordingly, here is a proposal in three parts pertaining to the tropical system of natal astrology. This proposal represents minimal delineation requirements and procedures. If you, the reader, have better suggestions or modifications that will improve overall effectivity, then all of us should be receptive.

1. A natal horoscope is correct when every house cusp, zodiacal sign and planet are in positions whose interpretations, by well known and generally agreed upon astrological precepts, fit the individual exactly, with no exceptions. No one said this condition would be easy to carry out, or that astrological precepts are uniformly accepted. However, questions or doubts of possible discrepancies are the first indicators of incorrect timing.

2. A natal horoscope is correct: a) when one can observe that the Ascendant sign agrees with the physical appearance, b) when every planet near the boundary of a house fits the house it is in, not the adjoining one, by correspondence with the indicated sector of the individual's life and c) when every pair of intercepted houses, if present, correctly shows an increase in the life's activities within those spheres of influence.

3. A natal horoscope is correct when at least one day-for-a-year progression, in either celestial longitude or in declination, coincides with each instance of every major event tested. While more than one aspect is usually present for a major event, at least one must be within four minutes of arc (not degrees) of the exact aspect angle. The four-minute limit might be subject to further debate, because it possibly ought to be less. It is not arbitrary, but based upon a considerable amount of historic evidence. The more confirmations of progressed aspects found within these limits, the better the confidence level that the horoscope time is correct. Also, the closer these aspects are to the theoretical angles, on average, the better the confidence level. However, one word of caution is apropos. We are looking for a high degree of exactness for all events without fail. It is better to find aspects for all events to be nearly exact than it is to rectify one and discover the aspects of other events are not as close.

A portion of these principles, while intellectually rigorous, could be deemed subjective, which leaves unwanted room for speculation. However, once learned, checking the ascending sign with the physical body and checking the progressed aspects with events are the easiest to do. Confirmations in this sequential order are usually the fastest, because once performed the other elements fall into place. The Ascendant verification can be conducted almost instantaneously, especially when the choice is between two, or at most three, signs. Usually some approximation of the physical birth time is available that places one in the right quadrant of the day. The Ascendant selection will provide a horoscope accurate to within 30 degrees on the Eastern horizon, or about two hours in time.

Progressed aspects will take longer to compute and verify, even with the benefit of computers. A series of confirmed progressions yields the greatest assurance of timing accuracy. One can refine the 30-degrees approximation, given by the sign on the Eastern horizon, to less than a degree. The reason is that numerical computations provide answers that are more readily confirmed than words or other means of expressing results. Also, the faster moving the horoscopic elements involved in a progressed aspect, the more accurate is the natal time. Thus, progressed aspects from the Midheaven, Ascendant, Moon, Mercury, Venus and Sun provide the greatest precision. Elements at the beginning of the list are the fastest moving. They become the vernier, so to speak, once the gross setting of the Ascendant sign is interpreted and refined. If one then obtains positive confirmations using the other stated criteria, that combination is the most powerful of all. A mathematical confidence level of probability that approaches one sigma is then achievable, which coincides with doubts that approach elimination.

Comments and Observations

If you are the client of an astrologer, you should expect such rigor in determining your horoscope. If not, you are being short-changed. It is the results that count, and better results can be obtained with more accurate horoscopes. Those astrologers who claim all they need is an approximate chart are simply begging the issue. Also, those who publish should require the same rigor of themselves. If not, then you can rest assured that the reader will be viewing an approximation of uncertain authenticity. The impression that some interpretations are correct, but not all, is a testament to the inexactness that unfortunately prevails. It is a virtual certainty, such questionable horoscopes can not meet the standard described above. Observe that a half dozen or more different horoscopes often appear in print for one important person. It does little good to excuse this situation by saying that everyone has a right to his or her own opinion. Of course they do, but the impression left with readers is that all but one published horoscope are in error, or every one of them is wrong. Logically, this makes all such writings suspect; it is the very situation that most astrologers would like to avoid in order to improve the acceptability of their profession. The results are that one must be constantly on guard against the unbelievable. This impression grows when the published horoscope does not correspond well with the personality of the person, the occupation or with important events. The natural question is why the author did not take the time to check progressions, at a minimum.

Another point is that when timing errors exist, false rationale is given to explain some of the interpretations. These contentions receive an undeserved aura of respectability that confuse and disrupt. The fundamentals of astrology then become embellished with ideas that are simply false. Consequently, the science and art of astrology receives another black eye. Students will sooner or later have to unlearn some of the things they have read, and that is a difficult process. So, an objective of this series of essays is to initiate changes by starting at the beginning of a standardization movement--with the sign on the Ascendant. That should at least correct one major error. What you often see in print today has not taken this first step.

Here are just a few other observations on this subject, and some may come as a shock.

1. In computing and verifying hundreds of horoscopes each year, prior to this undertaking, not a single one has met the three criteria expressed above when based upon a birth certificate time, a physical birth time checked against a standard such as broadcast on radio station WWV, the time shown in a family bible, a judgement of the time of first breath, the words of a relative, the mother, the father or the doctor who delivered the baby. You did read correctly. The number is zero. A few of the confirmations experienced to date were as close as ten to twenty minutes away, but never the same.

2. A horoscope cast for a different time than any of those described above was invariably confirmed by all three of the above criteria. Typically, that natal horoscope time was before the physical birth time. The average difference has been in the ten minute to forty-five minute range, but some have been over three hours before, especially for Caesarian births. Again you

read correctly. The percentage of confirmations using all three of the criteria has been 100 percent, with one possible exception when neither the time nor the day were certain. It seems to this author that a horoscope that works is to be preferred over one that does not work but adheres to a popular plausible theory. Additionally, a horoscope that checks on every count is to be preferred over one that checks on fewer counts. Yet, it is important to be open minded and receptive. If anyone knows that oxygen received through the nose or mouth of a baby fixes the time of the natal horoscope would that person please step forward and present his proofs, not opinions.

3. Despite the rigor embodied in the three criteria it is still possible to be fooled, because there are other factors involved in physical appearance. Also, a number of progressions are typically present for each major event, and those from the outer planets may hold for many days. After all, life is complex and so are horoscopes. For this reason, the first two criteria have been bolstered in practice by adding two practical requirements. In order to check the Ascendant, either the person whose horoscope is being cast must be present, or an adequate photograph must be available. A minimum of three dates of major events must be checked for close progressions whenever feasible. The larger the number of events that can be confirmed the better.

While contemplating physical appearance it should not be surmised that the Ascendant is the only factor. Most good astrologers know that the Sun establishes the skeleton and framework of a human body. Hereditary factors obviously come into play. For example, people from tribes that originated in desert regions tend to have larger and more aquiline noses. A majority of blacks and browns whose ancestors came from tropical regions have comparatively broad-based noses, absolutely beautiful white teeth and thicker than average lips, although not all by any means. Most orientals have black hair, and few blonds are found among the black, brown, red or yellow races. However, these factors do not appear to modify the astrological indicators. Race does not appear to change the general zodiacal traits. Yet an astrological factor, such as any planet sitting on the Ascendant, can have a major impact, especially one like Jupiter that invariably contributes weight. Hereditary factors are clearly present when one can see family resemblances. Heredity probably contributes to the size of the body as well, but not its nature. There are short Sagittarians and short Geminis, even though these tend to be comparatively tall signs. The Midheaven reflects how one's influence on society is perceived, which is a part of the human psyche. But experience shows that the Ascendant sign is invariably the strongest in fixing the shape and appearance of the physical body--especially the head. Knowing these traits can rapidly provide the first important confirmation. As previously stated, it is an excellent first procedural step in searching for the correct time.

4. Lest anyone believe that only one individual has had such thoughts on natal horoscope timing as those expressed herein, other sources will be cited. They are uniform on one major issue. All have expressed, in one manner or other, the idea that the soul enters the infant's body in the process of being born. The entrance of the soul rarely coincides with the time of physical birth--whatever that imprecise moment is. In fact, the well-known psychic Edgar Cayce clearly stated in one of his astrological monologs that souls enter physical bodies typically from three or more hours before to ten minutes after the physical birth.[1] It must also be stated that in other readings he spoke of widely different soul and physical birth times, some of them later and many hours apart. Nevertheless we are now immersed in a controversial subject. Most people are in one of three camps. They either believe in incarnation, in reincarnation, or that human beings do not have souls at all. The positions taken are generally strong, and that includes astrologers. The previously mentioned Isabelle Pagan wrote, ...“the

[1] Available from the Association for Research and Enlightenment, P. O. Box 595, Virginia Beach, Virginia 23451

truth of the doctrine of reincarnation is taken for granted," and ..."the Astrology which ignores that great teaching is apt to be too fatalistic and depressing." The late C. C. Zain wrote forcefully against reincarnation, but for human incarnation. Atheists might lean more toward an, oxygen in the lungs, theory than entry of a soul, but that is a deduction and not meant to be a general conclusion. However, a little known fact is that centuries ago a certain unknown astrologer (or astrologers) developed an algorithm to calculate the possible times when a soul could enter the infant's body, at any location on the surface of the earth. It has been handed down from one selected astrologer, evidently, to the next in each generation and is based upon the constantly moving positions of the Sun, Moon and Uranus in a complex relationship. Application of this algorithm invariably shows that one of those computed times meets the three criteria expressed above. Whether one believes in souls or not, it is far easier to select the right time after it is computed than to search for a completely unidentified time by trial and error. A knowledge of Ascendant sign physical characteristics and the use of computers to calculate the progressions makes this task faster and easier.

All of the horoscopes shown in this book were computed using the computer program called *INCARN*, that incorporates the incarnation algorithm mentioned above, and all were verified using the stated validation procedure. More information on the software is available upon request from the publisher.

Progressions employ the Naibod method, because it has consistently proved to be accurate, sometimes timing events to the hour and minute of the day, whereas other approaches have not been that effective. The Naibod method relies upon the exact day-for-a-year ratio of 365.25 days to 24 hours, or 15.28175 progressed days-per-hour added to the true natal time. The progressed horoscope is simply computed for the new time.

While transits are perfectly valid, once the correct natal horoscope has been determined, none have been mentioned in this book. The principal reason is to keep the explanation simple and unconfusing. Also, primary progressions are much stronger than transits, with regard to any major event, and they are invariably present when the event is of sufficient importance to be noted in a biography, or other commentary.

The convention used in referrence to progressed aspects is to describe a progressed planet making aspect to a natal planet or cusp, whether the latter is identified as natal or not. If the aspect is between two progressed planets, both are always identified as being progressed.

Plan for Subsequent Chapters

Using the tools, techniques and principles described above, one section will be devoted to each sign on the Ascendant. Each section will be illustrated with three horoscopes of public figures. In all cases, the horoscopes will be of people who are well known, whose photographs or images have often appeared on television, in newspapers or on film. It should be easy for the reader to compare the familiar images of these people with the sign appearing on the Ascendant. Outstanding minorities and women are included. Of course the challenge, as this task is being undertaken, will be to find a sufficient number of important people to illustrate each sign in the manner described. At least thirty-six will be required as indicated. Passive signs on the Ascendants of famous people appear somewhat less frequently than active signs, almost by definition. This makes the search for people with shy Ascendants more difficult to find and confirm than bold ones, because dates of events are less likely to be available. However, each horoscope will include the progression of a single confirming major event in the outer wheel, although other events will have been previously checked as well. The results of calculations will be given to the nearest tenth minute of arc, because the finer increments of precision can be better compared. It will also further the objective of increased accuracy. In addition, each confirmed horoscope will be discussed in relation to the one for the claimed physical birth time when available.

Remember, that all twelve of the signs do not ordinarily have to be reviewed for a single individual. When a physical birth time is available, that is your starting point. Usually the rising sign will either be the one indicated by a horoscope cast for the physical birth time or the one immediately preceding it. This becomes a choice between two adjoining signs. However, since a difference of more than three hours is possible, and the Ascendant passes through an entire sign within about two hours, one might have to choose among three signs. In fact, the number of famous people who have rising signs counted backwards to the third sign is rather amazing. Through practice, and the memory of repeated past confirmations, the correct rising sign begins to flash into the mind at each occasion. Another tip is that when the rising sign is the same as for a horoscope cast at the physical birth time, one should normally look for an earlier time and for an earlier degree on the Ascendant.

Before starting off with Aries we shall take a broad overview of the facial features typical for each rising sign. The face or head is the part of the human body normally seen first. It expresses the visible aspects of personality and other traits that are sensed. In some cases, specific areas of the head provide clues. The Sun will show up in the face structure too, to some extent, but it is the Ascendant we are trying to pin down. This can be done easily, after learning them, although any of the twelve different Sun signs will underlay each one. Therefore, an objective in this preamble will be to provide a broad framework of recognition regardless of which Sun sign is present. Nuances will be discussed within each section to come.

Furthermore, it probably would be a good idea to illustrate this preamble with drawings and the use of terms that will be applied. The intended meaning of words is extremely important, and illustrations can reinforce the most often used descriptors, such as oval, rectangular, square, elongated, rounded, triangular, etc. Not everyone might interpret these words in exactly the same way. Fortunately, astrology is good to us in this endeavor. The adjoining signs are distinctly different and they have finite boundaries in the tropical scheme of things, as opposed to the sidereal. No one, having 29 degrees plus or 0 degrees plus on the Ascendant, appears to show physical traits of the adjoining sign. The 29-degree Ascendant would be the more likely of these two to exhibit an effect, because most, if not all, of the next sign will fill the first house. But every indication is that the zodiacal signs have abrupt boundaries in relation to the Ascendant degree when it comes to physical appearance. The regions near the boundaries of each sign appear to be just as strong as the middle. Anyway, a suspicion to the contrary can be cleared up later by using the progression technique. The choice of Ascendant is simply not confirmed until a close progressed aspect coincides with every major event.

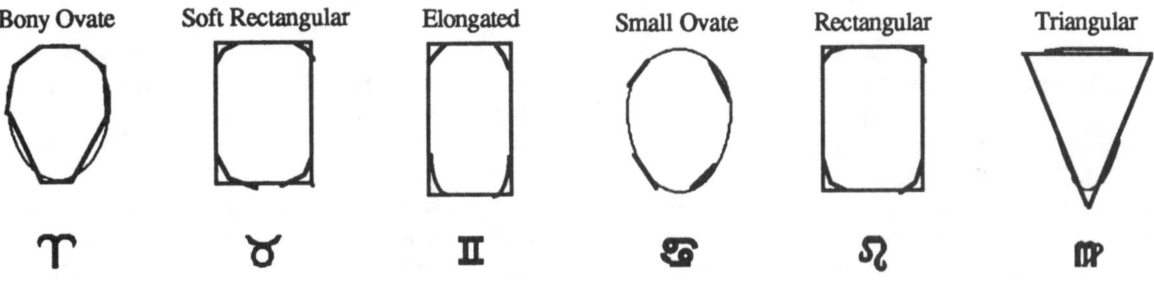

Figure 1. First approximations of head shapes versus zodiacal signs on the Ascendant—the first six signs.

Most people with Aries on the Ascendant have ovate, or egg shaped, heads, but they are bony (see Figure 1). This results in somewhat more angular features than average. The cheek bones are typically high, and the cheeks themselves are often hollow. A Taurus Ascendant can be easily distinguished from the Arian, because the head is more rectangular and the region of the jaws is fuller. In place of the bony angles, a greater softness or roundness prevails. Gemini ascending produces a more elongated head. That is, the distance from the top of the head to the chin appears to be longer than average, and definitely longer than Taurus. The height dimension predominates over the width. Cancer rising has an ovate head, which typically is somewhat smaller than the head of the signs on either side, although exceptions exist. It is wider at the upper jaw and temple region than at the top of the head. Leo switches back to a wider rectangle and a somewhat fuller face. The Virgo head is triangular. It is broad at the top and narrow at the chin. One can almost see the sharp angles, including the one associated with the usually straight, down-pointing nose.

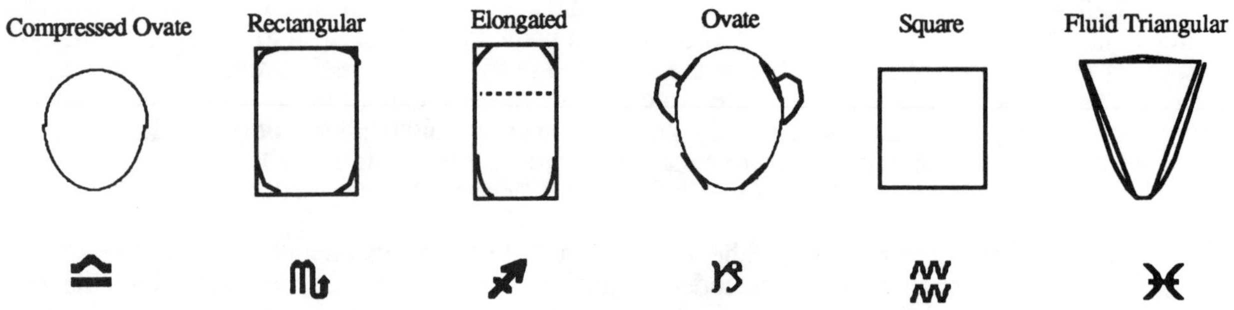

Figure 2. First Approximations of head shapes versus zodiacal signs on the Ascendant—the Next Six Signs.

The remaining six rising signs are quite similar in many respects to their counterparts (see Figure 2), yet there are detectable differences. Typically, the ovateness of Libra is somewhat more compressed than for Aries. The boniness gives way to softer, more balanced features. But more important, Libra is easy to distinguish versus Leo or Scorpio. The Scorpio rising head is rectangular, like Taurus, but with somewhat sharper features. The male Scorpio rising is typically hairy. The Sagittarian head is elongated, like Gemini. However, there is often a more distinctive shape of the forehead, either sloping back from protruding eyebrows or prominently full and convex. Capricorn has an ovate head like that of Cancer, but it may be somewhat more bony. The jaw often appears to be stronger. But the most distinctive physical characteristic of a Capricorn rising person is the absence of ear lobes, or very tiny ones. Aquarius rising almost invariably produces the squarest shaped head of any of the signs. It seems as wide as it is high. The proportions are much squarer than its opposite sign, Leo. Pisces rising is perhaps the most fluid in some respects. It is basically triangular, but with more curved lines than Virgo. Fluid triangular is the term applied. The limpid eyes may bulge or protrude, as can some Leo's. Pisces rising people almost always have unique skin qualities. One might use the terms translucent, liquid, watery or in some cases, pasty. Whatever, they are alert and aware of what is going on around them. Once observed and confirmed, there is no mistaking the Pisces rising sign. For that matter, there is no reason to mistake any of them.

CHAPTER 1. ARIES

Before launching into Aries, it might be well to distinguish first between the effects of the Ascendant sign and the Sun sign. After all, these are the two astrological elements that are strongest in molding the appearance. Astrologers have variously used the words individuality, personality and character to describe both. Unfortunately, Webster's dictionary is not much help, because it uses one or two words in this group to describe the third. Thus in the English language one can use all three terms interchangeably without necessarily being wrong. Individuality is defined in the most restrictive manner of the three, since scholars limit the meaning to a distinction or recognizable difference in qualities. Character is perhaps the broadest in meaning, since it combines the mark of an individual, attributes, qualities and personal traits. Personality is the totality of these same factors. Yet, in the astrological sense, the Ascendant and Sun are different. A separate term should really be available to describe each without interchangeability. Since there is no consensus on the right words, character will be used for the Sun and appearance for the Ascendant. The reasons are: 1) Character suggests origins, as for the Sun. It does not represent a totality of qualities, and 2) appearance includes physical, spiritual and mental traits observed by others, above the horizon, and by oneself, below the horizon. The Ascendant is at the dividing line of the sphere, and what it represents can be observed outwardly and inwardly.

From a physical standpoint, the Sun contributes the framework, or skeleton, of the body. It is the foundation upon which the flesh, hair, nails, muscles, skin and other parts grow. It is the source of human energy, as it is in our solar system. But the Ascendant represents the appearance as observed by all. The foundation may be broad or thin, tall or short, light or heavy. Also, the inherent internal psyche may be aggressive or shy, emotional or cool, active or passive. Thus what we see in a person has a foundation in the Sun sign with familial and racial attributes also present. Over that foundation is the veneer, shell, facade, expression, countenance and personification, of what can be observed, through use of the senses. The Ascendant represents that spectrum. One reason for presenting three famous people with the same rising sign is to portray variations in attributes caused by the different Sun signs. It would be wonderful to present twelve such variations. But that would be an even more difficult task, it would consume considerably more space and there is no certainty it would improve understanding.

Another very important point is that people exist at all levels of development. Hence, each of the rising signs produce variations on the same themes. There are crude individuals, without many social amenities. Others are refined, with complex and sophisticated manners. One cannot easily make blanket statements that apply to every extreme of civilization. Some people are country. Some are cosmopolitan. Some are primitive. Some are suave. What can be done, is to provide the general tendencies. How they fit is a question of advancement level in the psyche of the individual. Or it is a question of how experience and learning have been applied. The examples of famous people illustrating the signs will obviously portray a more cultured group than average. Perhaps in many respects, but not necessarily all, they represent a goal for people with similar rising signs.

Physical Attributes

Bony ovate is the term applied to Aries Ascendants. It is almost as though the bones were closer to the skin than average, or they jut out more. In men this gives a certain ruggedness.

They may have bushy eyebrows that add to the impression and a ruddy complexion. In women, who naturally show softer lines, it often leads to a distinctive type of beauty. The high cheek bones usually come with dimples. The neck often appears to be a little longer or thinner than average. The body heights of Aries rising men and women tend to be average to a little above average. However, genes can cause differences to occur. Even when the body is at rest, the eyes are typically active. Since Aries is associated with the head, it is not unusual to find a mole, scar or other mark in that area of the body. Also, untoward events can result in headaches.

Mental Attributes

"Me first," is often said by children. One of them with an Aries Sun or Ascendant probably was first and meant it. Restraint depends upon upbringing and acquired behavioral patterns of politeness. However, Aries rising is still the most likely to butt into any conversation and say what is on his or her mind. There is no intention to be offensive about it. This type of action simply results from an intrinsic feeling that the Arian is the pioneer and leader who needs to be heard. A story is often told about the Arian woman who walks up to the head of a line in a store and expects to be served right away, whether anyone else has been standing there longer or not. She then turns around and wonders what all of the commotion is about. Of course, this could have been an Arian man as well. But the average woman of this sign takes full advantage of woman's lib and any man's politeness. After all, they were already ahead. An Aries man or woman will formulate plans and expect others to conform. Many are like Tom Sawyer and manage to get someone else to paint their fence. Aries is the person who will make a purchase and feel no qualms about returning it, even though worn. When moods are negative they can have fits of rebellion against fate. But these are ordinary types. Among the more cultured people with Aries rising one finds great ambition, a motivation to investigate new and untried methods, courage, not being afraid to take a chance or to explore new territory and an ability to lead enterprises. These are among their most outstanding attributes. At all levels they are usually brisk and enthusiastic about what they are doing, sometimes having to guard against haste.

Example Horoscopes

It is the luck of the draw that the first two notables found with Aries rising are men. One has a Virgo Sun and the Second a Taurus Sun. Thus, the triangular features associated with Virgo underlay the Arian physical appearance of His Honor, David H Souter, newly appointed Associate Chief Justice of the United States Supreme Court. The broader features (head and body) of Taurus underlay the physical appearance of the brilliant actor, Sir Laurence Olivier. Both have what might be termed craggy physical appearances. We will start with David H. Souter.

Actually, this horoscope (See Figure 3 with Table 1), and all confirming progressions, were first computed without benefit of a reported time of birth. The day and place comprised the known input data. For this reason comparisons with a chart for the physical birth time cannot be given in the normal order. Recently, however, a journal published another version of his horoscope. The author gave 8:00 PM EDT as the physical birth time with 26 Aries 17 rising. At least the sign on the Ascendant is in agreement. Unfortunately, declinations were not listed, and only the wheel was shown. Also, as usual, no proofs confirmed the time.

A little logic and experience should tell you that any birth time given for an even hour or half hour has a very high probability of being wrong. The likelihood is that such a time is a crude approximation. If the sequence of horoscopes had been reversed, the proper place to start looking for a confirmable time would be earlier than 8:00 PM. At least the probability is much higher that an earlier time would check with respect to the three criteria. It so happens that the originally confirmed horoscope was for 6:51:23 PM true local time, which is independent of a one hour daylight saving time adjustment. It gave 15 Aries 15.5 on the Ascendant. The actual discrepancy in time between the two charts is about twenty-five minutes. That is highly typical. The horoscope for the earlier time appears in Figure 3 with the declinations in Table I. The progression for the single most significant event of those tested is in the outer ring. That event was the date of his appointment by President Bush to the position of Associate Chief Justice of the United States Supreme

Court. One would certainly expect significant progressed aspects for that date of July 23, 1990. But let us review the criteria against both horoscopes.

Criterion 1—Taking a broad view first, the question is, which horoscope fits a judge? Both show Jupiter in the twelfth house of service to others, and Saturn in the first. Yes, those could be the positions of planets for such a profession. Jupiter reinforces this conclusion by being a co-ruler of the ninth house, where legal events occur. The concentration of planets in the sixth house shows a pattern of hard work. That pattern fits the reports well. In this initial overview, neither chart has an advantage at the moment.

Table I. Natal and Progressed Declinations of His Honor, David H. Souter

Planet	Natal Decln.	07-23-1990 Appointment
♃	01 S 31.9	01 S 39.3
♀	02 N 16.5	20 S 31.2
☉	02 N 19.1	16 S 11.7
♆	03 N 47.5	03 N 08.1
☿	05 N 30.2	24 S 17.7
Asc	06 N 00.7	23 N 13.3
♄	09 N 00.7	07 N 39.5
☽	16 S 49.6	01 S 45.9
♅	17 N 54.0	17 N 28.5
♇	23 N 04.6	23 N 05.9
MC	23 N 12.8	12 S 42.4
♂	25 S 00.8	15 S 51.9

Criterion 2—In both horoscopes Aries is the Ascendant. The head of David H. Souter is a little more triangular in shape than for the average Aries rising person, but it is bony. The Virgo Sun sign has made its contribution. Published articles describing his personality traits check as well, and no reason exists to doubt the placement of the Ascendant in Aries from a behavioral viewpoint.

However, detailed differences exist between the horoscope in Figure 3 and the one cast for the physical birth time. The main differences are as follows: Uranus is in the second house

SEP 17 1939 6:35 PM EST
Melrose Massachusetts
42 N 27 36 071 W 04 03
6:51:23 PM TLT 23:34:40 GMT
Tropical *Placidus* *True Node*

Naibod Secondary
JUL 23 1990
23:34:40 GMT

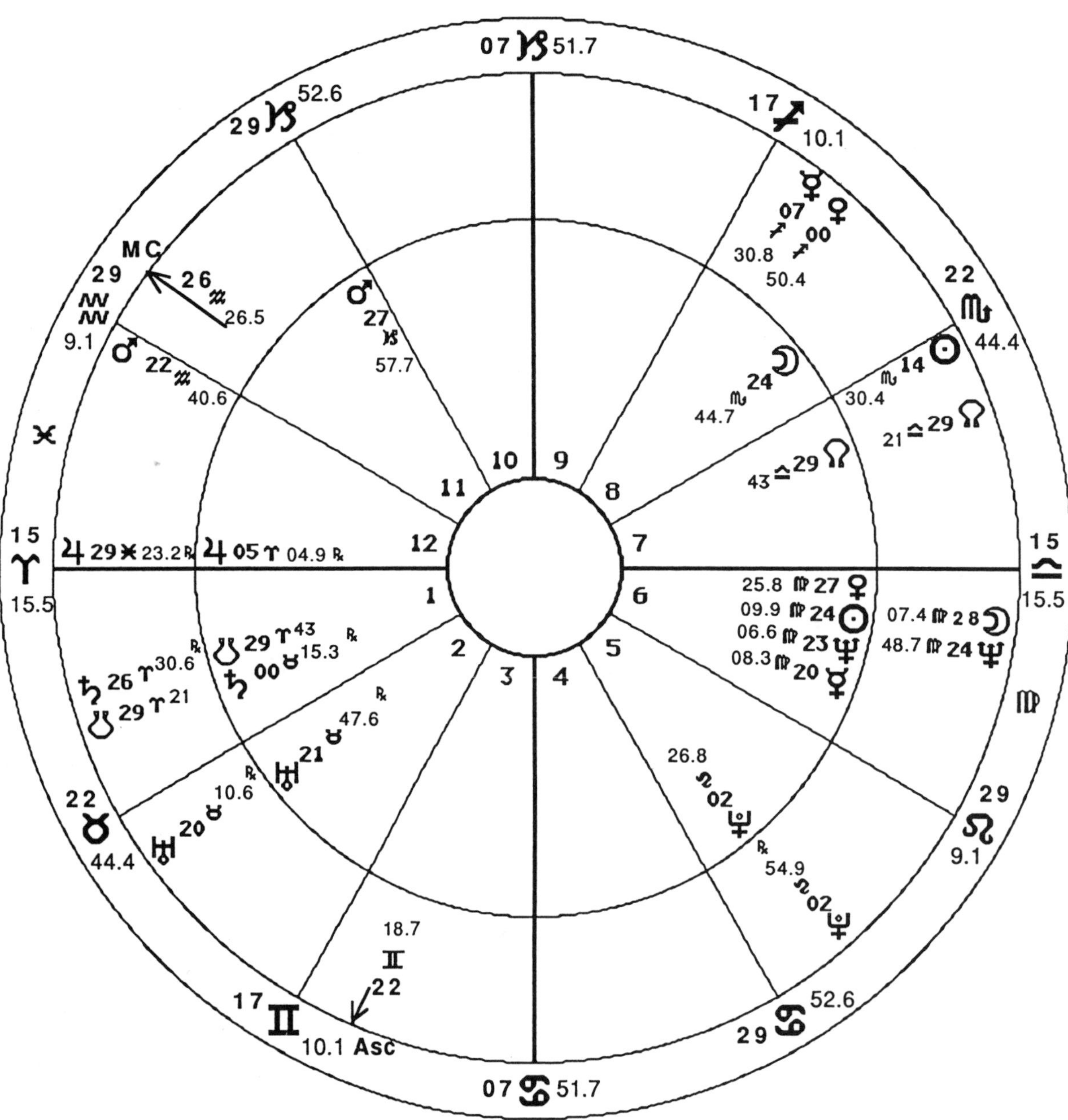

Figure 3. Natal horoscope of David. H. Souter with progression to date of appointment to Supreme Court of the United States

rather than the first; Pluto is in the fifth house versus the fourth; the Moon is in the eighth house instead of the seventh; Mars is in the eleventh house as opposed to the tenth; the sixth and twelfth houses are now intercepted, while no interceptions occur in the one for the later time. All the remaining planets, 6 out of 10, are in the same houses for both times, and the aspects in longitude remain unchanged. Declinations for the later time, if calculated, were not published. Therefore, they can only be indirectly compared. However, in the illustrated table the close parallel of the Midheaven with Pluto is very significant. It shows recognition related to his intensive efforts and resourcefulness. The same declination aspect does not exist for the later time.

Looking at the differences in house positions, one can ask a series of comparative questions. Is the Moon-Uranus opposition more appropriate for the first and seventh houses or for the second and eighth houses? If the first and seventh, then marriage accompanied by emotional upheavals and followed by divorce would be likely. Many disturbing concerns over partnership relations would be present. If the second and eighth, the only remaining indicator of marriage is Venus. Venus is the ruler of Libra and is inconjunct Saturn, combust the Sun, in a grand trine with Mars and Uranus and sextile the Moon. There is also a very close (combust) aspect of Venus parallel the Sun that adds heat. Marriage would be far less likely, but it should not be ruled out. Many concerns or decisions related to property, money and possessions would be present. That seems highly appropriate for a judge in civil matters and especially the judge of a supreme court.

Is Pluto more appropriate in the fifth house or the fourth? Is Mars more appropriate in the tenth house or the eleventh? These two planets are also in opposition. If Pluto were in the fourth house one would expect an extraordinary, diverse upbringing with parental clashes. If Mars were in the tenth house one would expect to find a martial type of individual, perhaps a military officer. When the Mars-Pluto opposition moves to the fifth and eleventh houses, the creative urges intensify. An enormous amount of energy is applied to meeting objectives. Conflicts permeate ideas and plans in these sectors, as might be expected in the life of a judge. Are the intercepted sixth and twelfth houses appropriate for a supreme court justice? You bet. They increase the activities toward service and the betterment of mankind. These interceptions are highly appropriate for a person whose very existence is to serve his country. On all counts where differences occur, the earlier horoscope positions appear to fit what we know about this man much better.

Criterion 3—Progressions to July 23, 1990, cause the 26 Aries rising chart to fall on its face. For this important date, when President Bush nominated David H. Souter, the only aspects close enough to be noteworthy are Uranus trine Mercury, within 2.3 minutes, and Neptune sextile Moon, within 4.3 minutes. Those outer planet aspects are the same in both horoscopes. Therefore, no advantage exists. However, in the earlier horoscope progressed Ascendant also parallels natal Midheaven, within 0.5 minutes, and progressed Midheaven sextiles progressed Saturn, within 4.1 minutes. Clearly we have one very significant aspect that is accurate to within 0.5 minutes (30 seconds), and the Midheaven-to-Saturn aspect came within our boundary conditions when he was confirmed. The horoscope in Figure 3 complies with our conditions, as it did consistently for progressions of other major events.

At this point, it is safe to say the horoscope portrayed in Figure 3 and Table I is acceptable and useful for further work. It might be further refined after many checks, but the likelihood is that the time would not change by more than a few minutes. In retrospect the discrepancy of twenty-five minutes in time caused forty percent of the planets to occupy new house positions, two houses to become intercepted, the longitudes and the declinations of the Midheaven and Ascendant to be radically different, and two aspects in declination to become recognized for their importance. The existing aspects in longitude remained about the same and the sign on the Ascendant did not change. This short revue indicates the typical cast of errors in astrology today. It is remarkable that astrologers working with the incorrectly timed horoscope can still derive so much benefit from the remaining parts that are correct. Is it a "mother, God and country" statement to declare that all delineations would improve if they used correct horoscopes?

In this first example of Aries rising the ovate head shape has a triangular frame underneath. The area of the face near the chin is narrower than usual. In the next example (see Figure 4 with Table II) the squarer frame provided by a Taurus Sun broadens the lower part of the face. In fact, Sir Laurence Olivier possesses an almost classic Aries rising head. It is bony, distinctive and expressive. Yet, there are those who would have you believe he has a Gemini Ascendant. The evidence is flimsy at best. The typical delineation would claim that a person with Gemini rising talks a lot. So they do. However, let us look at the source. Sir Laurence Olivier in his autobiography wrote, "But if the clocks did chime as I was born at 26 Wathen Road, Dorking, Surrey, on the morning of 22 May 1907, it would have been five o'clock that they were striking." Those are the dramatic lines of an actor. He then goes on to say that his father used to describe how he was frying sausages for Dr. Rawlings and himself when the doctor appeared in the kitchen doorway bearing a tiny but healthy-looking infant in his arms. Sausages on such an occasion could have been fried between midnight and noon. Also, the Sun rises quite early in Dorking in May. This description is typical of births timed without looking at a clock, and so many horoscopes are based upon such evidence. But even if the birth had been more accurately timed, the head was not elongated in the Gemini manner. Therefore, it is important to start looking backward through the signs. It cannot be Taurus, because then it would be rectangular. The next sign is Aries, and that one fits. It will be necessary at this point to verify this conclusion. Three Roman numerals will be used next and in subsequent reviews to indicate the three verification criteria.

I. Figure 3 and Table II show the derived Aries rising horoscope. The later, Gemini rising chart has 15 degrees 58 minutes on the Ascendant. If you rotate this Aries rising horoscope clockwise so that the third house cusp becomes the Ascendant, that would be an approximation of the other one. Every planet is in a different house, some shifting by two houses. The question is, which shows the life of this famous actor? Let us start with Venus, the patron of the arts. With those semi-sextiles from Saturn, Mercury and the Sun, the sextile from Pluto and the quintiles from Jupiter and Neptune there is no question about luck and activities related to an art form. It is noteworthy that the 3 Aries 49.5 rising chart also picks up a trine with the Midheaven. Fame has been added.

II. The Aries Ascendant has already been discussed from a physical standpoint. If one reads Sir Laurence Olivier's biography, Aries mental traits are evident as well. As for planetary placements, Mars in the tenth house was discussed in a martial context just a moment ago. However, Mars was alone in that scenario. In this horoscope Uranus is also present, both being opposite the Jupiter-Neptune conjunction and trine the Moon. So, Laurence Olivier was a pilot and Lieutenant during World War II. He was a military officer for a short period of his life At many other periods and in many other roles he acted the parts of martial characters. He wanted management and direction of plays and films, succeeding frequently during the later years of his life. This placement also confirms the somewhat antagonistic relationship he had with his father. Incidentally, the trine, Virgo Moon in the sixth house, shows popular and emotional personal accomplishments performed in an exacting manner. That especially applies to Shakespearian theater. With all of those aspects to Venus, Sir Laurence Olivier was surrounded by beautiful women most of his life. The Moon placement in Virgo says that his emotions were controlled, studied, distant and in many ways confined to his work. He married three times, the longest lasting 25 years. It was a tempestuous relationship with Vivien Leigh, and they were often apart. The two quintiles from Jupiter and Neptune to Venus correspond with this state of affairs. The sixth and twelfth houses are intercepted, increasing the work ethic and the ideals of service. He was knighted for his accomplishments and served in the House of Lords. The Gemini rising horoscope has most of the same aspects. By contrast, however, relations with his father would have been harmonious. He would have had many more flirtations and affairs outside of marriage, shown much less of a passion for work, experienced far more problems with respect to money, etc., etc.

III. Many progressions of events could have illustrated the closeness of pertinent aspects. His knighthood might be considered especially noteworthy, except the date was unclear. Also, much time passed between when he was first approached and when the ceremony took place

Naibod Secondary
MAR 17 1961

02:11:57 AM GMT

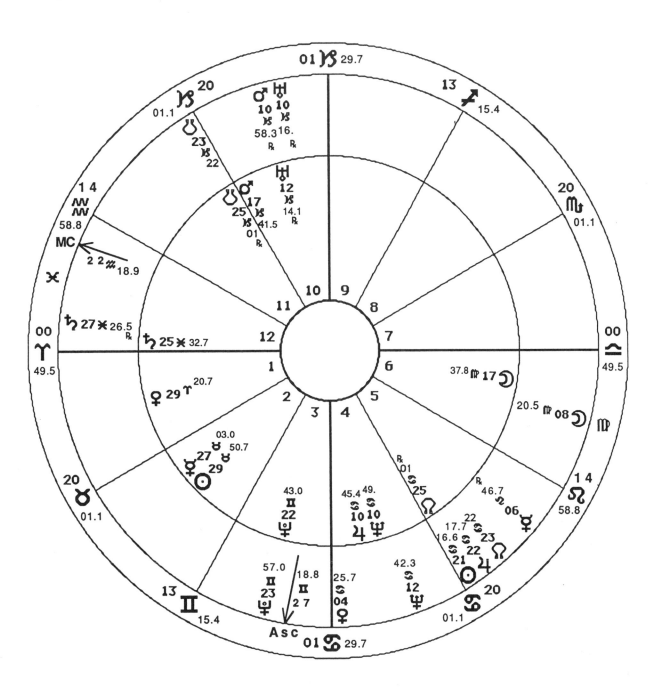

Figure 4. **Horoscope of the great actor Sir Laurence Olivier with progressions to the date of his marriage to Joan Plowright.**

Table II. Natal and Progressed Declinations of Sir Laurence Olivier

Planet	Natal Decln.	03 17 1961 Marriage
Asc	01 N 31.3	23 N 25.4
♄	03 S 37.1	03 S 04.6
☽	08 N 37.8	11 N 55.9
♀	09 N 34.8	23 N 13.9
♇	15 N 42.2	15 N 47.7
☿	19 N 31.8	15 N 01.9
☉	20 N 07.6	21 N 46.0
♆	22 N 10.8	22 N 01.8
♃	23 N 11.1	21 N 50.9
♅	23 S 14.8	23 S 25.5
MC	23 S 26.6	14 S 04.9
♂	24 S 26.7	28 S 31.8

Therefore, the date of his last marriage to Joan Plowright has been selected. Venus must be involved, and it is. Progressed Venus is contraparallel Uranus within 0.9 minutes. It was a hurried affair as though decided suddenly. Venus is also parallel natal Jupiter within 2.8 minutes. Both qualify in meeting our boundary conditions. A slow aspect, the parallel of progressed Uranus to the Midheaven was within 1.1 minutes. It was a newsworthy occasion. This is a case where three declinations pinpoint the event, while there are no noteworthy aspects in longitude. For those who ignore declinations condolences can be offered. The earlier horoscope passes all three criteria when declinations are properly considered.

As a general comment, the available biographical references on noteworthy people leave something to be desired. They are often haphazard with dates, quoting a year, or a month and a year, without the day. On the other hand, they can provide words and thoughts that fit the signs convincingly. Take, for example, Helen Reddy the pop singer. A female was needed to illustrate the Aries Ascendant sign as well, and many could have been chosen. However, so much of her biography was pure Arian that it became a natural choice. Her previously published horoscope shows Aries rising, but later as usual. Three prominent words stood out instantly, *I Am Woman.* This was a hit song on her second record release after coming to the United States from Australia. The title coincides perfectly with this rising sign What could be more fitting for Aries than the "I am" theme? It set the stage for her to become a leader in the women's liberation movement. See

OCT 24 1941 | 5:50 PM JAT
MELBOURNE | AUSTRALIA
37 S 50 47 | 144 E 59 59
03:48:08 AM TLT | 06:08:08 GMT
Tropical *Placidus* *True Node*

Naibod Secondary
FEB 19 1974
06:08:08 GMT

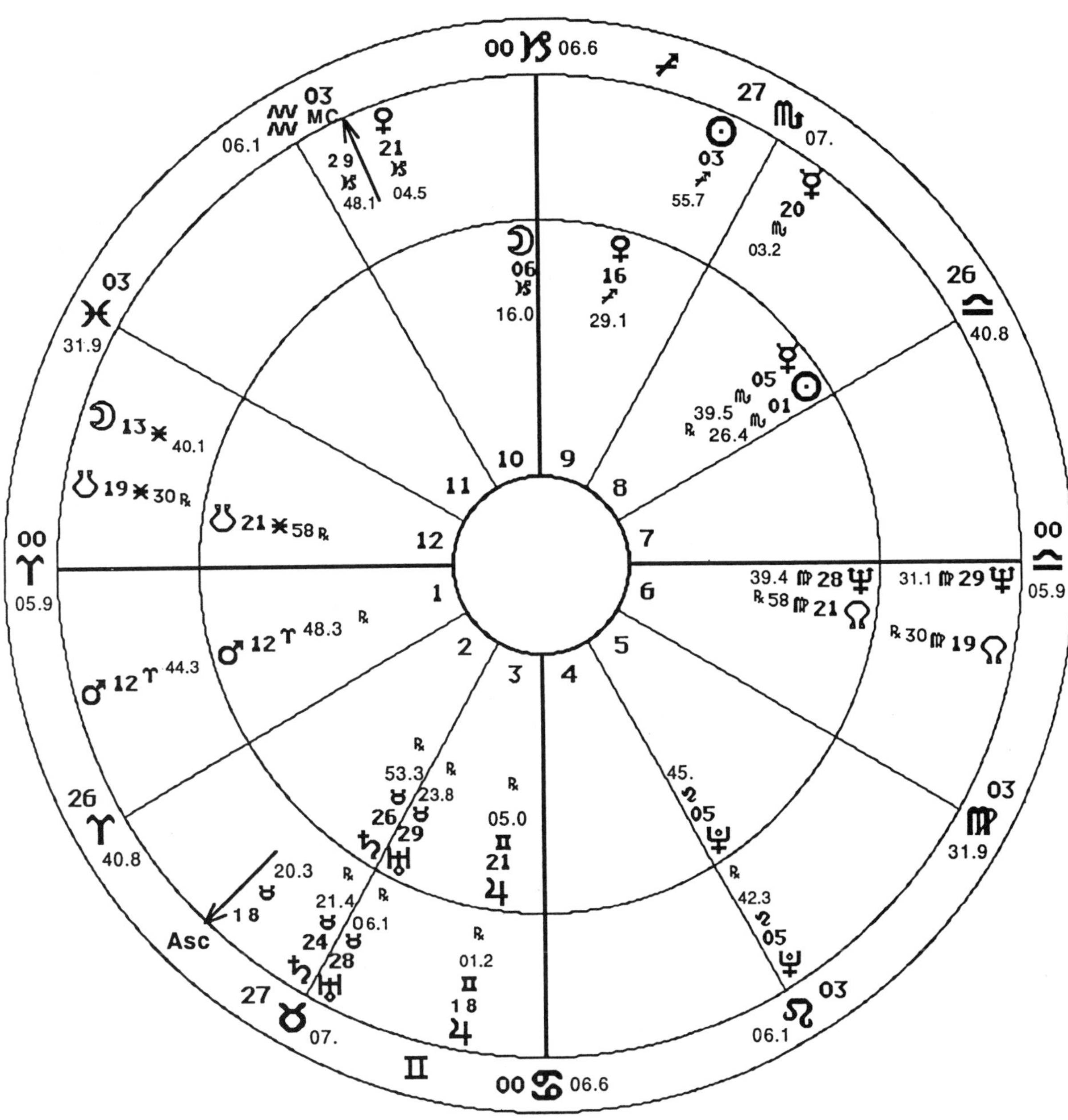

Figure 5. Natal horoscope of Helen Reddy with progressions to date of her first American music award.

Figure 5 and Table III for her horoscope and declinations. They include the progression to February 19, 1974, when she was named top rock/pop female artist at the First American Music Awards Show. *I Am Woman* was specifically cited. Her comments acknowledging this honor included a reference to God using the feminine pronoun, She. Her words created a due amount of notoriety, and the song was definitely Arian in context. Additional courage to say what she did might have been furnished by her Scorpio Sun. The extra dose of Mars and Pluto removed any fears that might have caused restraint.

Table III. Natal and Progressed Declinations of Helen Reddy

Planet	Natal Decln.	02 19 1974 1st Award
Asc	01 S 02.4	17 N 17.5
♆	01 N 51.1	03 S 04.6
♂	02 N 54.1	11 N 55.9
☉	11 S 58.6	20 S 56.3
☿	14 S 47.0	16 S 35.5
♄	17 N 10.0	16 N 35.0
☽	18 S 17.9	05 S 55.6
♅	19 N 48.6	19 N 31.8
♃	22 N 26.8	22 N 14.1
♇	23 N 10.8	23 N 17.4
MC	23 S 26.7	20 N 11.8
♀	25 S 27.0	24 S 48.3

I. The previously published horoscope had 20 Aries 58 on the Ascendant. This one has 00 Aries 05.9 on the Ascendant. The difference in time is about an hour and forty-two minutes. That is sufficient to move every planet to a different house except Jupiter and Neptune. If you rotate this horoscope so that the second house cusp becomes the Ascendant an approximation of the one for her physical birth time will be seen. You can be the judge, but Figure 5, with its declinations, fits a singer much better. Singing is a Venus art form. When in the eighth house Venus does not suggest that kind of career.

II. One only has to look at a photograph of Helen Reddy to see the bony features ascribed to Aries rising. The new position of the Moon on the Midheaven gives popularity, at least among some women, and the Mars first house location fits the rock/pop type of singing. It is trine Venus in the ninth house of performances. The third and ninth houses are intercepted. This indicates much travel and increased emphasis on shows, events, different scenes, unusual experiences, etc.

III. For a progression of an award event one would expect either a tenth house or a Midheaven aspect. On February 19, 1974, Helen Reddy had her progressed Venus in the tenth house inconjunct Jupiter within 0.5 minutes. That single aspect fills the bill nicely. Her Mars had returned to its own natal position in the first house within 4.0 minutes. This Mars aspect may have contributed to the assertive statements of the evening. But in addition, Mercury progressed was contraparallel Saturn progressed within 0.5 minutes. Could there be any doubt at this point? As if that were not enough, the slow moving Pluto was within 2.8 minutes of a square with Mercury. Feelings expressed that evening were harbored for a long time, and they have not gone away.

Now, if one had the opportunity to line these three people up on a stage, the common physical traits of Aries rising could be easily recognized. They would be readily distinguished from people who have nearby signs rising, or, for that matter, any other sign. Their boney ovate features would stand out. The objective has been to register a general image in your mind, and label it Aries. If recall of their appearances is not good, then access to their photographs in your local library may help. If you can find a copy of *Laurence Olivier, Confessions of an Actor, An Autobiography* published by Simon and Schuster in 1982, by all means check it out. His photograph is on the cover and one could not have a better example of Aries on the Ascendant. Also, if you like theater the book is most interesting.

CHAPTER 2. TAURUS

Physical Attributes

The term soft rectangular has been applied to the head shape of a person with Taurus rising. This means that the rectangle has rounded corners and the features are soft versus the boniness of Aries. The jowls are fuller. By comparison with the longer neck of Aries rising, the Taurus neck is shorter and larger in diameter. This thickness depends somewhat upon age, because youths normally start out in life with smaller necks. However, it is rare that a mature male with Taurus rising would not wear a shirt size larger than 16. By contrast with the neck, hands and feet are comparatively small and the fingers are short. The stature is typically short to medium. The body has more of a square build than Aries or Gemini, the signs on either side. It is usually strong in a young man or woman. This strength is typically retained to a more advanced age than other signs. The constitution is strong too, and that usually causes swift recoveries from illnesses when incurred. A virtue of this physical makeup is endurance. The body of the Taurus rising individual can survive under conditions where others would perish. In fact it is the nature of Taurus to endure. Yet good posture is not a strong point, and round shoulders are a tendency. It is the Taurus rising boy or girl who is often told, hold your shoulders up. So they do for a while, until their minds are turned inward to dwell upon other subjects. Because of a love for good food they may become plump as years advance, unless controlled. The female with Taurus rising frequently has even more rounded features than the male, and full round eyes that are often brown and heavily lidded, but not always. Their lips are more likely to be full, than thin. The nose bridge and tip might be somewhat broader than average as well. They can be very sensuous and a great comfort to have around.

It is very important to know the differences between the rising sign of interest and the adjacent rising signs, especially those preceding. In Taurus we have the rounded rectangular head. In Gemini we have the elongated head, much longer fingers and larger feet. In Aries we have the bony ovate features and the especially noticeable high cheek bones that often leave hollows below. When one is looking at this quadrant of rising signs there should be no mistaking the differences. Yet it is possible that the correct rising sign is further back. For the Taurus starting point it might even be Aquarius or Pisces. The physical appearances of these two signs will be described in greater detail later. However, the squareness of the Aquarian head and the more angular, liquid features of Pisces are the key points of distinction.

Having said these words a short review with real people is in order. One can start by looking at published horoscopes that show Taurus rising. Of course some might be rectified, but the greater likelihood is that each was cast for the purported physical birth time. Just a few that come to mind are Celeste Holm, Vivien Leigh, Pearl Bailey and Joan Sutherland among women, who are often harder to type than men. But, no, no, no, no. Proofs will not be given at this time. However, not a single one of these talented ladies appears to fit the Taurus rising mold. All appear to fit the molds of Pisces or Aries. None has the rectangular head absolutely required for Taurus rising, and don't be deceived by the stoutness in later years of Pearl Bailey. Some of this group have narrow, pointed chins and one could take a bet on Joan Sutherland, the fabulous opera star from Australia. With those facial features she has Aries rising. If you are not an opera buff and do not know what she looks like, just observe her photograph on the cover or in the notes of any record album containing her arias. Yes, her horoscope was checked, and Taurus is not the sign on her Ascendant. In fact, all were checked before citing these examples.

Mental Attributes

The symbol for Taurus is the bull, and people with Taurus rising can have dispositions that are similar to what one might imagine for this animal. In normal mode, which is most of the time, they are peaceful, gentle, stable and self reliant. In a provoked or aroused mode, the unevolved types, especially, can have outbursts of anger or passion. Extreme rath is exhibited on such occasions, and some have been known to charge. However, the Taurus rising sign usually causes the individual to be caring, affectionate, sociable and loving. They are exceptionally capable of faithful and enduring friendships. The character is strong and earthy. They have their two feet on the ground. Staunch builders of estates throughout their lives, the majority are reasonably prosperous. Most find a good purpose in life, and they accomplish much. This is the person other members of a family and friends turn to when asking for help. When there is a need, they are the most likely to be placed in the role of a guardian or trustee. No one else is as unshakable and practical. They are usually good at business and in the handling of money. The arts or agriculture are other pursuits where they often excel. One of the kindest remarks about Taurus is, they are the salt of the earth. The implication is that this sign represents an essential element without which civilization could not survive. Symbolically, it is fitting that bovines lick salt blocks. If other astrological indications do not act at cross purposes, they are dependable, reliable, determined and hard working. Taurians construct, and they can be pillars of quiet strength. It is not ordinary for them to toot their own horns, for they believe that actions speak louder than words. In some respects they fit the story about the tortoise and the hare. The Taurus tortoise does not often dazzle with flashiness, but the race is run from beginning to end. If they run fast it is straight toward the goal line. The touchdown is made. The project is completed. The mission is accomplished. Wise use of talents, materials, ideas, colors and methods cause what they build to last.

In youth, the natural tendency to be placid, trustworthy and steady, can cause then to be the butt end of jokes and ridicule. Some are slower than average. If naughty, they are usually the first to get caught, and they do not often have the quick tongue or the sharp adroitness to extricate themselves in the way other signs can. Later in life, if punishment is handed out, they simply absorb it. At all ages Taurus is indwelling and has strong convictions. An appreciation of what is beautiful in nature can provide solace and strength whenever the circumstances are momentarily unfavorable.

Much has been said about the stubbornness and possessiveness of Taurus. Stubbornness is fixedness of purpose, and it can be both an asset and a liability. The evolved Taurus rising natives accomplish what they set out to do. They are faithful to a cause and follow the rules. The word steadfast would be more applicable to their behavior than stubborn. Once a course is set the path will be continued without deviation. They will brook no interference unless shown and convinced there is a much better way. When others push to stop a project or to take a different route, they may be answered politely but ignored, unless a strong rationale proves that a change is warranted. Taurians who have experienced considerable opposition in life can become morose, and this can become habitual. More than most, perhaps, they are creatures of habit and determined in their ways. Good habits and routines are fine. However, hanging onto losing positions can become a detriment. Such stolidness is not always beneficial. In other ways they can become too fixed for their own good. Opinions can become biases. Sometimes their views render all opposing arguments impossible. Words from others that would cause a deviation from course simply roll off their backs. Yet, once Taurus rising natives make up their minds to change, they will do so thoroughly and completely.

The Taurus rising person spends considerable time in contemplation and meditation. They have goals in life and build for the future. All possessions are for sustenance at a later time, and they are taken care of. The desire is for a pretty, well designed, artistic, comfortable, harmonious future in keeping with the nature of the ruling planet Venus. Thus, Taurus rising makes money to fulfill this objective. When objects are bought, the first thought is that they should be attractive and should last. One would not want to keep something that was unattractive. Quality is of paramount importance. A Taurus rising male will buy one expensive, well made, stylish suit for the same price others would pay for two of lesser quality. However, it will provide good service for a very long time, and it will not look like it was slept in after the first few hours of wear. The Taurus rising female will acquire clothes made from the most exquisite fabrics. Again, they will own less to have better objects of beauty and utility that will survive. They prefer this approach over a quantity of clothes of lower ultimate value. Nothing is wanted that deteriorates rapidly, and the typical gaudy souvenir is not on their list of wants. When Taurians are selfish with their material possessions, it is because of interference with this objective of building for the future. They usually do not like to lend anything, unless to a loved one, because it probably will be returned worn, damaged or not as useful as it would be if retained and taken care of by themselves. Taurus much prefers to give something they own than to lend for this reason.

Thus, there is the complete range. On the one hand, we find the unreasonable, dogmatic, obstinate, self-centered, gruff and prejudiced types, indolent and sensual. When the favorable characteristics discussed in the above paragraph are negated, they are totally reversed. Then this native becomes sloven and could care less about possessions or keeping them in good condition. On the other hand, we find great artists who love beauty, or great builders and producers who have much to show for their efforts. They are sympathetic toward others and organized in their ways. What they do in life is usually regarded as worthwhile. In between are the solid citizens. The majority are the strong ones to whom others turn when in need.

Example Horoscopes

This first person selected to illustrate the Taurus rising sign is supposed to have Cancer on his Ascendant. Cancer is the sign you would get by simply and blindly casting a horoscope for 4:00 AM, July 20, 1920, in Kriminiez (or Kremenets in American atlases), Russia. This birth data is for the absolutely fabulous violinist, Isaac Stern. Here we have another rounded off birth time to the nearest hour. Should that not be a signal, a warning every time it is observed that the moment of birth is indefinite? Why should any astrologer cast final horoscopes and pin their delineations to such nebulous times? The good ones, you will find, don't. In fact a very good rule is, never cast a horoscope for an even hour given as the birth time. If you do it will virtually guarantee an erroneous horoscope. The only even hour horoscopes acceptable are those that have been validated, and those for zero minutes are extremely rare.

With that subject dispensed with, it is back to our example, Isaac Stern, who is even today doing so much for music, for younger musicians and for Carnegie Hall. Can you believe there was actually talk in New York City of tearing down Carnegie Hall for the likes of parking lots and more office buildings? It was Isaac Stern who was most prominent in coming to the rescue.

He plays frequently today in live concerts. PBS often broadcasts musical sessions with Isaac Stern as a guest soloist. He is often seen and heard playing with one of his protegees such as Yo Yo Ma. He is known for his good works. These characteristics are so strongly Taurian it is hard to imagine how anyone could mistake his rising sign for any other—that is, once you get the hang of it. Figure 6 and Table IV show the natal horoscope of Isaac Stern, who was brought to San Francisco at the age of ten months. He studied music exclusively in the United States and is accepted internationally as an American musician. His underlying Sun sign is Cancer. Therefore, Cancer characteristics are naturally present in addition to his Taurus rising sign. This Sun placement often tends toward slightly shorter than average arms and legs and in the heavier natives a more crab-like walk. They are always very strongly attached to the family.

Also shown in the outer wheel of his horoscope and in the declination table is one of many events checked for validation. The one selected was his October 12, 1937, debut at Town Hall in New York City. For that momentous occasion progressed Venus was parallel Jupiter with-

JUL 20 1920	11:34:00 PM EET	Naibod Secondary
KRIMINIEZ	RUSSIA	OCT 12 1937
50 N 05 16	025 E 46 22	
11:16:00 PM TLT	21:32:54 GMT	21:32:54 GMT

Tropical *Placidus* *True Node*

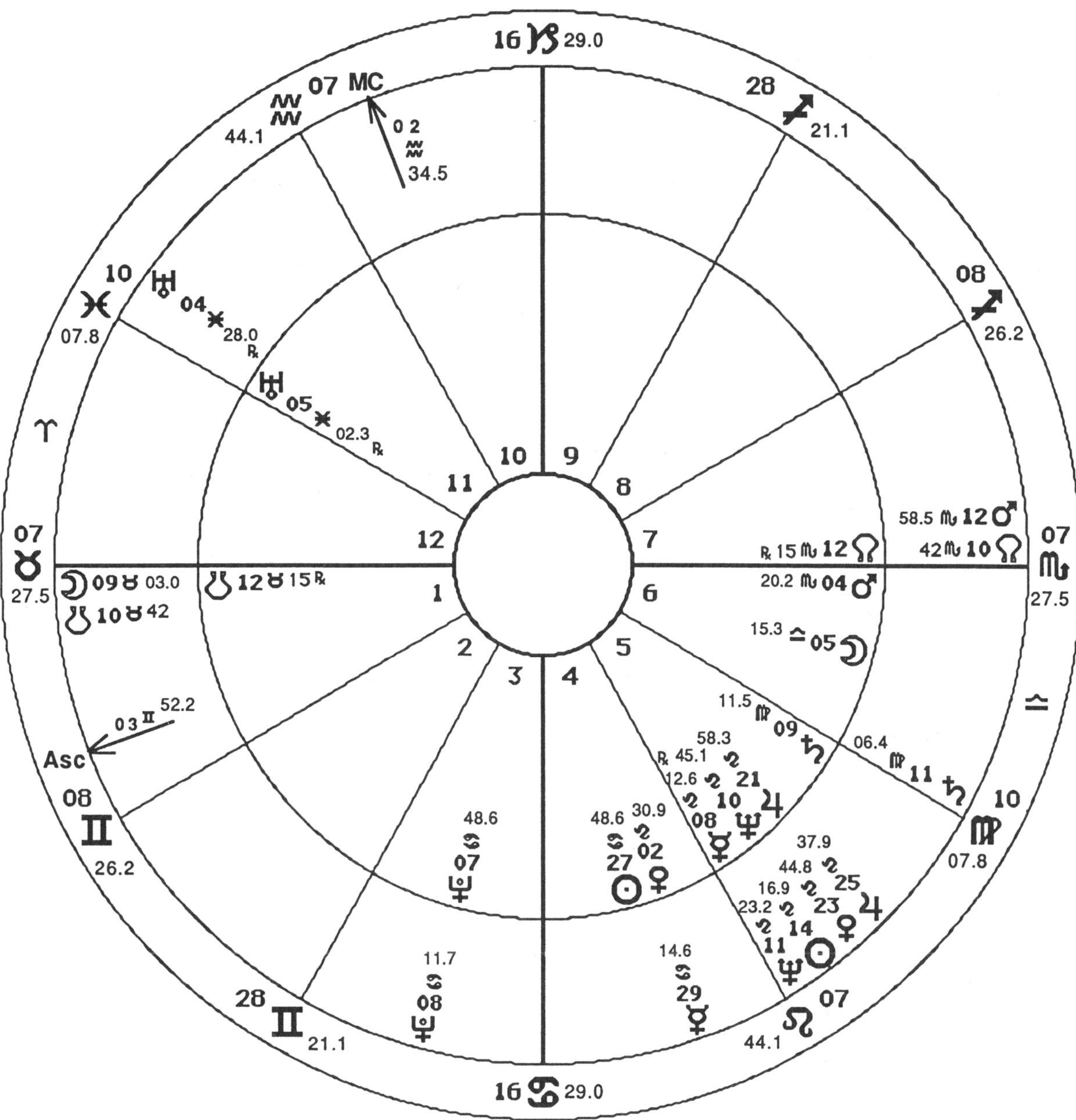

Figure 6. Horoscope of Isaac Stern with progressions to the date of his debut at Town Hall in New York City.

Table IV. Natal and Progressed Declinations of Isaac Stern

Planet	Natal Decln.	10 12 1937 Debut
☽	04 S 53.0	14 N 39.0
♄	09 N 46.3	09 N 02.1
♅	10 S 24.2	10 S 37.1
☿	13 N 52.1	17 N 08.4
Asc	14 N 00.3	20 N 55.9
♂	14 S 14.3	11 S 13.1
♃	14 N 57.6	13 N 45.3
♆	17 N 33.1	17 N 22.9
♇	19 N 39.9	19 N 38.8
☉	20 N 36.4	16 N 33.1
♀	20 N 42.5	14 N 56.9
MC	22 S 25.9	19 N 35.6

in 0.7 minutes (or 42 seconds). His progressed Midheaven was parallel Pluto within 4.3 minutes. Progressed Pluto itself was semisextile Mercury within 0.9 minutes and Midheaven was opposite Venus within 3.9 minutes. He himself did not feel that he played well on that day, but the reviews were supportive and prophetic of what was to come. However, let us apply the validation criteria in an orderly and pragmatic Taurian manner:

I. In all fairness, both the Cancer rising and the Taurus rising horoscopes have Venus in the foreground. Both indicate the strong possibility of a musical career. In the Cancer rising chart making money would be the principal objective of his work. In the Taurus rising chart the sixth and twelfth houses of service are intercepted. Thus, his objectives are focused much more strongly upon providing musical and cultural bequests to an appreciative public than to simply playing for them. His behind the scenes activities with regard to Carnegie Hall are a case in point. His work to benefit younger players is another.

II. Taurus rising fits Isaac Stern physically and with respect to his personality. Cancer rising does not. His Cancer Sun sign is evident in other ways, but it is not the principal molder of his body. One can look at any photograph to see the rounded rectangular features, especially those taken when he was young. They are like a template of what Taurus rising looks like. The

Cancer head would not be as rectangular, and it would curve back inward at the top. The combination of Cancer Sun and Taurus Ascendant support his good works.

The placement of planets in houses concerns us next. His is what Marc Edmond Jones called a bucket chart. Uranus is the handle planet, which provides a focus. The other planets represent the bucket itself and concentrate the energies and activities. All of these planets in the 11:16:00 PM true local time chart have moved backward from those in the 4:00 AM EET chart. To be perfectly honest an argument could be made for both horoscopes. The focus through Uranus in the Cancer rising chart would be in the ninth house of providing experiences to others. That is a plausible position. However, the major concentration of bucket planets would be in the twelfth through the fourth houses. The emphasis in life would be on himself, his possessions and his personal education and experiences. This would increase any Taurian tendencies toward apparent selfishness. Likewise, it would decrease the time spent with external contributions. Pluto in the twelfth and Uranus in the ninth would be the two main planets oriented toward providing musical experiences for others. Even so, that alignment is considerable.

In the Taurus rising chart Uranus has moved to the eleventh house. The main concentration of planets is in the third through the sixth houses. Here the main emphasis in life is upon recognizing his own capabilities, projecting his creative talents and pursuing those things that will benefit his community. These planets focus upon forward looking Uranus situated to act upon the dreams and pleasures of others. Jupiter, Neptune, Mars and Pluto now combine to increase the energies devoted to service because of the interceptions. Then, Mercury, Venus and Mars increase the amount of work, the effort applied and the assistance to subordinates. The sixth house Moon in Libra is a definite indicator of a career in the arts accompanied by strong emotions. Mars in the sixth house increases the activities applied and makes him a bundle of action, although sometimes accompanied by discord. It is most interesting that his biography talks about his whirlwind activities.

III. Every progression computed to the date of a major event produced close aspects in the 7 Taurus 27.8 rising chart. No close aspects emerged when testing three events in the 4:00 AM, 17 Cancer 20 rising chart, except for those produced by the outer planets. These outer planet angular aspects were almost identical in both, but not with respect to the houses. His marriage and several important engagements were tested. For a violinist, his debut is probably the best event to highlight. Those progressed Midheaven aspects in both longitude and declination are highly indicative—tenth house MC to Venus, the simultaneous contraparallel to Pluto in the third. The one aspect projected his art and proved to be a major milestone in building his reputation, the other made him extremely nervous of doing well. The Venus-Jupiter combination was there to pull him through, the greater and the lesser benefactors. In this placement they produced so much happiness. This reference is to the declinations, of course, that so many current astrologers are wont to throw away.

It is intriguing that one occasionally finds apologies for Venus being the ruler of Taurus. Stubbornness exhibited by some Taurian individuals is identified as one characteristic that might not belong to Venus. Yet, even that point is questionable when one considers the goddess of love can be blind in clinging to a relationship. One could interpret such behavior as a stubborn streak. Siderealists have also undermined Venus as the ruler of Taurus in explaining that tropical Taurus is sidereal Aries. They go on to talk about Mars being dictatorial, not Venus. But then avid Siderealists do not typically use planet rulerships, so that is a contradiction of sorts. They cite dictators with Sun in Taurus as examples. However, rising signs were not mentioned when referring to these obviously strong-armed individuals. Also, they give no examples of dictators who have the humanitarian, Aquarian Sun sign either. One current dictator, under house arrest, and with an Aquarius Sun, comes to mind.

Incidentally, an indictment of Sidereal Astrology is not intended. Sidereal Astrology has been found to have a place with respect to locations. The point is that attributing dictatorial tendencies to a Sun sign alone is like three blind mice describing an elephant. The whole horoscope must be interpreted, and the Ascendant is a prominent part of the whole horoscope. Since so many Ascendants have been in doubt, it is no wonder that confusion reigns with respect to astrological interpretations, including those of dictators. Once the Taurus Ascendant is positively identified, the Venusian qualities become highly evident. Many individuals with Taurus rising have careers associated with harmony, color, beauty, love and other traits of this planet. Even the rounding of the rectangular facial features can be associated with Venus.

But Venus is feminine, rather than masculine. It is less aggressive than the premier male planet, Mars. Those with Taurus rising are more likely to let their actions speak for themselves, than to push forward aggressively and constantly remind everyone who they are. At times, this leads to slower advancement or lesser roles until recognized. Thus, one finds that some individuals with Taurus rising are sufficiently prominent to be publicized, but not as apt to have biographies giving important dates. This makes finding good examples more difficult than average, especially when it comes to verification. But the best place to start is with people having published horoscopes claiming Gemini on the Ascendant. In many such cases Gemini is wrong.

The second person chosen for illustrative purposes did have a published Gemini rising horoscope. Only two dates were given in her American biography, the ones for her birth and her death. This eliminates momentarily the ability to run multiple progressions for proof of the correct time. On the other hand, her features are so definitely Taurian, and death for anyone is such a significant event, that it can hardly be accompanied by mild aspects. The aspects for this person were very strong, very close and highly indicative of the event. Also death, as an astrological incident, should be understood by those who would seek more light. This example is for the exquisitely beautiful Austrian actress Romy Schneider and her premature death in Paris. The reports stated that death resulted from natural causes. She was only forty-three years old when that happened in 1982.

Figure 7 and Table V show the horoscope of Romy Schneider for her planets in longitude and declination. One should look at her photographs or films first. Her rectangular head showed much roundness at the corners. Naturally the feminine curves are even more prominent than for a male of this sign. Her lips were full and sensuous. She was a blond with grey-green eyes. Her 5 foot 4 inch height and 110 pound weight were very typical for Taurus. This stature was much less than would be expected for the average woman with Gemini on the Ascendant. She was described as proud, hot tempered at times, impatient, but shy. She came from a theatrical family. Carrying on the tradition was probably at the root of her pride. Also, the underlying Libra Sun sign is not without that characteristic, or seeming impatience, when attempting to achieve balance. She was fourteen years old in her first film, *Wenn der Weisse Flieder Blüht*. Afterward she became type cast in one princess role after another until she rebelled. Thus, her career was not without controversy. She first came to the United States in 1958 to promote the motion picture called *The Story of Vickie,* in which she acted. She wanted very much to appear in more dramatic roles and eventually did. This was an actress of both continents, one who achieved recognition in Europe and the United States. She was criticized at times for taking so long to accept roles, and for not acting in more German films. She even sat out two years once until the right part came along. Her ability to speak well in the language of the country of the filming was a strong asset. It did not matter whether they were made in German, French or English, or one of the other seven languages she spoke fluently. Thus her acting was in the language of the script.

The horoscope that describes Romy Schneider has moved backward more than a full sign, from 28 Gemini on the Ascendant to 26 Taurus 05.4 on the Ascendant. This is the shift between her physical birth time horoscope and the natal horoscope that fits her behavior and appearance. Many planets have changed one or two houses, although not the Sun and the Moon. Both horoscopes have the creative fifth and eleventh houses intercepted. However, the Taurus rising chart shown is the one that concentrates five planets in the fifth house. We will apply our criteria, but must caution that only a single progressed aspect for verification was available. This makes it more speculative than desired.

I. Motion pictures and acting represent illusions. That is the domain of Neptune. Neptune is now in the center of the pack of planets in the fifth house, rather than over in the fourth with Mercury, where it would have alluded to parents and home life in place of the creative talents she

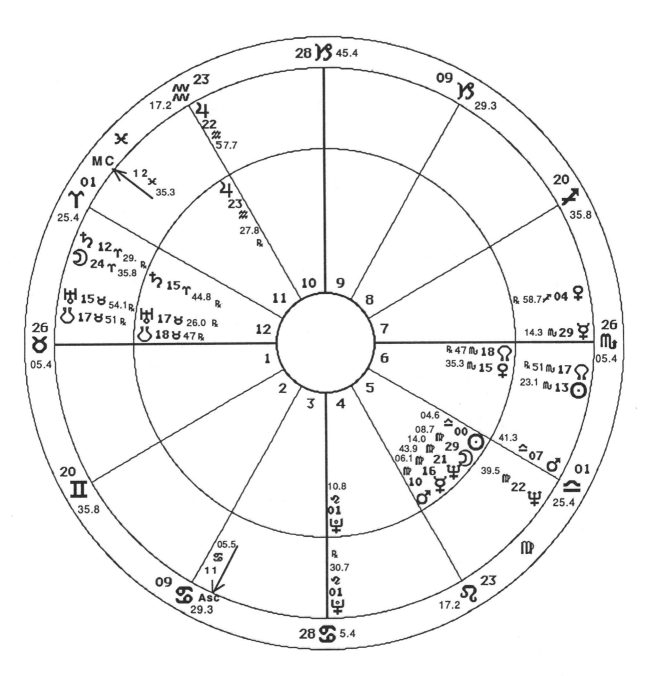

Figure 7. Horoscope of the Austrian actress Romy Schneider with progressions to the date of her untimely death.

possessed. True, the fourth house is cardinal and normally stronger than the fifth. But those fourth house planets together with Neptune form a powerhouse. Moreover, the adjoining Moon and Sun significantly increase energy. The Moon with Neptune and Mercury adds feelings and emotions to her acting career. The Taurus rising chart more accurately shows the person of an actress than the one of a tall, vivacious, constantly moving Gemini person whose attachment to films would be more cerebral than emotional.

Table V. Natal and Progressed Declinations of Romy Schneider

Planet	Natal Decln.	05 29 1982 Death
☉	00 S 01.8	15 S 51.6
☽	03 S 15.0	11 N 28.2
♄	03 N 40.2	02 N 26.2
♆	04 N 29.3	03 N 56.6
☿	06 N 53.9	21 S 45.4
♂	08 N 52.6	01 S 59.9
♃	14 S 50.7	14 S 55.5
♅	16 N 40.4	16 N 14.2
Asc	19 N 16.9	22 N 59.0
♀	20 S 21.0	26 S 18.8
MC	20 S 24.8	06 S 50.3
♇	22 N 58.9	23 N 00.8

II. Other planets will be examined. Jupiter was originally in the ninth house close to the Midheaven. It would be correct to say that such a position would provide an outlet for mutual expressions and expand the reputation. The inconjunctions from Pluto and Neptune focus upon Jupiter, adding considerable power, and Uranus, with a sextile, contributes technical compatibility. The emphasis of Jupiter in the Taurus rising chart is on eleventh house pleasures of others. The outlet of expressions with other people has now switched to Capricorn and its ruler Saturn, which is in the twelfth house of public accomplishments. So, which would you consider to be the better representation? Pluto has also moved from the second house of personal possessions to the fourth showing that her family was highly talented. As for the declinations, Venus is now on the Midheaven. That is more appropriate for an actress prominent in the theatrical arts than is a conjunction with Jupiter. The Moon is also contraparallel Saturn, which coincides with her tendency to be impatient.

III. Now let us look at this event of untimely death. The one aspect that simply jumps out at you is the parallel of progressed Ascendant with the fourth house Pluto within 0.1 minutes (or under 6 seconds). Pluto is in Leo, and Leo points to the heart. For death to occur, the fourth house is prominent, and so is the Ascendant or first house. The existence of self and of its inner influences exit, and these two domains have to be prominent under such circumstances. The progressed Midheaven was contraparallel Mercury within 3.6 minutes, which caused it to be a newsworthy event. The reports included some words of controversy. Progressed Jupiter, in declination, approached its own natal position within 4.8 minutes, relating to its rulership of the eighth house for the departure of the soul. Now having reviewed the important aspects in declination, we need to review the progressed longitudes for anything else of importance. Yes, there is one. The progressed Ascendant is 45 degrees from its own natal position within 0.1 minutes (again under 6 seconds). That is a very close aspect, and it is significant. Elsewhere, the Midheaven is semi-sextile Saturn progressed within 5.7 minutes, which is weak, but it added a certain stillness to the shock. Progressed Jupiter and Neptune were widely inconjunct, almost too far apart to be of major importance. They do portend the end of the acting career and both reflect the eighth house activity. Mercury progressed is sextile the Moon within 5.7 minutes. The public was informed of what happened. Progressed Uranus is also in wide opposition to Venus. But none of the rest of these aspects in longitude meet our requirement of being within 4 minutes for such a major event. They, do however, add their effects. The combination agrees with the report that death occurred from natural causes. It was probably caused by heart failure.

These have been two good examples of Taurus rising, one a male and one a female. The careers of both relate to Venus. It is probable that Isaac Stern has adequate personal possessions to satisfy his needs and that Romy Schneider received sufficient income to support herself in good style. However, neither appears to have concentrated upon a goal of making money in life. The creative arts appealed far more to both of them. One can observe their images closely to see what Taurus on the Ascendant looks like. Isaac Stern appears frequently on television (especially on PBS). Photographs of Romy Schneider are more likely to be found in biographies or in reruns of her movies. Perhaps these two celebrities do not follow the stereotype images which some would claim for Taurus rising. However, the physical birth time rising signs of Cancer for Isaac Stern and Gemini for Romy Schneider do not match, and they are simply not verifiable. Both appearances are in complete agreement with Taurus on the Ascendant.

Before leaving Taurus, one more example simply has to be included because of his importance to the world. When he was a boy in Ulm, Germany, his teachers said he was slow to learn and backwards. That is so typical of other people's opinions of a young person with Taurus rising. Yet, he had his own personal, inward kind of curiosity. When he was at the age of four or five he was shown a compass by his father. Later in his own words he said, "That this needle behaved in such a determined way did not fit into the nature of events which could find a place in the conscious world of concepts (effect connected with direct touch). I can still remember—or at least I believe I can remember—that this experience made a deep and lasting impression upon me. Something deeply hidden had to be behind things.....at the age of twelve I experienced a second wonder of a totally different nature: in a little book dealing with Euclidian plane geometry—this lucidity and certainty made an indescribable impression upon me." These recollections were of events that shaped his destiny. Much later it was said of this man that he made contributions to science unequaled by any other man. The reference, of course, is to Dr. Albert Einstein, whose horoscope is given in Figure 8 with declinations in Table VI.

During a six-month period, without restrictions imposed by formal schooling, he taught himself calculus and higher mathematics. This feat was sufficiently thorough and impressive to permit admission to the Polytechnic Academy in Zürich, Switzerland in 1896. So much for backwardness and slow learning in the eyes of others. One clue about rising signs can be learned from this episode. Cancer rising, on his published horoscope Ascendant, does not match the viewpoint of his early teachers. Taurus, two signs back, does.

Albert Einstein studied mathematics and physics. From 1902 to 1905 he wrote five papers that shook the scientific world. They were *The Special Theory of Relativity, The Quantum Basis of the Emission and Absorption of Light, Theory of Brownian Movement, The Inertia of Energy* and *On the Electrodynamics of Moving Bodies*. By 1909 he became Professor-Extraordinary of Theoretical Physics at the University of Zürich. Germany became engaged in World War I during his tenure. In 1921 he received a Nobel Prize. In 1928 he had a heart attack, although the date is not known. This required him to work at a less strenuous pace. By the 1930's Jews were being targeted by Hitler throughout North Europe and Dr. Albert Einstein fled to the United States. He settled at Princeton University in New Jersey at the Institute for Advanced Study. Meanwhile, he was troubled by certain aspects of his *Unified Field Theory* that did not appear to correlate. In a bit of Taurian humor he said, "If my theory is proved correct, Germany will hail me as a great German and the French will call me a citizen of the world. If it is proved false, the French will call me a German and the Germans will call me a Jew." On March 30, 1953, he formally announced that he had resolved the difficulties. This date was used for the progression illustrated together with his horoscope in Figure 8 and Table VI.

I. The question is, does this great human being fit the horoscope with 4 Taurus 29.2 on the Ascendant, or is Cancer rising even to be considered? Notice the sixth and twelfth houses intercepted. His life was devoted to accomplishments for mankind. His intuitive Pisces Sun and pioneering Aries Mercury and Venus in the twelfth house accentuate this posture. The Cancer rising chart contains an empty twelfth house. His physical appearance is Taurian, with his rectangular head and somewhat bulbous nose, typical for that sign when it is present. And remember the wild hair in virtually all of his American photographs. Neptune sitting on his Ascendant is directly responsible. Forget Cancer rising. Although similarities in head shapes exist between these two signs, the absence of any narrowness at the top eliminates the possibility for Cancer.

II. For a mental giant we look at not only the position and aspects of Mercury, but also of Uranus and Neptune. So Mercury is inconjunct Uranus. This planet of physics and technology is in the house of personal creativity and in the disciplined mental sign of Virgo. Neptune is not only powerful from its first house position next to the Ascendant, but it is trine Uranus. The intuitive faculties are enormously increased. Pluto is in the first house. The capabilities are extended again. Venus, the ruler of the Ascendant is in the twelfth house. That is a perfect placement for what we know about his career. Venus is conjunct Mercury and also inconjunct Uranus. It is semi-sextile Neptune and parallel Pluto. All of these contacts are supportive of harmonious thought processes. Mercury is contraparallel Saturn, which increases caution and fear of error. Haste in speaking or writing had to be guarded against. With Jupiter in the enlightened sign of Aquarius in the eleventh house, his students must have been in for numerous treats and an occasional shock from the squaring Pluto. Even Mars in the tenth house is in its most compatible sign, Capricorn. Despite the criticism of his youth and incompatibility with the primary educational system (or educators) of his locale, energies were productively applied to achieve success. Jupiter contraparallel his Ascendant conforms with the experiences of being forced to flee from time to time.

III. The March 30, 1953, event date is doubly important. First, it marked his announcement that he had resolved the difficulties encountered earlier with his *Unified Field Theory*. Second, only two weeks earlier Dr. Einstein had been honored by receiving notice that the Yeshida University Medical School in New York would hereafter be called the *Albert Einstein College of Medicine*. A Midheaven aspect would be expected under such circumstances. We are not to be denied. The progressed Midheaven is inconjunct progressed Uranus within 0.7 minutes. The progressed Ascendant is parallel Sun progressed within 2.4 minutes. The Moon is also in a wide, but approaching, semisextile to Venus. The very close aspects, however, more than adequately fill the bill for confirmation. The sometimes ridiculed Taurus rising native can indeed become the greatest in his chosen work. Here is Dr. Albert Einstein to show for this truism. The name of the

MAR 14 1879	08:03 AM CET	Naibod Secondary
ULM	GERMANY	MAR 30 1953
48 N 22 09	10 E 00 00	
07:42:08 TLT	07:02:08 AM GMT	07:02:08 AM GMT

Tropical *Placidus* *True Node*

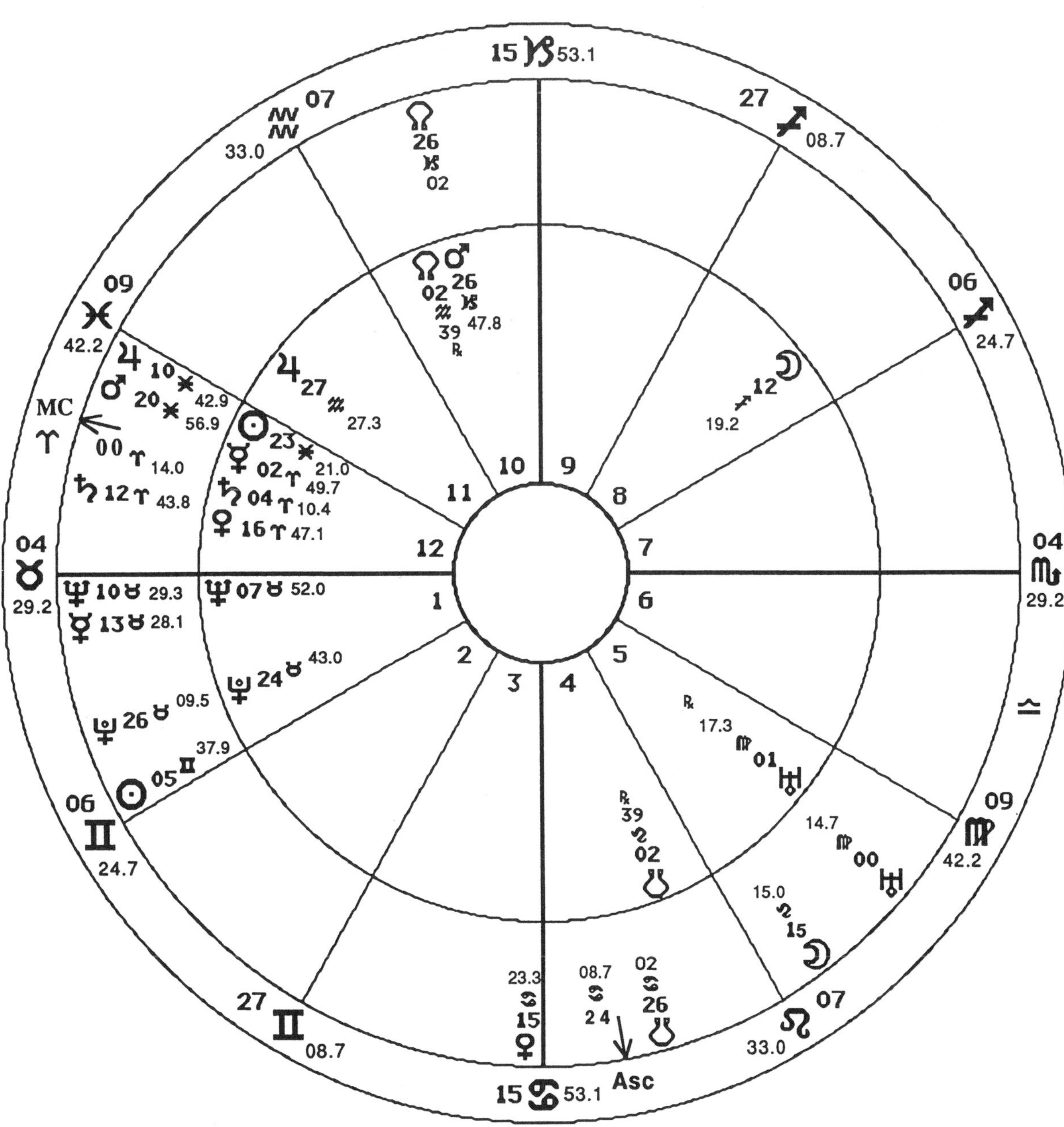

Figure 8. Horoscope of Dr. Albert Einstein with progressions to the date he announced resolution of his Unified Field Theory.

teacher who found it important to ridicule, and must have done so with sufficient purpose that the act was recorded in the annals of history, has long since been forgotten—and that is poetic justice.

Table VI. Natal and Progressed Declinations of Dr. Albert Einstein

Planet	Natal Decln.	03 30 1953 Resolution
♄	00 S 19.2	02 N 56.5
☿	00 N 44.5	13 N 22.6
☉	02 S 38.5	21 N 15.5
♇	05 N 39.1	06 N 08.6
♀	05 N 57.3	24 N 47.3
♅	11 N 46.3	12 N 06.2
♆	12 N 29.7	13 N 20.2
Asc	13 N 01.6	21 N 17.9
♃	13 S 05.0	08 S 29.0
♂	21 S 39.2	05 S 25.6
MC	22 S 30.7	00 N 05.6
☽	26 S 11.6	14 N 38.5

CHAPTER 3. GEMINI

Physical Attributes

The Gemini rising person has an elongated rectangular head with expressive features, alert eyes and usually a long nose. From the crown to the chin is a noticeably longer dimension than the width. In youth their bodies are thin, lithe, and they move with quick actions. This is one of the two tall signs, and they are especially agile. The other is Sagittarius. Saturn on a Gemini Ascendant could keep the person from being tall, but very few other circumstances would reduce the height. Later in life they may add a little flesh, depending upon eating habits. Their skin is of the type that usually tans easily. The fingers and feet are comparatively long. They love to talk, and their hands are active. They must always be busy with their hands. It can be writing, crafts, turning pages of a book, quilting, painting, playing music, gesticulating, throwing a ball, basket weaving, cooking—whatever holds their interest. Most of their interests are intellectual. If the underlying Sun sign is also thin, the chin is small and pointed.

When comparing the two adjoining signs with Gemini, distinct differences appear that aid in categorization. Gemini usually towers over Taurus and Cancer. Both of these other two signs have shorter heads, more rounded for Taurus and narrower at the top for Cancer. Gemini exhibits swift actions, while Taurus is slower and more direct. Cancer is also more cautious and deliberate. The length of the fingers and feet are a dead giveaway. Gemini rising could not get into the shoes or gloves of either of these other two signs. As usual the boundaries are exact. It is amazing how the physical appearance changes so drastically when the Ascendant goes less than a minute into the next sign.

Mental Characteristics

Gemini on the Ascendant is ruled by Mercury. Mercury is the messenger of the gods, the one that communicates. He also represents the intellect. Words are the main vehicle of communication, and words flow easily from most people with Gemini rising. The more advanced types can be highly intellectual. They are usually vivacious, exuberant, curious, imaginative, inquiring and often asking questions. They can be restless, high-strung, impatient and excitable. Some are good mimes and can easily imitate what others say. Others like to tell good stories. Most like literature and poetry. The person with Gemini in this placement is not happy unless busy and occupied using their hands. They are adroit in actions. Almost all take to education readily and they learn quickly. Reading, writing or talking on a telephone are common pastimes. Whatever the situation they never want to be fenced in.

One symbol of Gemini is a characterization of the Roman twins, Castor and Pollux (not the modernized symbol shown above). Thus, much is made of the duality of their personality. The Germans say *Himmelhoch jauchzend—zum Tode betrübt.* As usual something is lost in translation, but a near literal version is, high heaven rejoicing—with troubling doom. It refers to those who are full of optimism while simultaneously being dejected by doubt. Another way of looking at this characteristic of Gemini rising is to understand one of their greatest assets. That is to see the big picture—better than most. Of course the big picture includes both the beautiful neighborhoods and the slums, the wonderful potentials of a proposition as well as the risks, the saintly and the tawdry at the same time. It provides them with real insights into the duality of nature. They are better able to analyze a complex situation and come to a comprehensive solution than most. Others can handle only a piece of the same problem. Yet this ability to put an overview into words may be accompanied by doubts. Enthusiasm can be combined with trepidation. They can be overjoyed one moment and suffer a nervous breakdown the next. They can be the life of the party or perfectly fickle. It is easy for them to charm with words, and they like to have fun. If Gemini agrees to meet someone at a future time it is said with pleasure in their voice. But, it may or may not happen. Taurus looks at the same agreement as a commitment, and come hell or high water they will be there. Cancer foresees that such a meeting is to be kept for the potential emotional experience that follows. Meanwhile, for Gemini to show up, depends upon what is going on at the time. After all, the idea to have a meeting was simply a bunch of easily said words. If the present occupation is more interesting than the appointment, then other words can be used to offer apologies. Gemini apologizes beautifully. No problem. They simply like to keep their options open and have more than one choice. They are opportunists who prefer fulfilling their intellectual curiosity by selecting from a panorama of events at any given moment. If the current matter of interest and the arranged meeting do not coincide, so be it. This may be a bit hard on the Gemini rising native, but it is a frequent subject of their notoriety. Yet, when meeting regular commitments of teaching or performing in a series of programs they can be very fulfilling. They can also be the most fun of all the different signs.

The differences between Gemini rising and Taurus rising are pronounced, both physically and mentally. On occasion an Aries rising person might be mistaken for one who has Gemini on the Ascendant, but not Taurus. One example has already been given, and that was Sir Laurence Olivier. Another person reputedly with Gemini rising is Burt Reynolds, but he does not seem to fit the mold at all. Still another is Harry Belafonte. None of these actors and singers has any physical or clearly evident mental resemblance to each other, let alone to Gemini. A good test would be to attempt an identification of these people, based upon the information already given. Such exercises are an excellent way to hone one's skills at recognizing the correct rising sign.

Example Horoscopes

Two famous women will be given first, because they exemplify some of the finest qualities of Gemini rising. One is Lucille Ball, the second Julia Child. There are those who would tell you Lucille Ball has Cancer rising. As for Julia Child, she is one of the very few famous people having a natal horoscope timed a little after the birth time given and not before. The difference amounts to seventeen minutes (five degrees on the Ascendant) with no change in sign. But even that small shift caused planets to move to different houses. On the other hand, hers was another one of those birth times given to the nearest half hour. So if the blessed event occurred midway between when the big hand pointed straight up and when it pointed straight down, which one was the poor recorder supposed to choose?

But, let's get back to Lucille Ball. In the discussion above it was stated that Gemini rising is exuberant. So what did the young Lucille Ball do in one of her early outings? Why she put so much gusto into an Apache dance given at a local Masonic Review that she dislocated her arm. In *I Love Lucy,* her famous show with husband Desi Arnez, the Gemini clown came out hundreds of times for many years running. She was not a short statured woman, but comparatively tall. She was even tall for Desi. Her situation comedies constantly found her in trouble because of her big mouth. It is hard to imagine a behind-the-scenes Cancer on the cusp pulling all those shenanigans. Of course her underlying Leo Sun did not hurt her showmanship. That entire popular series from beginning to end was Gemini completely. The script, the actions and of course, the leading actress constantly made Gemini statements. Figure 9 and Table VII show Lucille Ball's horoscope and declinations. For proofs the three criteria are reviewed:

I. By now we should be getting used to seeing fifth/eleventh house interceptions for show people. After all they entertain. The fifth and eleventh sectors are the houses of fun. Personal entertainment is in the one, audiences are in the other. The Cancer rising horoscope does not

AUG 06 1911 | 01:03 AM EST | Naibod Secondary
JAMESTOWN | NEW YORK | NOV 30 1940
42 N 05 21 | 079 W 14 38 |
00:44:55 TLT | 06:01:54 GMT | 06:01:54 GMT

Tropical *Placidus* *True Node*

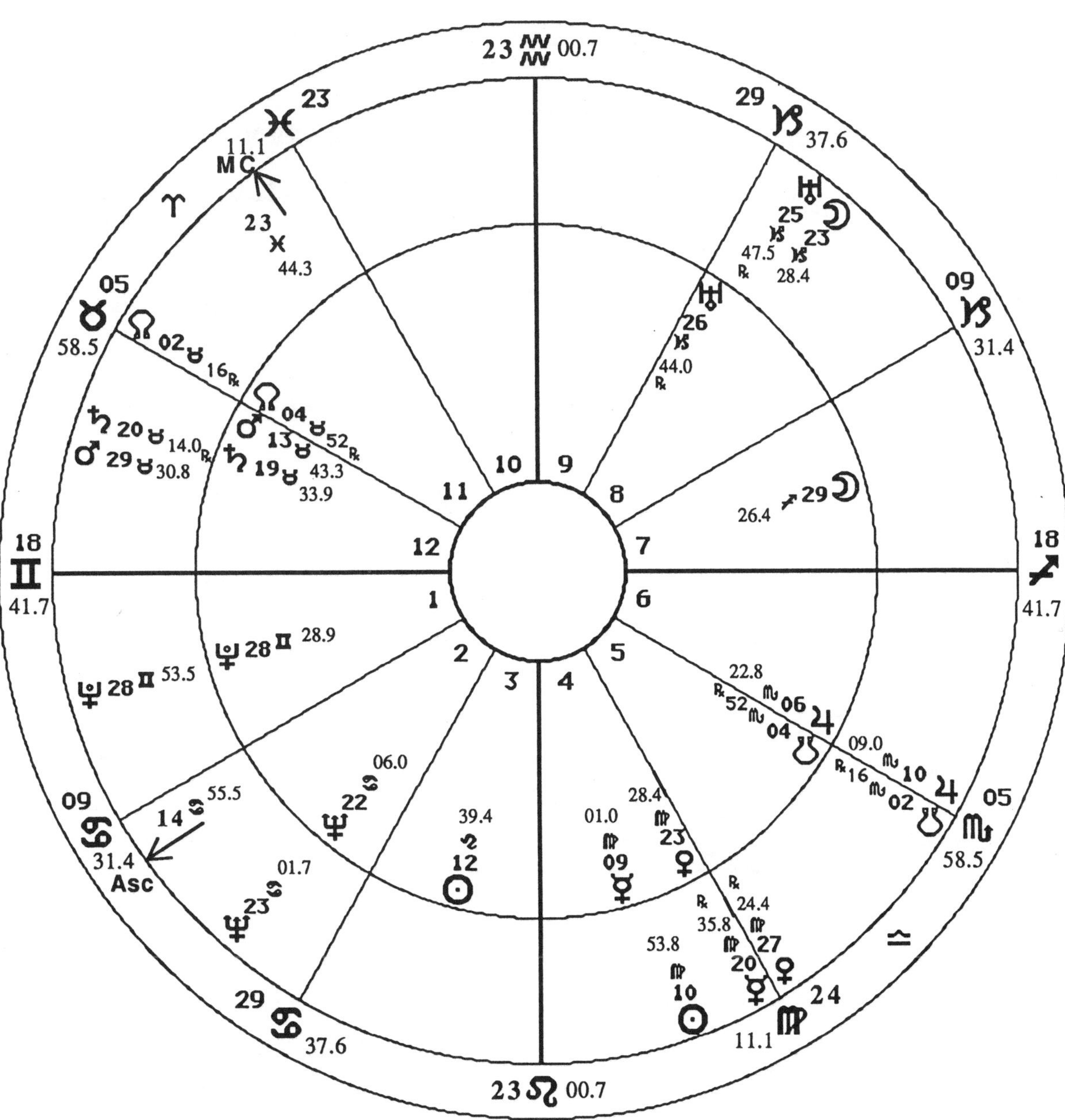

Figure 9. Horoscope of Lucille Ball with progressions to date of marriage with Desi Arnez.

have this highly repetitive signature. Moreover, Mercury and Venus are prominent in the fourth house. These are the planets of comedy, dancing and singing. They are strongly aspected, and enjoyment is written all over them. Again the ruler of the ninth house is in the twelfth. Many situations are concocted and performed in behalf of others. This is a horoscope that belongs to a cheeky person in the acting profession.

Table VII. Natal and Progressed Declinations of Lucille Ball

Planet	Natal Decln.	11 30 1940 Marriage
♀	00 N 01.8	06 S 20.2
☿	07 N 40.8	00 S 16.4
♃	12 S 40.7	13 S 59.3
♂	13 N 58.3	18 N 17.8
♄	15 N 24.2	15 N 28.6
☉	17 N 01.2	07 N 29.0
♇	17 N 05.1	17 N 03.3
MC	17 N 24.3	02 S 29.3
♆	21 N 04.4	20 N 55.3
♅	21 S 22.5	21 S 32.9
Asc	21 N 20.7	22 N 37.1
☽	27 S 32.3	26 S 22.6

II. If Figure 9 is rotated so that the third house cusp becomes the Ascendant, an approximation of the Cancer rising physical birth time horoscope can be observed. Most of the planets are shifted one or two house positions. Venus is now weak in the third house. Mercury is in the house of personal possessions. Mars is in the tenth, while the Sun is in the first. Saturn in the eleventh would show fears of being a comedian or standing up in front of an audience. The Moon, co-ruler of the first house, is in Capricorn and the sixth house with Uranus. This sign placement for the Moon is not a comfortable situation for employment, as the emotions, ambitions and technical ideas would clash. It looks much more like the horoscope of a person who wants organizational authority or to run her own business. These planetary placements do not indicate the profession of acting. Amusing other people would be a highly unlikely occupation.

The Gemini rising horoscope points to entertainment. Besides the activity-increasing interceptions, jolly Jupiter is now in the sixth house of work. The strongly placed Venus is in a T-square with Pluto and the Moon, but it is also semisextile Jupiter, sextile Neptune and trine Uranus. Those favorable aspects turn that strong "T" into an implement of enjoyment. Mercury, the ruler of the Ascendant, makes several harmonious aspects with the T-square planets and some of the others. Pluto in the first adds extra ability to extricate herself from predicaments. Many opportunities were written into her scripts to do just that. The fit is perfect.

III. Many recorded events were available for verifying the horoscope of Lucille Ball with 18 Gemini 41.7 on the Ascendant. The one chosen for illustrative purposes was her marriage to Desi Arnez. That had to be a strong relationship, because it was the foundation of not only a matrimonial association but also the Desilu Company. So what do we find in the progressions? Well, for starters there is the exact trine of progressed Moon to Venus on November 30, 1940. Other aspects of note were the inconjunction between progressed Neptune and her Midheaven within 1.0 minute. Neptune is a co-ruler of the seventh house of matrimonial relationships, and the inconjunction foretold the opportunities in television with a partner. Progressed Mars was also inconjunct the Moon within 4.4 minutes, and the slower moving progressed Jupiter was contraparallel Mars within 1.0 minute. This match was not without later conflicts. Overall there are a number of aspects that correspond to the progressed event and meet our test of accuracy. All the other dated events were found to have corresponding aspects that agreed with their nature.

Now Lucille Ball was an entertainer par excellence. The six-foot tall Julia Child is also an entertainer—a cooking entertainer and educator. Well, what do you know? Those few minutes difference in time of birth caused her intercepted houses to shift from the sixth and twelfth to the fifth and eleventh where they belong. She is not a government servant. That was the role of her husband. Rather, she devotes her performances to the enjoyment (and education) of others. She makes French cooking interesting, simplifies it and in the process has lots of fun.

Julia was born in Pasadena, California. She went to Smith College and majored in History, an appropriate subject for Gemini rising. When she was thirty-four years old she married Paul Child, who became a member of the American foreign service. He was a gourmand in his own right, and his occupation took them to Paris. There the educational instincts of Julia arose again. Not one to sit still in a lonely apartment while her husband was off to work, she enrolled in the famous *Cordon Bleu de Paris* school of culinary arts. There she started to pick up the basics of French cooking. She enrolled in a Berlitz language course to learn French. This enabled her to understand lessons more easily and to converse with her teachers and fellow students. After these initial experiences with learning in France she studied under master chef Max Fugnard, who was an assistant chef at *Escoffier*. Their relationship was a lasting one. She met Madame Simone Beck and was honored by being invited to become a member of the prestigious *Le Cercle des Gourmettes*. Such organizations are not taken lightly in France. They are a matter of national pride. This organization is for the most famous female chefs, and to be invited to join was a superlative honor. These two women, together with another member, Madam Louisette Bertholle, joined forces to author a mammoth cook book. It was at first unsuccessful, possibly because of its size. Therefore it was later pared down and finally released under the title *Mastering the Art of French Cooking*. The trim English language version was printed in the United States by Alfred Knopf in 1961. That volume became extremely successful. Meanwhile, the three women had opened a restaurant by the name of *L'École des Trois Gourmandes,* which has survived.

But Julia Child had to leave France when her husband was relocated back to the United States. Returning to Boston, the idea for the television series *The French Chef* evolved and the program made its debut on February 11, 1963. So that is the date of the progression that is highly appropriate for illustrating the authenticity of Julia Child's horoscope. It has 10 Gemini 57.3 on the Ascendant, not 5 Gemini 54, which was the chart previously published for her using the nearest half hour birth time. Half hour birth time horoscopes are almost as bad as even hour ones. But in this case the two horoscopes are similar. The later time causes Saturn to be further away from the Ascendant, where it did not limit her stature. The earlier time had Saturn so close to the

Ascendant that one would wonder how Julia grew to six feet.

Julia Child has a Leo Sun with Gemini on the Ascendant. The best qualities of those signs have been displayed often on her television show and in interviews. She set out to show ordinary people that French cooking could be easy to master in the home kitchen. Not all of it had to be complex and difficult. In doing so she communicated in a way that few have done before, and Gemini loves to communicate. The essence of her message is that the French always use fresh ingredients and fresh herbs. So what could be simpler? In giving this message she comes across as a delightful, knowledgeable person who occasionally makes mistakes like the rest of us while demonstrating. So she is a human being after all. Her *faux pas* become fun. One would love to have the opportunity to sit down and eat diner with her. Meanwhile, the rigorous review of her horoscope (Figure 10 and Table VIII) is in order.

I. The change to the correct time with its new intercepted signs (fifth and eleventh) is the main cause of Julia Child's ability to entertain. A drastic increase in ability to entertain represents the key difference between the previously published reference chart and the one computed for her moment of incarnation. Her own husband calls her a natural clown. As stated before, the other chart would have pointed her in other directions, probably to government service more in line with Paul Child's former occupation.

II. About the only other change between the two horoscopes is Mars. Mars has slipped from the fifth house back into the fourth. In both cases Mars is in another mental sign, Virgo. This change relieves any tendencies toward verbal strife as a function of her own creativity and passes it back to the domain of her home life. Mars is now only one of four planets in the fourth house and well aspected. It is parallel Mercury, which gives her the quick wit. This is one well-adjusted person. But more important to our objectives, those two categories of change both favor the illustrated horoscope.

III. The debut of *The French Chef* occurred when progressed Mercury was exactly parallel her Moon. What could be more appropriate for a show that appeals to the public? The progressions for this date appear in the outer ring of her horoscope (Figure 10) and in the last column of Table VIII. Progressed Jupiter was also sextile the Moon within 1.9 minutes. All that fifth house-eleventh house creativity harmonized. Both aspects are commensurate with the event and meet our test of being within 4 minutes of perfect. Progressions were separately calculated for the date of her marriage, her graduation from college and other events of consequence. All checked as they should. These same progressions were in the earlier chart, but the Mercury aspect was further away. Even though the change in timing is in minutes, all of the progressed events simply did not tally as well.

This brings up another point that should perhaps be discussed a little more. When two potential birth times are close together, many of the aspects for each event will be the same. That is especially true of those being formed by outer planets. The best solution under these circumstances is to find an event for progressions that involves the Ascendant, Midheaven or inner planets, including the Moon. This is because these elements have the highest velocities and they will move the furthest in the shortest length of time. It does not matter whether the aspect for the event is formed from one of these elements or to their natal positions. The differences will usually be sufficient to make a decision as to which time provides the closest aspect. The Ascendant and Midheaven, however, have special significance. Along with the lights, they are of greater importance than the others in matching major events. A special honor known to society can usually occur only when the Midheaven is involved. A change to the physical body, whether an accident, an operation, a miraculous recovery and often a permanent relocation, almost invariably involves the Ascendant. An advancement in position almost certainly is accompanied by an aspect of the Sun, and it may include the Midheaven if important enough. Those are the extraordinarily important events in life. When these planets and cusps are a part of the day-for-a-year progressed aspect picture, then the most momentous and memorable of events are the ones being encountered. Lesser events involve lesser planets. At any rate, even tenths of a minute of greater accuracy in the aspect do make a difference in the selection process.

AUG 15 1912 11:47 PM PST
PASADENA CALIFORNIA
34 N 06 55 118 W 06 33
11:58:41 PM TLT 07:51:08 GMT
Tropical *Placidus* *True Node*

Naibod Secondary
FEB 11 1963

07:51:08 GMT

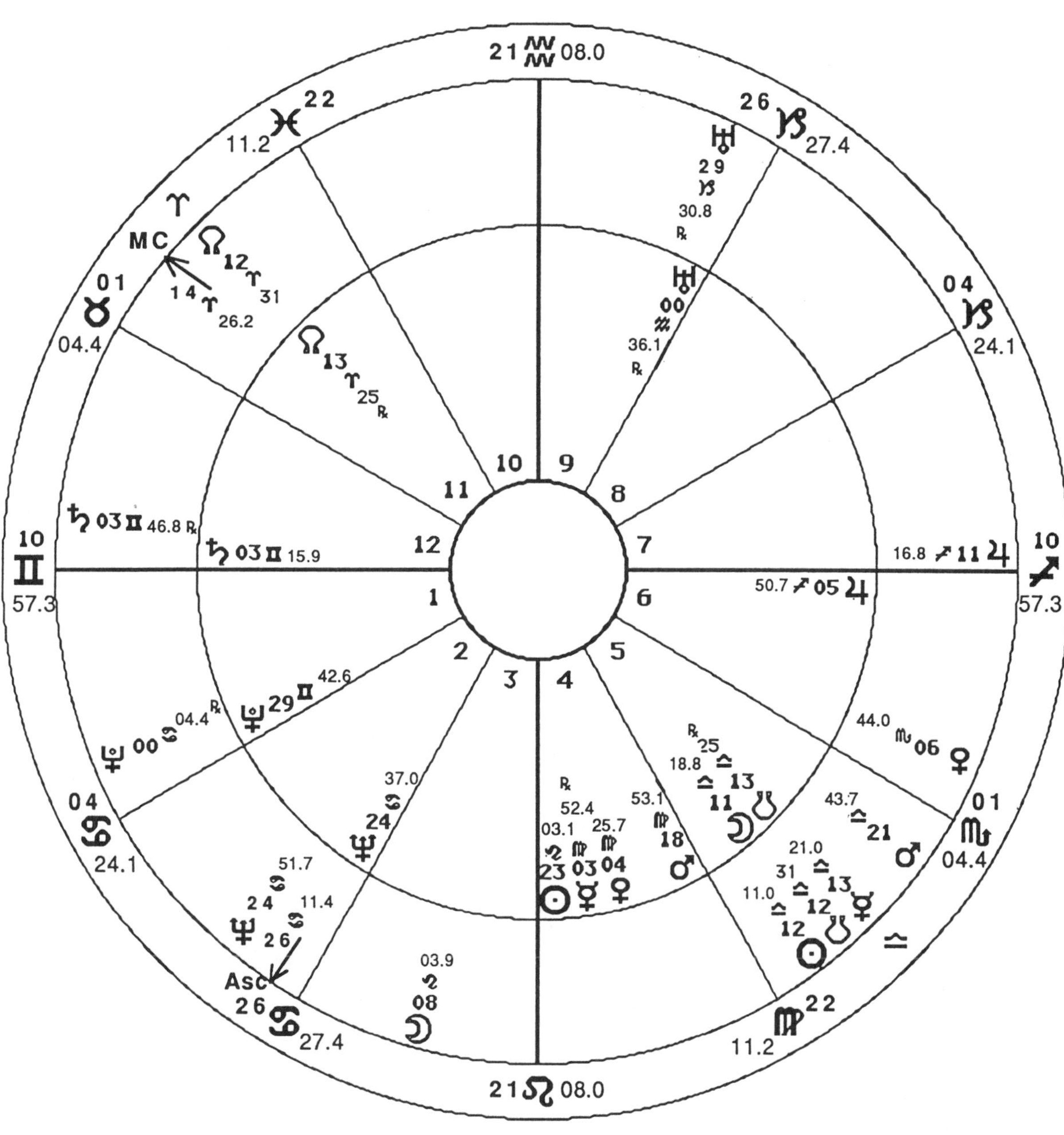

Figure 10. Horoscope of the *French Chef* hostess, Julia Child. Progressions are to the date of her debut on this show.

Table VIII. Natal and Progressed Declinations of Julia Child

Planet	Natal Decln.	03 11 1963 Debut
☽	04 S 17.7	22 N 51.3
♂	05 N 11.1	08 S 05.2
☿	05 N 40.7	04 S 17.7
♀	11 N 14.3	13 S 39.4
☉	13 N 50.5	04 S 49.1
MC	14 S 27.8	05 N 41.7
♇	17 N 22.7	17 N 18.6
♄	18 N 49.5	18 N 47.2
♅	20 S 37.4	20 S 50.5
♆	20 N 42.7	20 N 29.1
♃	20 S 45.6	21 S 45.4
Asc	22 N 06.0	20 N 55.5

For a male example of Gemini rising why not another comedian? After all comedy is one forte of Gemini, although not the only gainful occupation. One easy place to start is among the published horoscopes that show Cancer rising. We look for a tall person with elongated rectangular head. Of course, that is not the average physical characteristic of Cancer rising. Those statements apply to the sign preceding. Also, Cancer is rarely into comedy except to privately retell a joke, while we already know that Gemini is. This process does not take long. *Voila*, Jerry Lewis fits this picture as though made to order. His published horoscope is for fifteen minutes after noon on March 16, 1926. The validated Gemini rising horoscope is given in Figure 11 and Table IX. Need anything more be said about using his mouth for humor. He was a slapstick comedian in a similar manner to Lucille Ball. Although one is male and the other female, their physical and mental attributes are alike and should be easily recognizable. The similarities are striking. Thus, we apply our criteria again.

I. The first important question is, could this be the horoscope of a comedian? One fact is that the fifth and eleventh houses are not intercepted as with others in this line of work. However, both Mercury, the ruler of the Ascendant, and the Moon are in the eleventh house. That contributes a great deal of strength. Both planets are themselves strongly aspected, which increases

MAR 16 1926	10:41 AM EST
NEWARK	N. J.
40 N 42 10	074 W 10 21
10 AM 43 44 TLT	3:40:26 GMT PM

Tropical *Placidus* *True Node*

Naibod Secondary
JUL 25 1946

3:40:26 GMT PM

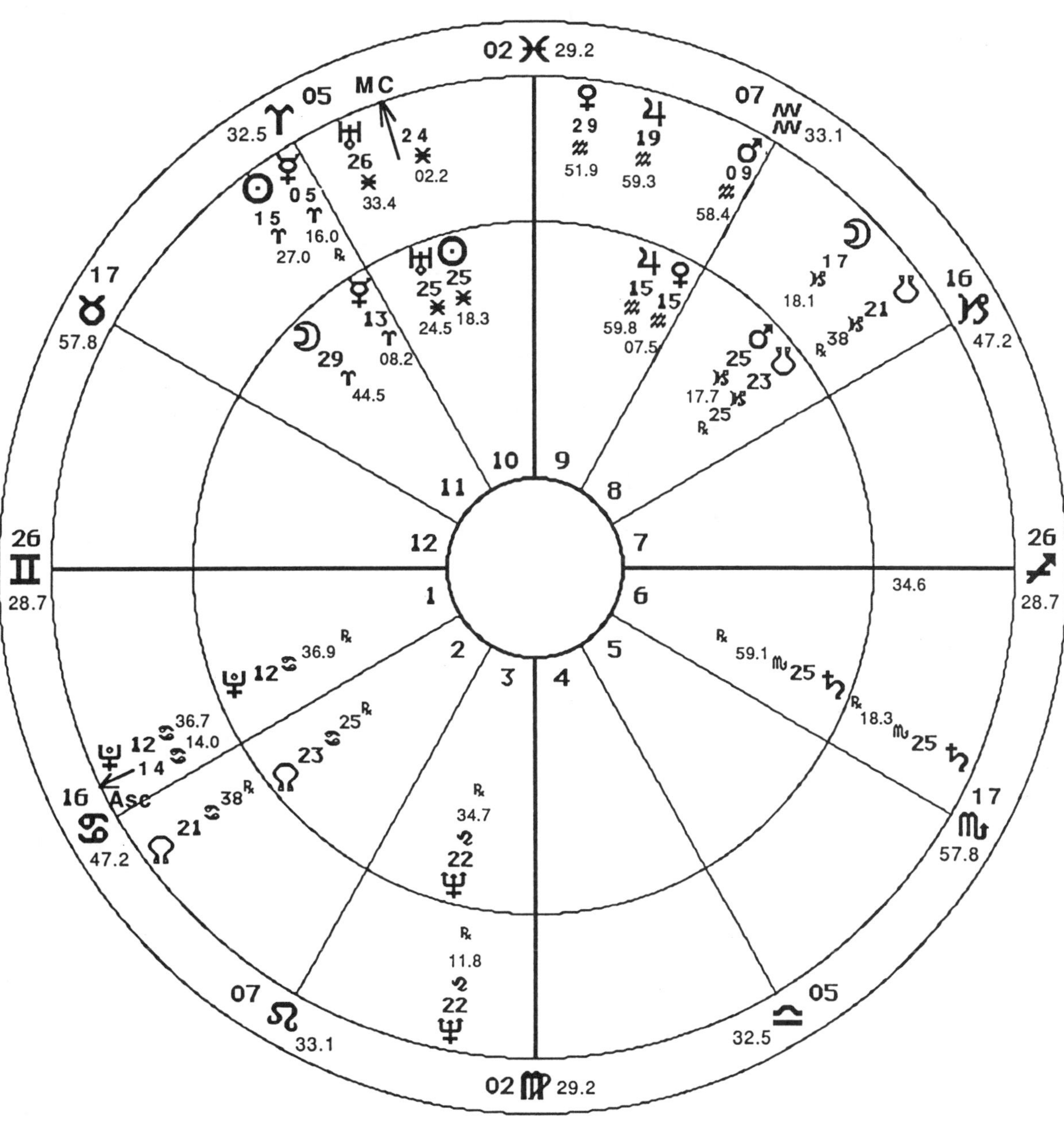

Figure 11. Horoscope of the comedian Jerry Lewis. Progressions are to the date of his first performance with Dean Martin. The show became extremely popular.

the energy in this house. The eleventh house is where pleasure is given to other people. So, the answer is, yes it could. Moreover, this sector is even stronger than at first meets the eye, as will be shown by a review of aspects in the next section.

One would hesitate to provide an affirmative answer for the Cancer rising horoscope. Reticent Cancer is not known for spontaneity with words unless more active planets are present. Being at 17 Cancer, you can visualize the physical birth time chart by a one house rotation. Call the second house cusp the Ascendant and find the Midheaven two degrees after Uranus. That looks more like the horoscope of a short statured technologist or a person perceived to have revolutionary ideas.

Table IX. Natal and Progressed Declinations of Jerry Lewis

Planet	Natal Decln.	07 25 1946 1st Perf.
☉	01 S 52.0	06 N 05.1
♅	02 S 29.2	02 S 01.9
☽	06 N 40.1	21 S 57.9
☿	07 N 34.4	03 N 32.5
MC	10 S 35.6	02 S 22.2
♀	11 S 44.1	09 S 50.9
♆	14 N 22.3	14 N 29.8
♃	16 S 34.8	15 S 24.3
♄	17 S 00.2	16 S 47.5
♇	21 N 10.7	21 N 12.7
♂	21 S 53.5	18 S 52.6
Asc	23 N 24.1	22 N 41.3

II. Physically, Jerry Lewis is six feet tall. That is perfect for a Gemini Ascendant with the underlying Sun in Pisces. Between the two horoscopes it appears that every planet is rotated by one house. We can concentrate on certain known factors. For example, Jerry Lewis has had a long lasting marriage blessed with six children. With Libra on the cusp of the fifth house, its ruler, Venus, is conjunct the prolific Jupiter in the fixed sign Aquarius. That fits. Jupiter is also a co-ruler of the seventh house of marriage. If Saturn were in the fifth house restraint in having children and a holding back, or a sage quality with respect to creative developments would be expected. Mars in the seventh square the Moon would precipitate emotional arguments with his mate and other associates. That is not known to be an accurate generalization with respect to his wife. It is true that Jerry Lewis and Dean Martin eventually separated as a working team. But the T-square of Saturn with Neptune, Jupiter and Venus, plus the inconjunct of Saturn with the Moon, can readily account for that event. Yet, the Mars-Moon irritation remains. This pattern affects the income of others and his projected image. He was the fall guy over material things, both on stage and off.

A very powerful combination exists in Jerry Lewis's horoscope. This is the close mutual reception of Mars and Saturn. Mars in Capricorn, the ruler of Scorpio, is sextile Saturn in Scorpio, the ruler of Capricorn. These two planets are in each other's signs, and Mars is exalted. They affect the sixth and eighth houses in a highly favorable manner. Also, Mars is co-ruler of an entertainer's important eleventh house. Thus, Jerry's work in show business has always contributed income to his partners. The Sun-Uranus conjunction bolsters this situation. Also, Mars and Saturn are inconjunct the Ascendant, forming an arrow that goes straight toward his very being. These are fortunate alignments.

Jerry often played the part of the naughty brat. Mercury is square Pluto and sextile the Venus-Jupiter pair. All kinds of things were made fun of, and again that combination worked. Children are said to have been tickled with his performances, and Jerry said it was because he got away with things they were punished for. In the Cancer rising chart this kind of mischief would have resulted in a more serious impairment of professional reputation. All the known personality traits and career activities correspond to the Gemini rising horoscope. The placements of planets in the Cancer rising chart are questionable.

III. The next step is to check the closeness and meaning of progressed aspects. An obvious choice is the date of Jerry Lewis first going on stage with Dean Martin, although that was an impromptu get together. Both discarded their prepared scripts and adlibbed. The performance that evening of July 25, 1946, was a resounding success. However, the formal formation of the team was yet to come. Thus, we might expect to see some indications of their spontaneous program plus more powerful aspects approaching. And that is exactly what we find. Slow moving Saturn has come to within 0.6 minutes of a perfect sextile with Jerry's all important action planet, Mars. The spontaneous progressed Uranus is square the Ascendant within 4.7 minutes, which alludes to the physical strain. But what is most intriguing is the progressed Midheaven approaching the parallel of Uranus. It is 7.0 minutes away on the date of their first performance when ovations caused the potential to be recognized. Within a little over a month this aspect would be exact. And thus the team was formed that brought joy to many people over many years. The progressions did their jobs with respect to the event. Other progressions for different events did likewise, and all met the less than 4.0 minute criterion.

CHAPTER 4. CANCER

Physical Attributes

The term small ovate has been used to describe the head size and shape of Cancer on the Ascendant, although some might call the face moonlike or round. Much depends upon the weight or fullness of the body. That in turn depends upon the underlying Sun sign and positions of planets with respect to the rising degree. What is most noticeable is for the top of the head to be narrower than at the temples. The size of the head is usually small to average, but this can be modified as well by other elements. In some cases the head is actually large. It is possible that because the Moon, who rules Cancer, is the largest reflector of the Sun's light to an observer on earth, the effects of the sign the Sun is in are more pronounced than for the other rising signs. At any rate the variations in body height and head size are noticeable. Characteristics given in this paragraph are typical. However, if the Sun is in Gemini or Sagittarius, the person will probably be tall or taller. If in Taurus or Scorpio, the one with Cancer on the Ascendant will be of average height, and so on. The hands and feet are normally medium in size. Some people with a Cancer Ascendant have been observed to have comparatively short legs versus the proportions of the body. Others are simply well proportioned. A heavy Cancer may walk with a crab-like gait, but that is not a noticeable trait if the person is light in weight or slender. The mouth tends to be wide, rather than narrow. The lips are sensitive as opposed to thin and tight. This is a feeling, sympathetic, prudent type of person, and these characteristics are conveyed by the appearance.

Even though more variations may occur than average, Cancer on the Ascendant is still easy to differentiate versus the signs on either side. The greater difficulty is two signs back with Taurus, because of several similarities in physical appearance. Fortunately, a tall sign intervenes. Cancer does not have the elongated head of Gemini or the rectangular head of Leo. It is rounder and has that narrowness of breadth at the top. Cancer does not have the long fingers of Gemini or the extra size of the chest cavity found with Leo. However, if the Sun is in either Gemini or Leo the differences may be less noticeable. Those placements still do not change the basic Cancer characteristics or eliminate them. Cancer rising will usually provide a quieter demeanor than the surrounding signs, and less of a likelihood to dominate conversations. They do enjoy talking one on one, but it is not necessary for them to be more than a participant in the conversations. These outer appearances, combined with the mental ones, contribute to the necessary confirmations.

Mental Attributes

Cancer is a cardinal sign desirous of control and authority, but also naturally reticent, often meek and very sensitive. Individuals with this sign on the Ascendant normally prefer to avoid confrontations whenever possible. This causes them to exert influences behind the scenes more often than not. They can reverse or change positions easily. The emotions are typically strong. In fact the emotional nature is often stronger than the physical. This leads to receptiveness and close relationships, but not always the strongest constitutions. The attachment to the family is most evident. The family comes first, and tight bonds with their own children are uppermost. A Cancer woman can be adamant in protecting her children. In fact the symbol of Cancer is the breasts of a woman. Hence, this is a feminine sign, often shy and retiring. In the female sex, those with Cancer rising are usually loving matriarchs who prefer small family gatherings to large crowds. The family meal together is a major enjoyment. In either sex one or two guests would usually be the preferred option over going to a large party with many strangers. At work their team comes first.

Cancer rising is ordinarily modest. However, there is a strong feeling of selfhood that looms beneath the surface. Even when timidity shows they are not easily persuaded to accept another person's opinions. They like to be needed by other family members, and at times they can be conspicuous by their absence. In the less developed types, irritability and backwardness may appear over small upsets. Sentimentality may be overdone. What seems to be a lack of courage can also be observed, especially when the retreat is silent. With higher education and a more dominant position in life, the Cancer rising person can overcome fears of speaking before large audiences and develop a capability to impart their thoughts with considerable feeling. They then become masters of their own moods. When in the teaching profession, for which they are well suited, a closeness with some students generally transpires and they are popular. It is possible for them to impart the fruits of personal experiences and to convey feelings of joy, sorrow, compassion or despair. As the situation arises, they love to capture the interest of others, to stimulate imaginations and to sway opinions. Yet they are typically conservative, discreet, diplomatic and conventional. The self-assertiveness is tempered with caution that never, or rarely, allows an act that would draw ridicule.

The memory is retentive and history is often a poignant and likable subject. Cancer also loves to recall childhood scenes. Pleasurable events may be vividly remembered and spoken about on numerous occasions. By the same token, injustices rankle for long periods of time. The Moon always likes popularity, and occasions with that ingredient are also good remembrances. Friendships are usually longlasting and accompanied by warmth and affection. Relatives are close and the attachment to the home and parents is rarely inharmonious, unless stressful aspects clearly show the contrary. Even then the emotional ties are strong. The main past experiences are not simple statistics. They are felt in the heart.

Thus, the differences between people with Cancer rising versus those with nearby signs are sharply contrasted. Gemini rising is the talkative, mental one who babbles on. Deep emotionalism is not an ordinary trait with them. Further back, Taurus is compatible with Cancer on the emotional and conservative side, but the main differences are with respect to the way plans are adhered to and the manner in which life's foibles are handled. Leo is far more forward in actions, authoritative or regal in attitudes, and possessive of a more rectangular face with chunkier body.

In putting these guidelines to use it is difficult to imagine how Merv Griffin, Arnold Schwarzeneger or Richard Burton among men would have Cancer on their Ascendants. If you don't think so either you are right, although horoscopes for physical birthtimes show otherwise. It is also highly unlikely that Cher, Farrah Fawcett or Judy Garland have Cancer rising for the same reasons. If you believe several of these famous people have physical characteristics and personalities that are similar, you are right again—but it is not due to Cancer. Consider how their appearances do correspond with previously described signs. All indicate earlier than reported birthtimes.

Example Horoscopes

It is fitting that the first example horoscope is of a foreign actress who had this to say about the film industry in the United States, "Hollywood is fun, but I'm a little afraid of it, and a bit ashamed sometimes of the way important work in the world is downgraded. I didn't say no to the money or roses or the cars, but I do try to remember that the work is what is important. The roles you play. The work is what you went on the stage in the first place for." Those were the words of Liv Ullman when being interviewed by Tom Donally, of the Washington Post in 1973. Did you get the feeling that what she said was expressed in the manner of Cancer rising? The trait of being withdrawn was embodied in the first sentence. Yet here was an actress speaking, who had completed four award winning performances in a row. That was a feat unequaled at the time.

Liv Ullman was the protege of the great film director, Ingmar Bergman, and that doubtless had something to do with her success. The four superb performances were in *The Hour of the Wolf, Shame, The Emigrants* and *Cries and Whispers*. She said, "Every time Ingmar Bergman talked to me I blushed and panicked." Such a confession would be true of Cancer rising more than any other sign. She later spoke about being overwhelmed, because after an introduction to him in the streets of Stockholm by a girl friend he wrote a letter. An invitation was enclosed for her, a Norwegian, to come to the island of Farö where he offered her a starring role in the film he was producing there. You need to be in Scandinavia for a while to understand the complexities of Swedish-Norwegian relationships and the significance of why her nationality was even brought up. But to say that she was shy and timid is an understatement. She also showed her Cancer rising traits when sent to Hollywood for the first time in 1971, on an errand to accept an honorary award for Ingmar Bergman. It was a matter of observable trepidation.

Liv Ullman's horoscope is shown in Figure 12 and Table X. These two illustrations portray the longitudes of her planets in the houses and the declination respectively. It is interesting that she was born in Tokyo, Japan, while her family was there. Her father was an engineer and the family had exited North Europe during the time of the Nazi invasion. They eventually travelled from Japan to Canada, where Liv spent most of her girlhood. Her father lost his life in Canada by walking into an aircraft propeller. Mother and two daughters did not return to Norway until after most of the Germans left.

Many events were checked to provide assurance that this indeed was the correct natal horoscope. The one chosen for illustration purposes was calendarized in her biography as a month and year without a day. That was the biographer's style in discussing most of her noteworthy experiences. Such biographical styles drive those interested in astrology up the proverbial wall. However, this one is interesting in that it portrays an initial failure. Cancer does not necessarily give up because of an obstacle, but would not continue on the same track. She had wanted to attend the Oslo National Theatre School. On this first attempt she was rejected. Thus, a day late in July was selected for this happening, because it is known that she applied early in that month. The fact that she changed directions for the time being, by asking her mother to send her to an acting school in London, is typical of Cancer behavior.

It might interest readers to know that in searching for Cancer rising natives to illustrate this chapter, all with Leo rising published charts were reviewed first. That approach causes the probabilities to be so much higher. Thus, our three verification criteria will be applied to one of those mythical, quiet little lions that doesn't roar—and for that matter, doesn't exist.

I. Our overview question is, could this Cancer rising horoscope be correct for an actress with the accomplishments of a Liv Ullman, even if they were extracted by a superb artist? Well, well. The highly repetitive and creative fifth/eleventh house interception appears again for a person in show business. Then look at the closeness in declination of Pluto and Sun with respect to her Ascendant. This is one Cancer rising lady who has a considerable amount of depth and resourcefulness, characteristics that Ingmar Bergman doubtless understood when he met her. Of course, perceptions of ability were in addition to her attractiveness. Yes, this could be the horoscope of a very good actress when properly directed by Jupiter trining her Moon. The embodiment of Jupiter, ruling the sign on her Midheaven, was Ingmar Bergman. He harmonizes with the Moon, ruling the sign on her Ascendant that represents herself.

Liv Ullman is 5 feet 7 inches tall. She is slender, has blue eyes, reddish-blonde hair and freckles. Probably 5 inches of her height can be attributed to Sun in Sagittarius. When looking for clues of a Cancer Ascendant, long hair in women often makes it difficult to see the narrowing at the top of the scull. However, it is there. The broader face and body, wider shoulders and deeper chest cavity of a Leo rising person are not present.

DEC 16 1938 | 07:20 PM JAT | Naibod Secondary
TOKYO | JAPAN | JUL 31 1956
35 N 42 58 | 139 E 42 57 | 08:29:48 AM GMT
05: 48:40 TLT | 08:29:48 AM GMT

Tropical *Placidus* *True Node*

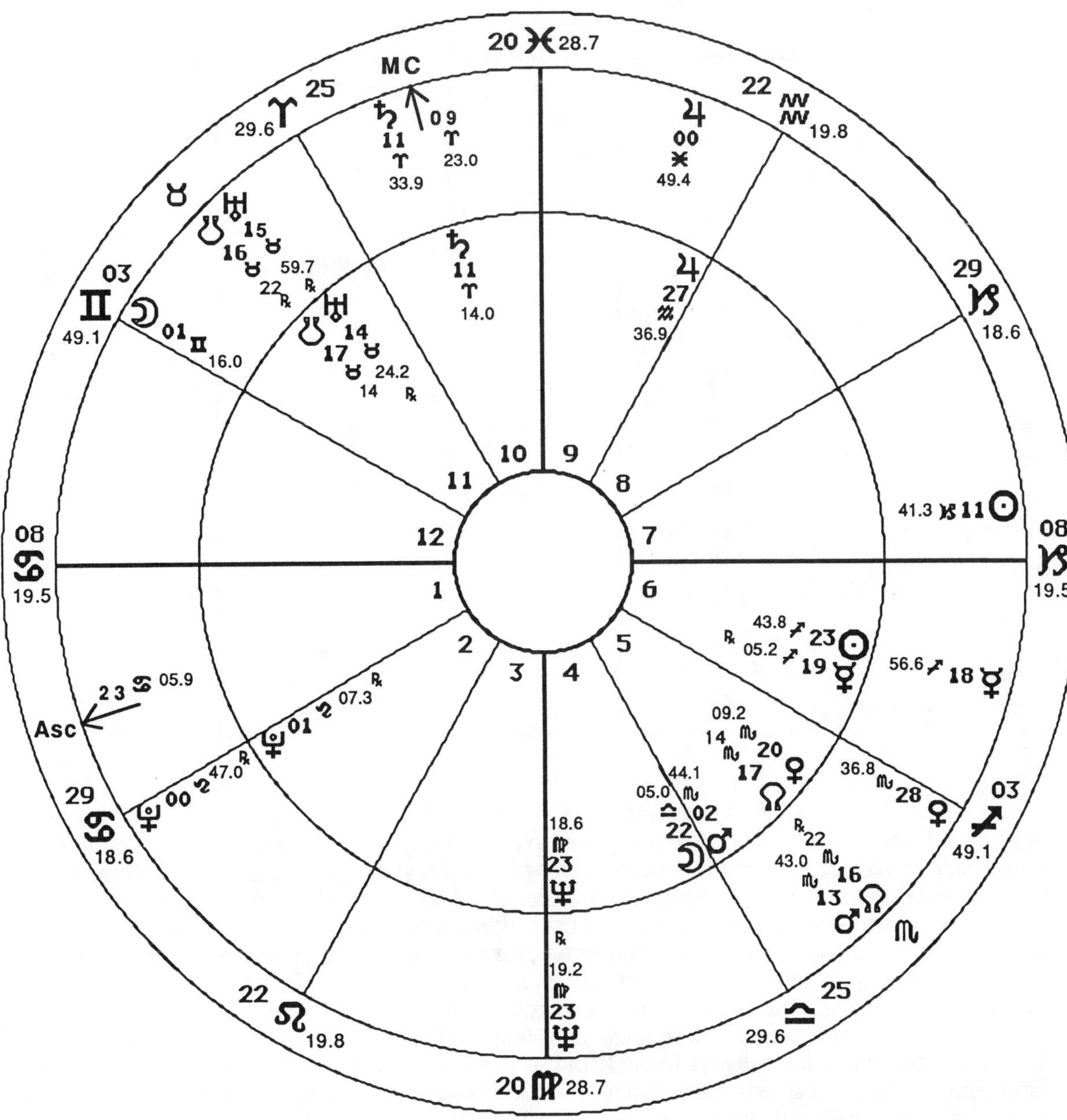

Figure 12. Horoscope of the first actress to have four award winning performances in a row, Liv Ullman. Progressions are included for the date of her initial attempt to enter Oslo's National Theatre School.

Table X. Natal and Progressed Declinations of Liv Ullman

Planet	Natal Decln.	07 31 1956 Competition
♄	02 N 05.0	02 N 17.0
♆	03 N 42.8	03 N 43.3
MC	03 S 46.5	03 N 43.2
☽	10 S 40.2	19 N 08.0
♂	11 S 28.0	15 S 04.6
♃	13 S 16.5	12 S 07.6
♀	15 S 08.2	15 S 50.3
♅	15 N 48.5	15 N 41.7
☿	20 S 41.9	21 S 05.3
Asc	23 N 11.1	21 N 28.1
♇	23 N 11.6	23 N 18.0
☉	23 S 17.8	22 S 55.9

II. Pluto is on the Ascendant by declination. Hence, a comparison with the previously published 1 Leo Ascendant horoscope equates to the same type of influence. Pluto is conjunct the Ascendant in that chart. Only Leo simply does not fit the young, outwardly timid woman whose talents were drawn from her. With Leo the greater necessity would be for a director to guide or channel her energies with reins pulling back or to either side, but not pulling forward.

In the Cancer rising horoscope Pluto has moved to the second house, where it provides a faculty for earning money. Neptune has moved from the third to the fourth. It is very interesting to recall a remark made by Liv Ullman that she often romanticized about her father after his death and even composed letters to him in heaven. Neptune in the fourth house would easily do that. The concentration of four planets in the fifth house focus across the way upon Uranus, and those interceptions result in an enormous amount of creative energy. The life work in cinema and on stage are conveyed by these powerful alignments. In the Leo rising chart, only the Sun and Mercury are in the fifth, with no planets in the eleventh. The strength to fascinate other people while acting is not as strong. Sun and Mercury in the sixth, on the other hand, confirms her own attitude about hard work. Mercury is further in agreement with the type of work she was engaged in. Jupiter in the ninth increases prospects for travel, which unquestionably occurred. Saturn there would constrict such activities. But Saturn in the tenth brings fame slowly. It did take a while. Even her eventual acceptance at Oslo's National Theatre School was not immediately forthcoming. Her eleventh house dreams of acting were fulfilled, however, by the sudden (Uranian) chance meeting in Stockholm. All of these placements seem to fall into place.

III. Our day of the month is uncertain for the first application to Oslo's theatrical school. It might be in error by one or two weeks. However, it is necessary to proceed with our best guess. The biography simply recorded that Liv Ullman applied in July of 1956. The 31st of the month was used for the progression on the basis that it might correspond more closely with the time of being turned down. It proved to be more than satisfactory. Her progressed Midheaven was parallel progressed Neptune within 1.1 minutes. The progressed Midheaven would have shifted by only a few tenths of a minute during the month. That is very good in terms of accuracy and no other aspect would show the nature of the event as well. Neptune is theatre. Her reputation was on the line. It was thwarted by her Midheaven coming shortly into a contraparallel with its own natal position. Thus the personal disappointment. If an astrologer ignored the declinations it is relatively easy to see how an explanation might be contrived based solely upon longitudes. An inconjunct of progressed Sun and Saturn occurred near the first of the month. A much wider opposition of progressed Mars to Uranus is present, but four or more years must elapse before it is exact. The Sun and Saturn definitely relate to the third and ninth houses where schools are found. The inconjunct would be labeled an opportunity, which it was. However, the progressed Sun-Saturn aspect, together with the declinations, paint a much more complete picture. Considering our progressed date is only defined within thirty-one days, these aspects meet our test conditions during that period. Furthermore, the sequence of aspects suggests that the original turndown was probably preconceived.

A male example of Cancer rising is Neil Simon. He is a double Cancer, meaning that his Sun and Ascendant are both in that sign. Thus, his physical appearance and personality reflect Cancer without strong modifications from a different Sun sign. In fact the main additional influences, although not close enough to change his appearance, come from Pluto and the Sun being close to his Ascendant. Pluto causes him to be more energetic, resourceful and magnetic than would be the case without this placement. Sun increases self-esteem. Yet his photograph shows almost pure Cancer. The head is ovate with a pronounced narrowing at the top. He works at his typewriter. This is not on stage directly, but behind the scenes. His influence on theatre has been great.

If it were possible to have Neil Simon and Liv Ullman in the same room together, one could instantly see the similarities. He is only slightly taller than she is. Their facial features are nearly identical in an astrological sense. Of course their origins are different. One is male, the other female. Their professions are not the same, although related. Yet their similarities would be visible for all to see.

Neil Simon has been a prolific playwright. His writing career began when he was in the Army Air Force assigned to Lowry Field, Colorado. He became sports editor of the base newspaper. This eventually led to writing comedy for television. By 1959 he was already at the level of an Emmy award nomination from the Academy of Television Arts and Sciences. In the meantime he started to write plays. *Catch a Star* had twenty-three performances. This was followed by such major successes as *Come Blow Your Horn* with six hundred seventy-seven performances and *Little Me* at the Lunt Fontanne Theater with two hundred twenty-three performances. Then came *Barefoot in the Park*, which first opened at the Biltmore Theater on October 23, 1963. It had one thousand five hundred and thirty two performances. *The Odd Couple* played for two years at the Eugene O'Neil Theater. It was followed by *Star Spangled Girl*, and his outpourings continued. Many of his plays are being revived and performed in little theaters across the country.

It must be confessed that no previously published reference horoscope was found for Neil Simon and no birth time was available. His appearance is simply that of Cancer. This narrowed the choices down to those early morning hours on July 4, 1927, when Cancer was in the East. The band of an astrological sign on the Ascendant is about two hours wide. The task was to find the one time that could provide a verifiable natal horoscope. Since no comparisons can be made with a horoscope for an unknown physical birth time, the validation must proceed as though one were there. You can judge for yourself how good the appropriateness of this horoscope is.

I. The playwright profession of Neil Simon must be reflected in his horoscope. The one for 04:48:37 AM true local time does. It is illustrated in Figure 13 and Table XI. Mercury is in the first house and Mercury is the planet of writing. It is strongly bound in a grand trine with Saturn, Jupiter and Uranus. The latter two planets are just past his Midheaven, where what he is in life can be viewed by the world. The fifth and eleventh houses are intercepted and he has been known to write funny lines. Those are the houses of creativity, comedy and playwrights. There is no question about his impact upon the stage and television.

II. The planets will be reviewed for their placements and fit. First, let us look at the most powerful aspect in declination. That is Venus parallel Neptune within 2.2 minutes. Here is art and drama together. Those are the basic elements required for involvement with plays, theater and television. Since in longitude those two planets are in the second house they of course represent his principal source of income. Mars is there too, which provides even more energy and some strife. Neil Simon is known to have acquired above average wealth in life. He does own the Eugene O'Neill Theater, and that property fits the nature of Venus and Neptune. Venus is both parallel and conjunct Neptune, causing the relationship to be doubly strong.

Table XI. Natal and Progressed Declinations of Neil Simon

Planet	Natal Decln.	07 15 1943 ARMY
♃	00 S 03.3	00 N 07.2
♅	00 N 40.1	00 N 38.7
MC	02 S 39.4	04 N 09.8
☽	11 N 35.3	00 S 17.3
♀	13 N 33.6	06 N 56.8
♆	13 N 35.8	13 N 25.8
♂	16 N 54.0	13 N 35.4
☿	17 N 42.0	16 N 05.7
♄	18 S 35.1	18 S 31.2
Asc	22 N 44.4	20 N 49.8
☉	22 N 57.5	20 N 49.4
♇	21 N 24.4	21 N 22.5

JUL 04 1927 | 4:45 AM EST
BRONX | NEW YORK
40 N 48 58 | 073 W 51 54
4:48:37 AM TLT | 9:44:04 AM GMT
Tropical *Placidus* *True Node*

Naibod Secondary
JUL 15 1943
9:44:04 AM GMT

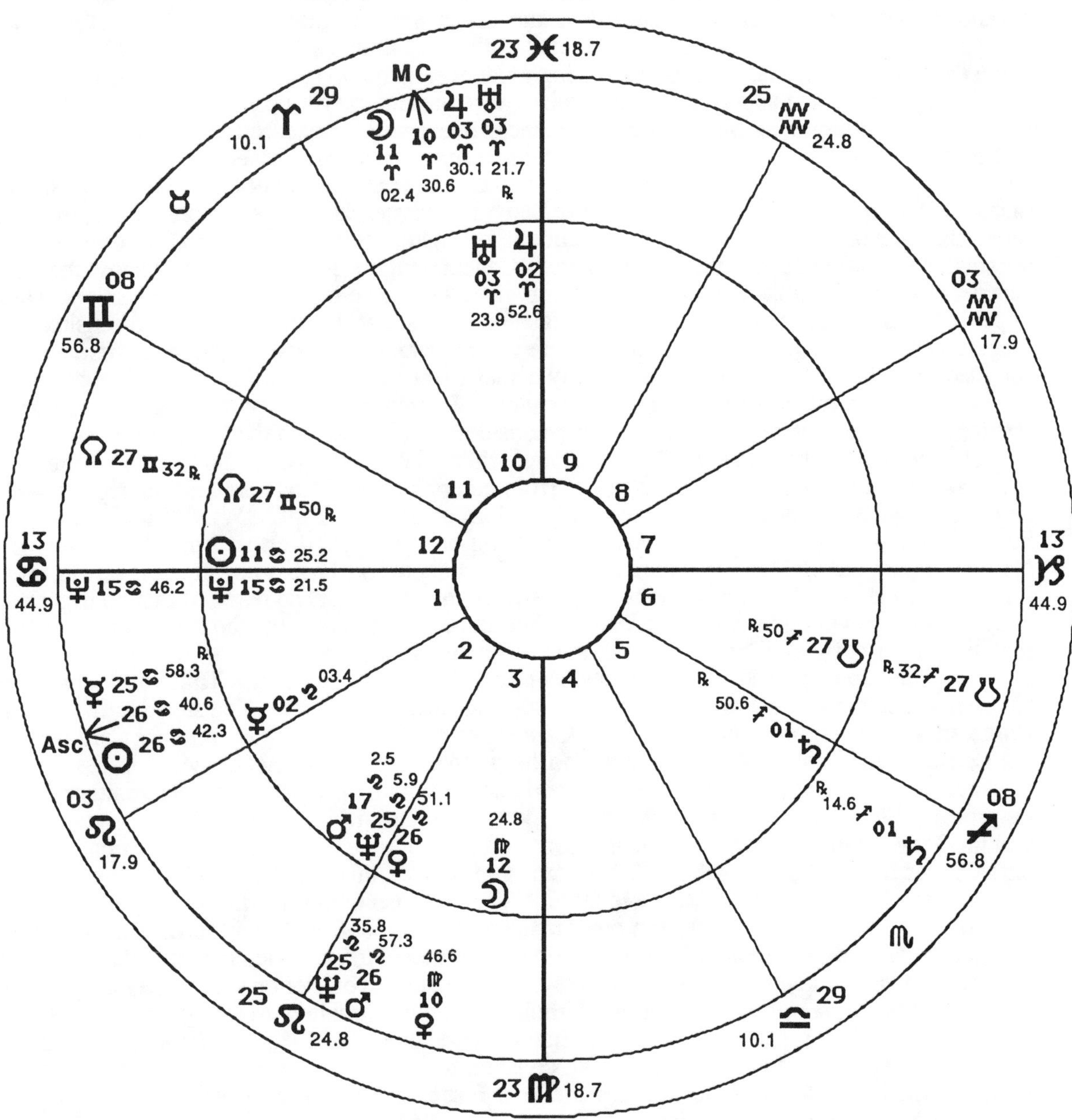

Figure 13. Horoscope of Neil Simon, the prolific playwright. His progressions are for the date he entered the U. S. Army Reserves.

III. Neil Simon has written so many plays that an opening for any one of them is almost routine. Accordingly, they can hardly be judged major events for this man. To someone else, the first day of a play might be a momentous event. To Neil it is another day. Therefore, a little searching had to be undertaken in order to find an event of big enough impact to be significant for illustrative purposes. While his biography only gave the month of July and the year of 1943 for his entrance into the U. S. Army Reserve, a mid-month day was selected for the progression. To anyone joining a service, a relocation is expected. That is exactly what his progression shows, a parallel between his progressed Ascendant and his progressed Sun within 0.4 minutes, a progressed conjunction of the same two elements within 1.7 minutes and progressed Mars parallel Venus within 1.6 minutes. That is convincing evidence. Other events were progressed (to necessarily fuzzy dates), and appropriate progressions were present in every case.

If anything, Neil Simon is classic Cancer rising with respect to his physical appearance and personality traits. However, it is important to show variations, especially a very important person with Cancer rising who has a large ovate head instead of a small one. The next example matches that objective nicely. An underlying Leo Sun enlarges the bone structure. Also, by virtue of strong planetary placements on his Ascendant, one can observe extra height and other characteristics that would not be directly attributed to Cancer. Figure 14 and Table XII show the horoscope of General Norman Schwarzkopf, a large man with large face, but nevertheless one whose upper head narrows in typical Cancer rising fashion. He shows the compassion and sensitivity of that sign irrespective of his occupation. There is no question that, his army, comes first, and one can place a high confidence bet that his family comes first too.

I. Mars must be prominent for a general. Prominence can occur in a number of ways. Extra power is present when the planet under consideration is placed in the first, fourth, seventh or tenth house, when aspecting the Sun or Moon, when ruler of the Ascendant, ruler of the Midheaven or when having many aspects to and from other planets. Being in a cardinal sign provides an extra push. So what do we find for General Norman Schwarzkopf? Why Mars is in his first house in a cardinal sign. It is opposite the Moon and semi-sextile the Sun. Moreover, it is conjunct Pluto, parallel his Ascendant and trine his Midheaven. That is power. It is power fitting for a military leader. The fourth and tenth houses are intercepted. The result of that configuration is even more power and the urge to lead. What is observed is not just the horoscope of a high ranking military officer. This is, after all, the horoscope of a general.

How appropriate it is that he has been called Stormin' Norman. That hot poker, Mars, has been dipped into the water of Cancer. Sizzle and steam gush forth. The storm brews. So he isn't a small, reticent man like others with Cancer rising. He is larger and more forward because his Leo Sun established a big skeleton and helps to overcome shyness. Mars is parallel his Ascendant, and that adds masculinity to the body and action to his disposition. Hereditary factors have probably contributed to his larger size. Even the square from Jupiter to the Ascendant, Mars and the Moon (who rules the Ascendant) can increase body size. Thus, the modifications of a pure Cancer rising sign are explainable. But most important, this horoscope belongs to a general.

II. Pluto is conjunct Mars and leonine Venus is also in the first house. Pluto especially, sets Norman Schwarzkopf apart from other officers. When confronted with problems this planet shows a tremendous capability to derive solutions, to plan and to use efficient techniques. Venus in this location is very good for show and display. He became the officer on stage. Mercury and the Sun indicate a degree of wealth, but not without encountering delays from the opposing Saturn. Neptune in the third house suggests somewhat idealistic and dreamlike experiences in youth and early schooling. However, being in Virgo, constant reminders call attention to essential details. Jupiter in the fourth house is the handle planet of a T-square. It focuses a considerable amount of energy into what the self represents. This Jupiter resulted in an expansive and relatively joyful home life. Resources based upon sound principles from the Saturn trine were available when necessary. Moon in the seventh causes certain effusive relationships with other people. Uranus in the tenth house provides a reputation for being technically advanced, and promotions have come as suddenly as might be expected when in the solid, earthy sign Taurus. The dominant parallels are among Mars, the Ascendant and Pluto. The career is military. Mars causes a proneness to accidents when so placed, but the call to arms in this case is unmistakable.

III. Many progressions were used to verify that this horoscope was correct. Verification was obtained before a birth time was known. Only later did Beth Koch, Data Exchange Committee Chairman of the American Federation of Astrologers, obtain a 4:45 EDST report of physical birth time. That is equivalent to 3:45 standard time and not far from the one selected for the natal horoscope illustrated. The later time would have thrown Mars into the twelfth house where it would be weaker and result in a highly unlikely military career. Bookkeeping might have been more appropriate for a fictitious person with such a natal horoscope.

Table XII. Natal and Progressed Declinations of Gen. Norman Schwarzkopf

Planet	Natal Decln.	05 28 1970 Injury
MC	01 S 01.8	13 N 15.1'
♃	06 S 51.0	09 S 26.2'
♆	08 N 02.0	07 N 32.3'
♅	11 N 25.7	11 N 06.8'
☉	12 N 00.4	01 S 17.4'
♄	14 S 43.9	15 S 30.2'
☿	15 N 02.3	11 S 04.7'
♀	19 N 18.6	05 N 23.6'
♂	22 N 04.4	16 N 51.2'
Asc	22 N 25.7	16 N 25.2'
♇	22 N 35.1	22 N 31.0'
☽	23 N 04.3	23 N 21.9'

Perhaps, because the last thought of the preceding section was about the possibility of injury, that type of event was selected to illustrate one of the many progressions that have met the accuracy criteria. It might not be as positive an event as the commencement of the offensive against Iraq to free Kuwait (where progressed Mars was trine the progressed Uranus within 0.2 minutes), but in one sense it is more personal. Receiving a wound, whether minor or not, is a first hourse affair. Both Mars and Pluto qualify as planets related to wounds. Thus, on May 28,

AUG 22 1934 04:30 AM EST
TRENTON NEW JERSEY
40 N 12 47 074 W 44 58
01:43:17 AM TLT 06:48:17 GMT
Tropical *Placidus* *True Node*

Naibod Secondary
MAY 28 1970
06:48:17 GMT

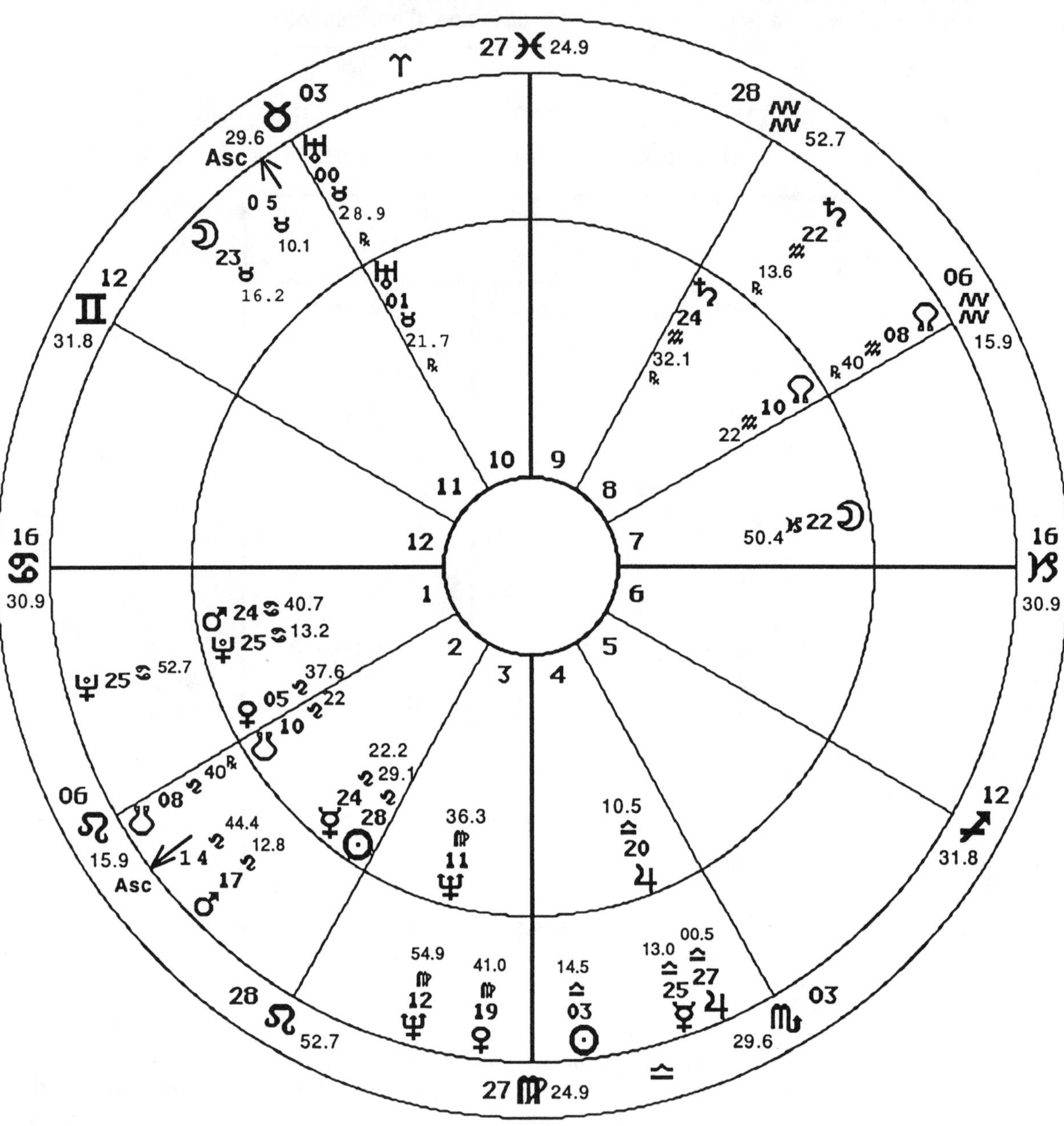

Figure 14. Horoscope of former General Norman Schwarzkopf. His progressions for a mild injury in battle are also given.

1970, Normal Schwarzkopf did receive a minor injury. Progessed Mercury square the first house Pluto within 0.2 minutes fits this scene perfectly. Mercury relates to the helicopter. First house Pluto relates to the individual's body. Incidentally, progressedd Mercury was also contraparallel Uranus progressed within 2.1 minutes. Most events of significance have more than one aspect meeting the accuracy requirements. They usually add information. Life has many turns and twists, and these supporting aspects add finer detail.

Three well-known Cancer rising people have been presented. Two are highly typical. One was an example of how the basic sign characteristics can be modified. It is worth repeating that the Ascendant comes first in establishing the physical appearance. The all important Sun is second. The underbody, or chassis, is Sun sign related. Planets aspecting the Ascendant are third. Those planets within less than one degree of a conjunction or parallel have the strongest impact. When all of these elements are present, the task of selection may or may not become more complex and more difficult. Often the conclusions are more definitive once the right choice has been made. A warrior is not the number one profession of Cancer rising. However, as modified by the cited additional elements, and considering the highly important interceptions, a person such as General Norman Schwarzkopf is the kind of warm, sympathetic warrior who feels for the soldiers under his command—and especially those who lose their lives.

CHAPTER 5. LEO

Physical Characteristics

Leo has a rectangular head, usually of full size. The eyes are typically large and round. They may protrude, noticeable especially among women, or simply be large and wide spaced. The chest capacity is big in both men and women, and the shoulders are broad. The body might be termed solid or chunky, but that depends upon the weight. The waist may be narrow in youth, but as with most signs it tends to expand with age. At all ages the upper part of the figure has breadth and fullness. The bones are large, and the body is normally medium tall to tall and solid. That is to say, of all the signs, only Gemini and Sagittarius rising might be taller. The men especially, walk with long strides. The knees may be knobby. Older Leo rising natives tend to lose hair and especially among men show signs of baldness or actual baldness. The posture is usually good, and the overall body appearance might be called cheerfully imposing. Another characteristic among most people with this sign rising is to exhibit a commanding and confident presence.

On either side of Leo are signs that can be easily differentiated. Virgo's features are triangular. The region of the jaw is always narrow with Virgo, and wide with Leo. The Cancer head is typically, but not always, smaller. Even when large, the Cancer head is narrower at the top, whereas Leo's is wide. It would be extremely rare to find a Leo who did not show self confidence and determination, even when of a quiet demeanor. With Cancer one would more likely find shyness, or reticence, especially upon first meeting strangers. A public figure with Cancer rising may be more forward and open than average for this sign, but a sensitive reserve is then present that is unlike the noblesse of Leo. From time to time self-deprecation comes out in Cancer, while that characteristic has never been observed when Leo is on the Ascendant.

Mental Characteristics

Leo radiates the joy of life, especially when in congenial surroundings. Most have cheerful and sunny dispositions. They can be joyful, hospitable and generous. When Leo gives, the largess is big. Most are optimistic, not pessimistic, and outspoken. When crossed, they may be quick to anger. However, they are also quick to forgive. This is the fixed fire sign, and vitality is applied to projects undertaken. They usually see the project through. The sign of the Lion Ascending likes to be the center of attention and typically assumes authority. When this occurs, dominance of a situation is simply unquestioned. With subordinates the attitude is masterful, but sometimes condescending. Obedience and devotion are expected, if not demanded. When best efforts are not given, or when a Leo is crossed, their indignation will know no bounds. After all, the attitude is one of a noble person such underlings are dealing with, and they need to be made aware of it. When the shoe is on the other foot, Leo rising natives are the way they want their employees to be, loyal and cheerful. Noticeable traits when dealing with respected superiors are these: they will be correctly courteous, constantly trying to make a good impression and conspicuously saying only the right things to further advancement. When respect is not present, or an end to employment is in sight, they can be haughty and arrogant. In these cases the boss is a damned fool.

One generally finds a person with Leo on the Ascendant to be honorable, frank, hopeful, occasionally impulsive, fearless and strong—both physically and mentally. If deeply ill or sickly, the effect may be devastating and cause a huge reversal of strength. This is the sign ruled by the Sun, and the Sun is considered to be the spark of life. Thus, when the spark is dim, life is in the balance. When the spark is bright, life is to be cherished. The normally healthy person with Leo on the Ascendant is ardent, energetic, inspirational, lavish with philanthropy, and generally fortunate. They are usually confident, but flamboyance is not necessarily their style. Yet, this mode should not be ruled out among those with other aspects to support it. Usually more to their liking are quiet authority, natural leadership and being a calm recipient of accolades. Among their best traits is giving to others or to just causes without restraint. Altruism frequently reaches its highest level with this sign, although anonymity would not be insisted upon. Even among quiet Leo rising types, they would ordinarily seek management of affairs, businesswise or otherwise. They like the idea of being the heart of an organization or movement. However, the married woman with this sign rising may be more than content to play the role of queen, as opposed to absolute leader.

With this information and knowledge, it is interesting to compare some famous people who are supposed to have Leo on their Ascendants. Lauren Bacall, Judy Collins and Anita Bryant are among those who qualify according to their physical birth times. Well, it is possible that one of this trio does. But, if you really want to find Leo rising look for those with Virgo supposedly on their Ascendants. Zza Zza Gabor comes to mind as one example who definitely does not have Virgo in that place, although her birth year is very much in question. Victor Borge, the classical music comic, is another. These examples should be good practice for astrologers or for people interested in people.

Example Horoscopes

Now let us look at some Leo Rising horoscopes that can be verified with the data available. What better place to start than with Mikhail Gorbochev, the very epitome of Leo on the Ascendant. His characteristics were just described in the preceding paragraphs. There is his large, rectangular head, now balding. He is a big man. He speaks with a commanding presence. He was at the helm of his country until after this section had been first written, in a position of authority. Although recently stepping aside, he has proven that he is not a quitter. But these are repetitions. Observe his horoscope in Figure 15 and Table XIII. This horoscope stands out so clearly as belonging to Mikhail Gorbachev it is hardly appropriate to make further comments about a later one with Virgo on the Ascendant. In no possible way could this determined and authoritative figure have the sign of the virgin on his Eastern horizon.

There have been several contacts between American and Russian astrologers in this 1991 period of casting aside the cold war. The Russians are responsible for furnishing his 07:16 PM time of birth. It is not known whether this time is for the Sun or for a zone two or three hours later than Greenwhich Mean Time. However, the issue is unimportant except for understanding how far in advance the soul's entry may occur. The difference here is over four hours, or three hours if an earlier zone time was intended. It is the moment of the soul's entry that fixes the natal horoscope. Whether an atheistic viewpoint of life by the subject might reject the idea of a soul is irrelevant. The natal horoscope with 0 Leo 06.6 on the Eastern horizon checks. The main inaccuracy, if one exists, would be associated with the location.

The Russians also provided the latitude and longitude of Mikhail Gorbachev's village of birth. He was born in Privolnoye, Krasnogvardeisk District of the Stravropol territory. This should not be confused with the city of Privolnoye, as some astrologers have done, which is over 1300 miles to the west and north. Unfortunately, Russian maps to the outside world are notoriously inaccurate. Available library sources do not possess atlases that show the small village of Privolnoye, or even the Krasnogvardeisky District. Hence, the coordinates could not be scaled to the nearest second of latitude and longitude. The 45N02 latitude and 041E59 longitude is a little west of the city of Stravropol, and appears to be reasonable. Fortunately, an error of a minute or so in either latitude or longitude will cause a tolerable shift in time. Rectification can later correct any small errors. Picking a city in the wrong Russian state, however, would provide an erroneous birth time of larger proportions.

We know that this Russian leader is articulate, well educated and confident. According to Serge Schmemann of the *New York Times Magazine*, "He typifies a style and substance of upcoming generations in Moscow." He was the youngest man since Joseph Stalin succeeded Lenin in 1924 to assume USSR leadership. For twenty-two years he served as a Communist Party official in the Southern district of Stavropol, where he was born. He became Agricultural Secretary of the Central Committee in 1978 and a full member of the Politburo in October of 1980. During that period he became a disciple of Yuri Andropov in carrying out economic and social reforms. This policy continued when he succeeded Konstantin Chernenko as general secretary on March 11, 1985. Since that time he has been responsible for fostering peaceful coexistence in the spirit of detente during the 1970's. Then came glasnost and perestroika in the 1980's. His actions must be termed radical, in the nature of having a strong Uranus placement. Observe what his natal horoscope computed for the moment of soul entry shows:

I. We are looking to confirm the map of a leader with radical ideas. The Sun of this horoscope is in the impressionable sign Pisces, and the Ascendant is just into the royal sign Leo. The sixth/twelfth house interceptions identify intensive service to country and they are loaded with planets. Sun, the ruler of the Ascendant is in the eighth house, where the major concerns are for economic and social reforms. Mikhail Gorbachev was facing monetary crises even as these lines were written. Uranus, the revolutionary planet already anticipated, is strongly placed on his Midheaven in the pioneering sign Aries. The influence of Uranus is intensified by its close parallel with his Midheaven. No alternative horoscope has confirming forces so clearly displayed as this one. It is clearly the horoscope of a national leader with revolutionary ideas.

II. Other placements and aspects will be reviewed. None seem out of place. First, it is obvious that he is bald and stocky. Leo on the Ascendant agrees. There is his Moon in Leo contra-parallel Saturn, located in the sixth house. Saturn stalls and tries to maintain the status quo. Gorbachev's biggest problems were related to subordinates who did not follow orders. Over their miscues he becomes overwrought and angry. This is precisely what newspapers have reported. Leo is also on the cusp of the second house, ruled by the Sun, and Neptune is there. His personal residences are quoted as being lavish. The Sun is benefited by that strong trine with Jupiter seeking expansion. His material wealth is greater than most of his peers. Sun is opposed by Neptune and that aspect suggests thefts and undercover activities. Venus and Saturn in the sixth house indicate hard work in a pleasant setting. Both being in the sign Capricorn causes increased ambition. Mercury in Aquarius contributes words of aid to the underdogs of his nation. Uranus at the zenith always portends a revolutionary, one who changes the order of things. Jupiter, Pluto and Mars in the twelfth house inspire major actions in behalf of his country. As for any person proposing major changes in a nation's direction, especially one with Mars in the twelfth house, his ideas are met with both favor and opposition. Note the President of the state of Russia, Boris Yeltsin, who has been both a thorn in his side and a benefactor.

That was a fairly swift circuit around the wheel, but in every case the planetary placements appear to be correct. A review of any Virgo rising chart would be a waste of time, but you are more than welcome to try.

III. The occasion of Mikhail Gorbachev's election as General Secretary of his party was chosen to be the progression used for illustration purposes. A Midheaven aspect must be present to celebrate an event of this magnitude and nature. The progressions for that date were computed, and the output did not disappoint. A progressed Midheaven aspect was present. Its parallel with the Moon within twenty-four seconds appeared, as though by magic. These two horoscopic elements fill the bill in conformation of the event. Moon is in the first house. He himself was honored, and the victory must have been euphoric. It was assisted by a much wider semisextile from progressed Mercury to the Midheaven (6.1 minutes). The progressed Sun also happened to be trine Neptune within 5.0 minutes. These supporting aspects contributed nuances, but not the main theme. Neither conforms with our 4 minute criterion, but remember the latitude and longitude may be just far enough away to cause these aspects to shift out of the prescribed tolerance. The Midheaven-Moon aspect does fit anyway.

Table XIII. Natal and Progressed Declinations of Mikhail Gorbachev

Planet	Natal Decln.	03-11-1985 Elected GS
MC	04 N 41.7	21 N 19.6
♅	04 N 43.0	05 N 52.9
☉	07 S 28.4	12 N 57.9
♆	10 N 38.5	11 N 03.1
☿	13 S 39.0	17 N 21.9
♀	19 S 22.8	01 S 40.1
Asc	20 N 08.3	07 N 41.2
☽	21 N 20.0	24 N 13.6
♄	21 S 37.7	21 S 12.8
♇	22 N 18.2	22 N 22.0
♃	23 N 17.7	23 N 01.3
♂	24 N 25.3	20 S 19.1

Leo rising characteristics in a male figure of international repute have been provided. Though the Ascendant is just into the first degree of Leo, the possibility of Cancer rising is nil. By now the differences in physical and mental traits should be obvious, although it is still possible to be fooled by complex interplanetary relationships. Pinpointing the rising sign is the all important first step. Acknowledging the placement of every planet in its rightful house is next. But finding a series of close progressed aspects for significant events constitutes the best final confirmation of a time yielding a horoscope with the acceptable Ascendant sign. For Gorbachev's important moment his Midheaven-to-Moon parallel was the one aspect that has every earmark of being correct. Still, a cautious word needs to be injected. With any uncertainty such as the location, plus the large quantity of aspects possible, it is important to check and double check. Many confirmations of the specific time being tested increase the probability of correctness. Hence, other events were checked, such as his induction into the politburo in October of 1980. The aspects were right for this event as well. It is believed that this horoscope needs minor rectification, based upon a more

MAR 02 1931 | 02:18 PM EAT | | Naibod Secondary
STUROPOP | USSR | | MAR 11 1985
45N02 | 041E59
02:06:51 PM TLT | 11:18:55 GMT | | 11:18:55 GMT
Tropical | *Placidus* | *True Node*

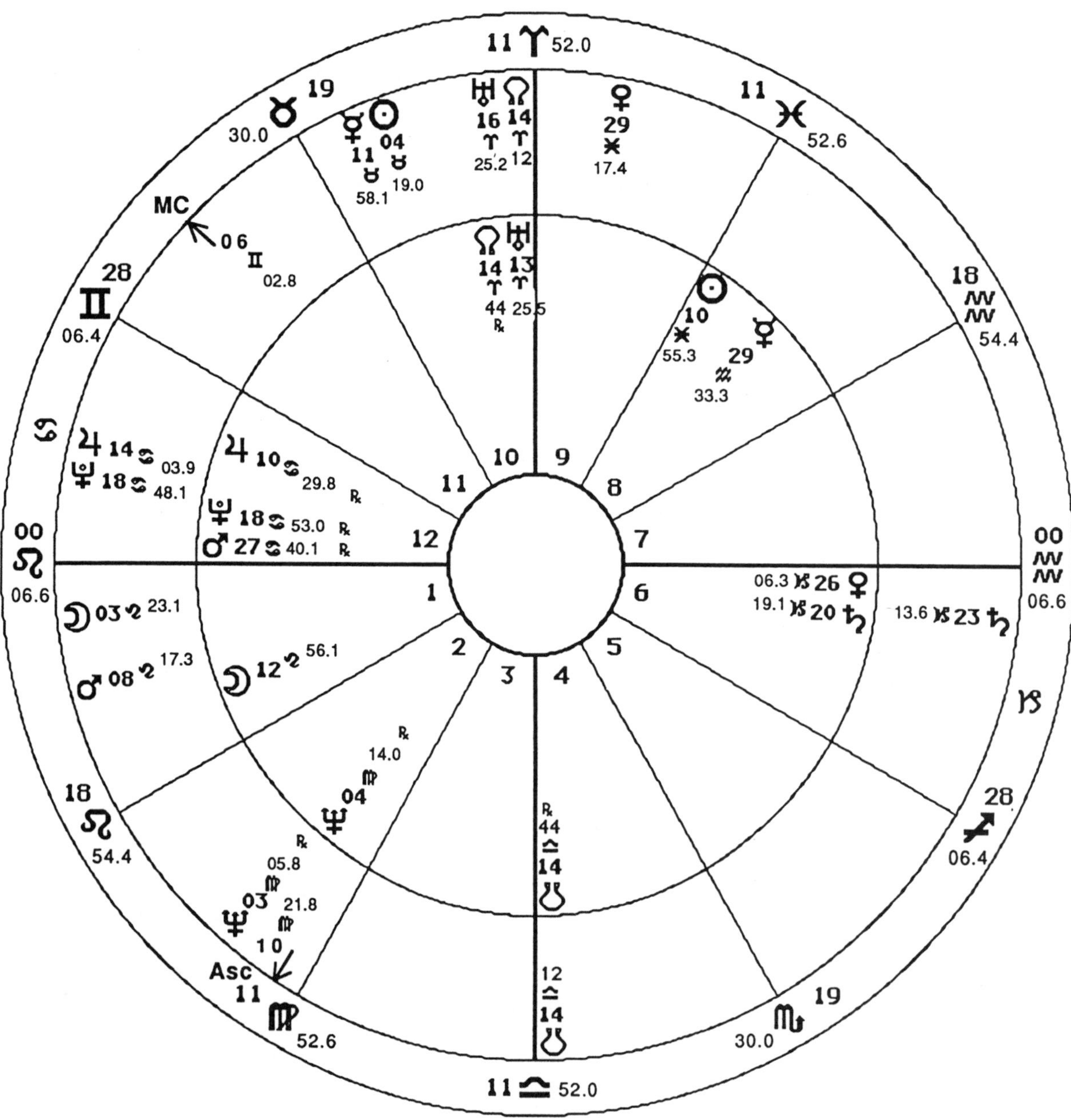

Figure 15. **Horoscope of Mikhail Gorbachev with progressions to the day he was elected General Secretary of the Communist Party.**

accurate birth place, but it will stand up when compared with the timing of future news items reported in the press.

This chapter was completed before the coup of August 18, 1991, however not before the book was finished. Therefore, it was deemed highly appropriate to run the progressions for that date and report the results. They were progressed Mars inconjunct Sun within 1.7 minutes and progressed Midheaven contraparallel Pluto within 3.7 minutes. Clearly, force was used in confining Gorbachev to his vacation *dacha*. It was used in trying to usurp his position as president and replace him with former Vice President Gennady Yanagev. Progressed Sun was also weakly sextile Jupiter, which agrees with the weak health reason given by the old line communist power group for his removal. Gorbachev could very well have ill health—in the pit of his stomach—with stressed Mars and Pluto in Cancer. It has since been reported, though, that his wife, Raisa, suffered the greater health problems.

So far, mostly white Caucasian celebrities have been used for illustrative purposes. Just to show that rising sign characteristics are independent of race, an oriental female with Leo on the Ascendant of her horoscope will be described next. This is Yoko Ono, avant guard artist and wife of John Lennon of *Beatles* fame. She was selected, not only because she has Leo rising, but because it is important to show that race does not alter the basic physical characteristics. Also, several significant dates of important events were available. It is interesting that Uranus also plays

Table XIV. Natal and Progressed Declinations of Yoko Ono

Planet	Natal Decln.	03 20 1969 Marriage
♃	05 N 00.6	06 N 49.0
♅	07 N 29.1	08 N 09.5
MC	08 N 42.7	19 N 50.0
♆	08 N 57.5	09 N 19.6
♂	09 N 45.0	13 N 50.3
☿	10 S 02.2	02 N 19.0
☉	11 S 46.4	02 N 04.6
♀	17 S 37.8	01 S 56.3
♄	18 S 23.3	17 S 24.6
Asc	19 N 29.4	10 N 45.1
♇	22 N 39.8	22 N 45.0
☽	26 S 50.7	05 N 23.9

FEB 18 1933 08:09 PM JAT
TOKYO JAPAN
35 N 42 58 139 E 42 57
04:14:49 TLT 06:55:57 AM GMT
Tropical *Placidus* *True Node*

Naibod Secondary
MAR 20 1969
06:55:57 AM GMT

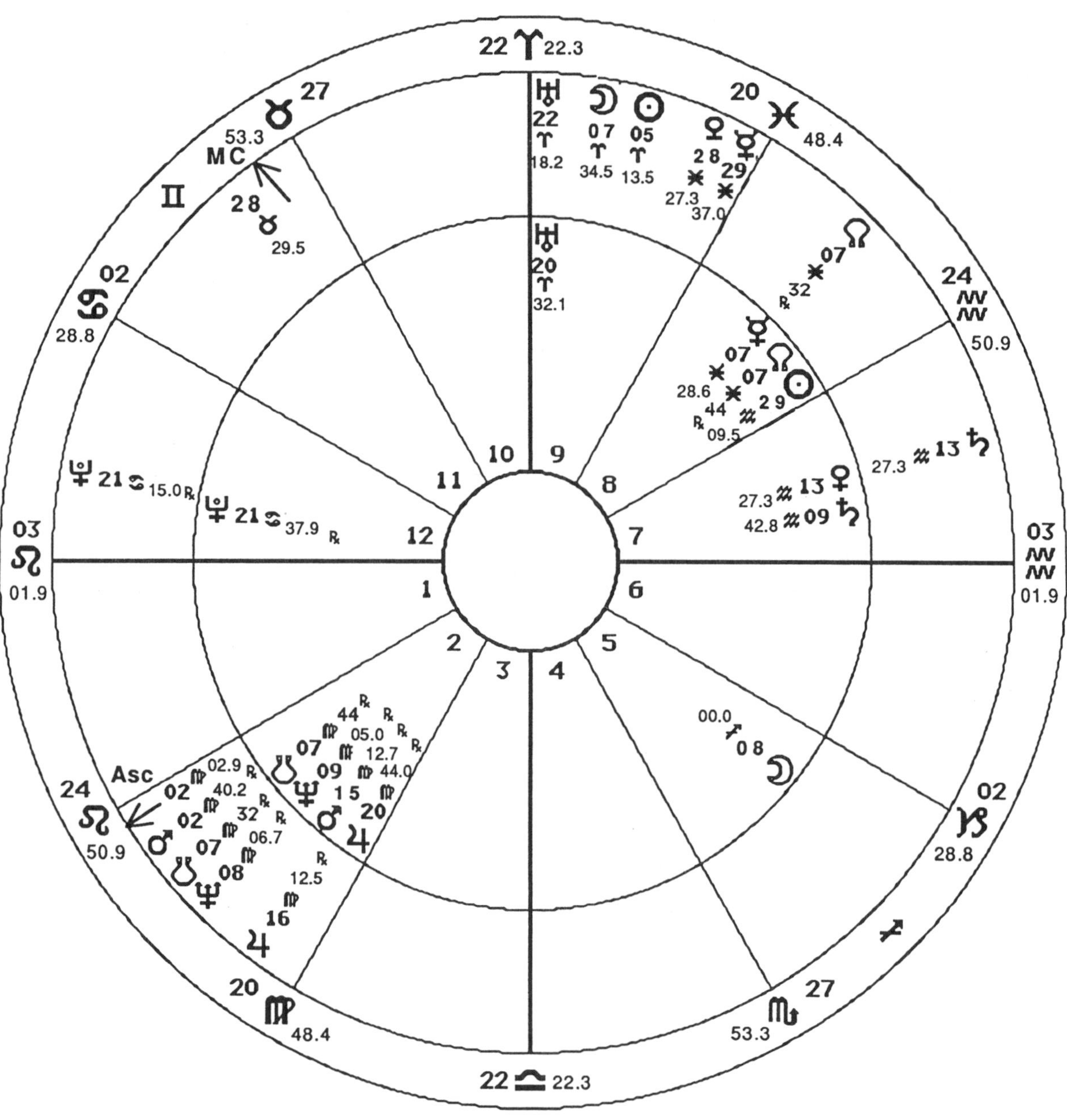

Figure 16. Horoscope of Yoko Ono with progressions to date of her marriage to John Lennon.

a prominent role in her chart.

Yoko Ono has been described as short but not small. Ergo, the Japanese of the Tokyo area are short as a race compared with mixed race Westerners (or Americans). Also, Saturn contra-parallel her Ascendant might have a small effect in containing growth, although it is just a fairly close aspect. She has a large frame for her height, and her rectangular face points to Leo, as opposed to Virgo. This is decisively so upon further examination.

For those who might not know much about her background, Yoko Ono was born into a prominent and comparatively wealthy Japanese family. Her first name, Yoko, means oceanchild. Because her father traveled considerably, she traveled with him. Ultimately she established roots in New York and became a friend to artists. Also, she became creative in unique ways and using a quantity of different media. Mysterious lights, peculiar sounds, smells and illusions were combined in ways contrived to shock. Some critics have belittled her work. Others simply regard it as far out. Dale Denmark of Newsweek (November 8, 1971 issue) wrote that she was,"....an early friend of John Cage, a crucial member of the *fluxus movement*, which cooled off the first free-for-all happenings and turned them into quiet, personalized events. She has been a continuing influence on other artists through her concerts, performances, films, paintings and writings. In every case, that influence has been reductive and meditative." Her notoriety ascended when she married John Lennon of *Beatles* fame. This act spelled the demise of the *Beatles*. From that moment the two of them pooled resources on such works as *The Dream is Over, Come Together, Give Peace a Chance* and *Imagine*.

Yoko Ono is another person with a prominent Uranus. That must follow from the nature of these creations that were filled with sensations, sex, peace wishes, rock music and other radical concepts of this attention-seeking group. Nothing has been too outrageous to say or do. The shock motive was uppermost, and in later offerings that approach has not changed. A typical composition had the title, *Woman is the Nigger of the World.*

Now, it should never be considered that Leo rising would not be ostentatious. That sign on the Ascendant can be very much so. However, before even looking further, it is certain that a prominent Uranus would carry ostentation to its limits. Thus the task is simpler. Upon discovering that the Sun sign is in Aquarius as well, the new age is suddenly upon us. One can feel sympathetic over her tragedies while looking for the horoscope that tells this story. It was readily selected without hesitation and is presented in Figure 16 and Table XIV.

I. Uranus, within less than two degrees of a conjunction with the Midheaven, fulfills the most realistic expectation. It is still in the ninth house where shocking experiences are provided to other people. The fifth and eleventh houses, where shows are created and performed, are intercepted as for so many whose primary purpose in life is to act or to present. This is a splay horoscope that exerts energies in many directions. Yes indeed, it fits.

II. The placement of planets in this horoscope is interesting to behold. One of the first noticeable aspects of great power is the parallel of Neptune to the Midheaven. Thus, two outer planets of extranormality (or paranormality) are sitting on top of her horoscope. The heavy preponderance of planets in the second and eighth houses relates to talents of her own and others, besides money matters. The Sagittarian Moon sits in the fifth house of original ideas. Venus and Saturn in the seventh house of marriage are inconjunct Mars and Neptune, not the most propitious of aspects. She was married several times. The sextile Moon receives bliss, but other heavy aspects are oppressive. Sun, the ruler of the Ascendant is void of course in the eighth house of death to her partner. Pluto, in the twelfth house, seeks acceptance of her art.

To be fair, it should be mentioned that others have cast Yoko Ono's horoscope with Libra on the Ascendant. That would make Uranus prominent in the seventh house, where it would speak of the Uranian qualities in her mates. One was Toshi Icheyanagi, a musician. Another was Anthony Cox. Then there was John Lennon, also a musician. It could be said that Uranus fits each of them in a way, but an Aquarian Venus and Saturn fit even better. The Libra chart simply does not show the Uranian nature of Yoko Ono herself. Any doubt of this magnitude is sufficient grounds for rejection

III. A dramatic incident took place in Yoko Ono's life when John Lennon was assassinated in the streets of New York. That terrible act occurred on December 8, 1980. The Oriental viewpoint toward death is known to be different from the Western viewpoint, and the astrological aspects could reflect this perspective. However, her progressions for that day were not out of line. Progressed Moon and progressed Mars were conjunct. Mars pierces. The event must have had a severe emotional impact. Progressed Mercury was semisquare Saturn, and progressed Ascendant was parallel progressed Jupiter. Such a moment could have been used to illustrate a confirmation of this chart, because these aspects met the accuracy requirement. However, in case anyone might argue that death of a partner is indirect, another was chosen.

A more pleasant happening was her marriage to John Lennon on March 20, 1969. This is the date of the progressions shown in Figure 16 and Table XIV. On that date her seventh house progressed Saturn was conjunct Venus within 3.1 minutes. Progressed Midheaven was parallel progressed Venus within 2.2 minutes. These are more than sufficient forces to cause a marriage to take place. Another date of possibly her most successful performance was checked as well, although not illustrated. On January 10, 1972, a nearly exact progressed Sun trine Moon occurred. Then progressed Uranus was still close to her Midheaven, and one of the features of this performance was musicians sustaining high notes until she finished eating an apple. This "original" idea received an ovation at the Cannes Festival.

In some respects Yoko Ono's horoscope dwells more upon an uninhibited Uranus at the apex than it does Leo rising, although all the parts have a place in painting the complete astrological picture. Irrespective of the nature of her expressiveness, the Leo Ascendant is commensurate with her personality. Leo enjoys display and show. That is her primary mode of operation. But it should also be recognized that Leo rising is conservative when the horoscope so ordains. Mikhail Gorbachev exemplifies the more conservative side.

One who might be classified between these opposite poles was Ernest Hemingway. This big, bear of a man had a risque side, besides being a fantastic writer. A male Leo is almost invariably a man of large proportions. Virgo rising might be tall, but not the big hunk that he was. His on the even hour, 8 o'clock in the morning reported birthtime would yield a Virgo Ascendant. By now it is sincerely hoped that the reader is sufficiently knowledgeable to question any even hour birth time, especially when the physical makeup appears to correspond with the preceding sign. Ernest Hemingway, with his Cancer Sun, could not have grown so big any other way unless Jupiter was pushing him up. Jupiter is not close to the Ascendant in the horoscope of Figure 17 and Table XV. Therefore, bodily size must be attributed to the Leo rising sign exclusively.

Ernest Hemingway started writing as a cub reporter for the *Kansas City Star* in October, 1917. World War I brought travel to Europe, and by June 4, 1918, he reached Schio, Italy, near Milan. He was assigned to driving ambulances. Only a month later, on July 8, 1918, he was wounded in the legs and feet. This was followed by a period of hospitalization. Six months later he was on a ship bound for home. However, the experience of writing in the field, the excitement of traveling and the lure of danger had gotten into his blood. In successive years he went to Toronto, married his first wife, Elizabeth Hadley Richardson, and covered the Greco-Turkish war of 1922 in Constantinople. His job as feature writer for the *Toronto Star Weekly* permitted him to roam Europe from a Paris hub. By May of 1923 he visited Spain, where he gained further experiences that found their way into some of his great novels.

What we have in review is a fearless war correspondent who turned to the writing of novels. His travels were extensive. They provided many opportunities for making contacts with women and wine. His circle of friends grew to include other writers, teachers and sophisticates of the early twenties who were bent on changing the style of literature and art. These included Ezra Pound, F. Scott Fitzgerald, James Joyce, Gertrude Stein, Max Beerbohm and many other drinking buddies. His frequent moves to new locations and personal experiences provided scenes in his best selling works, and his craftsmanship was outstanding. The novels he wrote became best sellers.

We also know that he was a sportsman and often faced dangers. He was frequently in-

JUL 21 1899	06:07 AM CST	Naibod Secondary
Oak Park	Illinois	OCT 29 1926
41 N 53 32	087 W 49 38	12:05:32 PM GMT
06:14:14 AM TLT	12:05:32 PM GMT	

Tropical *Placidus* *True Node*

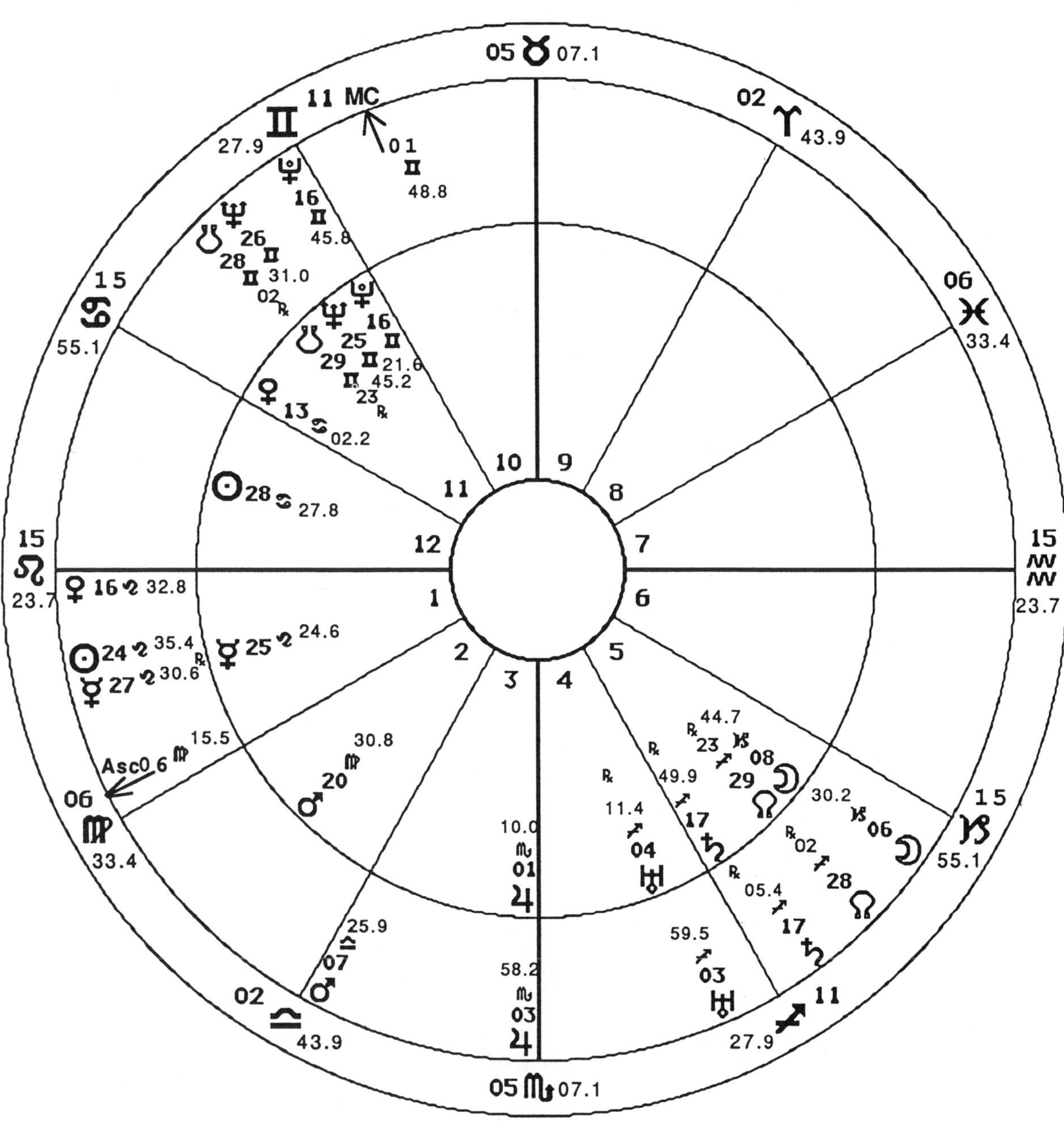

Figure 17. Horoscope of novelist Ernest Hemingway. Progressions are to the date of publication of his first great book, *The Sun Also Rises.*

Table XV. Natal and Progressed Declinations of Ernest Hemingway

Planet	Natal Decln.	10 25 1926 Famous Book
♂	04 N 24.5	02 S 37.0
♃	10 S 49.4	11 S 53.0
☿	12 N 20.5	07 N 58.6
MC	13 N 14.1	20 N 32.2
♇	13 N 14.5	13 N 13.4
Asc	16 N 13.8	09 N 13.3
☉	20 N 28.8	13 N 20.0
♅	20 S 54.0	20 S 52.2
♄	21 S 30.2	21 S 31.1
♆	22 N 08.4	22 N 09.2
☽	22 S 18.2	22 S 32.1
♀	22 N 56.9	16 N 55.2

jured but usually managed to have a mother figure present, among the females he knew, to nurse him back to health. Altogether, he married four times. He wrote in a house in Key West, Florida, during 1928 and 1929. He spent two years in Africa during the 1930's and several more covering the Spanish War. There was a stint in China with wife of that period, Martha Gellhorn, who was a writer herself and in some ways a competitor. This was followed by a period in Cuba, a land that he dearly loved. He covered the invasion of France during World War II and participated with the resistance forces until he caught pneumonia. After severe illnesses, and a debilitating stay at the Mayo Clinic he ended his days in Ketchum, Idaho, taking his own life.

I. Verification of Ernest Hemingway's horoscope requires that the above overview corresponds with no reason for doubts. The only real question is not whether the rising sign is Virgo or Leo, but which of the many Leo rising degrees is the correct one to select. He was a large, barrel chested man. His biographer, Jeffrey Meyers, wrote, "In 1922, before he had replaced gentleness with toughness, Hemingway was a tall, handsome, muscular, broad-shouldered, brown-eyed, rosy-cheeked, square-jawed, soft-voiced young man." He went on to say, "The essential [point] that is always missed is the great sense of fun he exuded and how much fun it was to be with him. His enormous appetite for life flowed over everyone around him." These words describe Papa as a Leo. Virgo is out of the question when Cancer is the Sun sign.

Any degree of Leo might be on the Ascending angle to have those things written about him. However, boundaries are established by two planets. One is Mercury, which belongs to a writer when in the first house. The other is Jupiter, which causes the writer to be prolific when in the third house. With 15 Leo 23.7 on the Ascendant, both boundary conditions are met. That might seem arbitrary to those who have not worked with the horoscopes of authors before, but those two planets happen to be in the right spots and many other indicators are in full agreement. Note also the concentration of planets in the fifth and eleventh houses, where creative juices flow and where the public finds enjoyment in the stories.

II. Looking at the other planets one by one, and their aspects, simply provides a stream of additional check marks. One of the very first things to notice is the almost exact parallel of Pluto and the Midheaven. If fame had not come, something would have been wrong with the choice of his birth time. A person blessed with a Pluto-Midheaven parallel is almost certain to acquire fame. Other aspects to these two components hardly matter, they simply provide the tone. Another interesting formation is the T-square, with Mars the handle planet, in the second house. It is also in the sign Virgo, and that adds to his technical prowess as a writer. This Mars says in effect that he earned money covering the subjects of war. He reported on World War I, The Greco-Turkish conflict, the Spanish Civil War, and World War II, to name a few. War was an integral part of many of his novels. Mars gets hurt at times, and his wounds attest to that. He was often injured. Mars is also ruler of the ninth house of foreign travel, and these wounds were incurred overseas. Mars likes outdoor sports, including big game hunting. Being square to Neptune and Pluto in the eleventh house and square to Saturn in the fifth house embroiled him in many debates among his friends. These debates were frequently conducted with bottles and their contents at hand. Moon in the fifth house says that he thoroughly enjoyed a good time; but opposite Venus, it sometimes resulted in emotional partings with those of the opposite sex. Moon contraparallel Neptune also did not help. That aspect tells about his heavy drinking and strong suicidal tendencies. His father before him was a suicide. Sun in the twelfth house shows a desire to leave a legacy and considerable effort to make sure that is what happened. He even fabricated stories to enhance his image. Every planet position and aspect seem to add, not subtract, from the total picture. They are like bricks and mortar that solidify the image.

III. Fortunately, authors are in the inner circle among biographers. Therefore, biographies of famous authors are better than average, and they give dates. Every date provided the necessary close aspects. At the instant during World War I when he was wounded, for example, progressed Mars and progressed Moon were parallel and the progressed Ascendant was contraparallel Jupiter. Either Mars or Pluto is invariably active when the flesh is pierced. Aspects involving either Saturn or Uranus were present for each of his three marriages. Many times were available for illustration purposes. The final choice was the date of publication of *The Sun Also Rises*. That novel was his first great success, and it brought him instant fame. That should not be unexpected when his progressed Midheaven was parallel his Sun, and his progressed Sun was parallel his Midheaven—both at the same time. The second aspect was slightly beyond our 4 minute range, but for goodness sakes—this was a double set of aspects between the same two astrological elements. They convey a double confirmation of the event. Of course, a close progressed semisextile between Jupiter and Uranus was also present. This was most fortunate for his publisher. However, those who disregard declinations would miss most of the fun and the main points for that date of October 29, 1926. It is likely they would have been attending a different party—the one where it would be most difficult to find agreement between the stars and what really happened. Either the progressions would be ignored altogether or a mental concoction would have to be voiced in the way of an explanation.

It should be easy to see the similarities in head shapes, body structures and personality traits among the people given as examples of Leo rising. One was an oriental female and the other two were males in totally different professions. Many similarities can be found in their natures, although each one's manner of expression is different. Definitely, none has any resemblance to Virgo, which comes next.

CHAPTER 6. VIRGO

Preliminary Observations

For whatever the reason, during the first part of the nineteen-ninety decade there has been a run on Virgo Ascendants of VIP's. Writing astrologers have published a wide assortment of horoscopes claiming the sign of the Virgin to be on the first house cusp. Either imagination is at play, or the incidence has been larger than normal. A few examples are President George Bush, Sadam Hussein, former President and General Dwight D. Eisenhower, etc. If you truly have Virgo on your Ascendant some pride might be felt at being included in such company. Yet, do not be depressed if this myth is exposed. The truth of the matter is that Virgo does not appear to have generated any more or less celebrities than any other feminine rising sign. Masculine signs are more forward and aggressive than the feminine. Therefore, they are more likely to attract attention and tend to predominate. Statistically, the quantity of celebrities with feminine signs rising appears to be less than those with masculine signs rising. Virgo happens to be feminine, and so there are not as many to chose from. The authors who believed Virgo graced the horoscopes of the VIP's they wrote about were probably sincere, but the sad truth is that their indiscretions and lack of attention to details reflect badly upon our great study of astrology. When Virgo is a leader, the probabilities are higher that the profession will be in research, or will make use of detailed facts more often than one in which people are commanded from a position of power. Exceptions do exist, as for example General Schwarzkopf with his feminine rising sign Cancer. However, the planets then align themselves in such a way as to apply the necessary forces. The published Virgo rising horoscopes named above lacked such forces and they contain serious mismatches between the planets and the houses they should be in as well.

Physical Characteristics

Virgo on the Ascendant features a triangular head. Almost anyone who studied geometry knows that a triangle has three sides and it does not look like a four-sided rectangle. Thus, the Virgo head is wedge shaped, having a top, a left slanting side and a right slanting side. The intersection of the two sides forms a point. Virgo chins may not necessarily be as sharp as a point, but they are narrow and sometimes appear to be chopped off as though scissors had cut them off. The mouth is usually small to average in width, and the lips are likely to be thin rather than full. Another feature is the nose. It is usually straight, or very slightly arched, and down pointing. The bridge is thin. Exceptions do exist, but not often. The stature is typically medium to tall, although once again weight is often added with age. The body in youth is normally wiry. Almost every Virgo rising individual is conscious of health and germs. Time is set aside for exercises, sports or other activities to keep their bodies in good shape. The Virgo rising body displays an attitude of preciseness, of knowing many facts and of a desire to be faultless. Yet, they can be witty in their own fun-seeking way of twisting facts for this purpose.

Before Virgo is Leo. After Virgo is Libra. Leo has a rectangular head, and Libra has an ovate one. The possibility of making a mistake among this trio should be remote. The Virgo triangle is distinctly different.

Mental Characteristics

The sign Virgo on the Ascendant is symbolized by the image of a Virgin holding a stalk of wheat (stylized modern versions do not always show the wheat). The intension of the symbol makers was to convey the idea of a youth, in this case female, who examines every aspect of life in detail, always wanting to be right. The wheat symbolizes nourishment, and the Virgo person is forever conscious of what constitutes good nourishment. Sometimes ideas are approached with equal weight in the material world, where they are really unequal, as is often the case with academics. Correctness to a Virgo person applies to everything, regardless of other priorities. Being pure and faultless is a goal. Having good health and being germ-free is another. Cleanliness is an important virtue. Some Virgos have a fear of germs and they will take precautionary measures to avoid contacts that might cause them to spread. But to go further, Virgo is a mutable earth sign. Thus Virgo favors practicality and productivity. They easily go along with the rest of the crowd. They often do the hard, detailed work for less than average credit. The secretary-treasurer of an organization is a typical position. They usually are good students, good with numbers and their minds are reservoirs of facts. A Virgo rising boy who likes sports will know the batting averages of ball players or other statistics. A Virgo rising girl who likes clothes will be good at needlework, if she makes them, or will show extraordinary discrimination and good taste in the choice of dresses, if she is in a position to buy them. They are rarely showy or ostentatious. The single word that best describes their behavior is probably discrimination. When highly developed they have marvelous powers of subjecting every thought to the crucible of their own criticism, separating the wheat from the chafe. The best practical choices are then made.

An undeveloped or negative Virgo rising person can be critical of everyone and every thing. The nose-prying maiden aunt, or elderly unmarried French concierge, come to mind. These are the spinsters who continually talk about other people's business, but may have led disastrous lives themselves. Every procedure must be done their way. Only one right way exists and it is theirs. They invariably see flaws. Their opinions of others are frequently disdainful. Worst of all, for such opinionated individuals, is to receive criticism about themselves. Because of this concern with always making the right choice, many of them wind up unmarried.

The advanced or positive Virgo rising person is reserved, fastidious, knowledgeable, capable and funny or comic. They usually keep their distance and are not imposing toward others. They are often well read and do not suffer many illusions. Learning, maintaining a sound body, making the best judgements and a stream of good accomplishments characterize their lives. Performing any task requiring attention to details is well within their grasp. It is not likely that they would spare themselves when helping out. Either private or public resources are handled simply and frugally. Most of the time their expenditures are wise. If a choice of marriage partner is ultimately made, Virgo will work hard at making the marriage a success and will normally be very good with the children. Elaborate rituals, however, are usually regarded as a waste of time. To do good things and be faithful to ideals is important. To examine every proposition in the light of its real value is even more important. Madison Avenue and tinsel do not necessarily represent good values, and not even in their food do they ordinarily like a profusion of condiments.

Do you now see why there is reason to be skeptical of Virgo rising for the VIP's in question? President Bush doesn't like broccoli. That dislike does not a Virgo Ascendant make, although he does pay attention to physical fitness. It is not known whether Morgana King, Arthur Schlesinger, Henry Fonda or Julie Andrews dislike broccoli either, but such taste preferences would not guarantee Virgo Ascendants any more than their reported birth times. It requires more evidence than that. The necessary evidence starts with a triangular head.

Example Horoscopes

One who has such a head, and personality, is Jacques Yves Cousteau, the famous French oceanographer. Skin divers around the world are indebted for their sport to this man. He was their "pioneer, foremost promoter, prophet and poet," according to *Time* magazine. He was co-inventor of the Aqua-Lung and developer of such technically logical innovations as a one-man, jet-propelled submarine. Conshelf I, II and III implemented the first manned undersea colonies. He was a researcher amassing vast amounts of valuable information on marine life, biology, botany and ecology. He wrote numerous best selling books on these subjects and was responsible for award-winning films. Best of all, these outpourings enabled millions to share his discoveries. It is proper at this point to ignore any suggestion of ascending Libra that appeared in a published horoscope for him. The information gathering pursuits are pure Virgo. The physical look of this man is Virgo with very little modification from his Gemini Sun sign except to increase height.

Jacques Cousteau was born in the small village of Saint Andre de Cubzac, which lies on the East bank of the Dordogne river not far from where it joins the Garonne in the region of Bordeaux. His was another father who traveled frequently and Saint Andre was a temporary stopping place. Being moved from school to school, Jacques became a bored and indolent student. In fact he became a mischief maker. Eventually he was expelled from his *lycée* for breaking 17 windows. After being sent to a much stricter school in Alsace he began to apply himself. Upon graduation he joined the French Navy, rose to the rank of Second Lieutenant and made a round-the-world voyage on the *Jeanne d'Arc*. Afterwards he was assigned to the French Naval Base in Shanghai where he became engaged for the first time in map-making along the Indochina coast. He decided to be a navy airplane pilot, but broke both arms prior to receiving his wings. His recovery was accompanied by the typical Virgo approach of a calculated exercise program to strengthen his muscles.

By the time World War II was under way Jacques Cousteau was assigned to the French naval base at Toulon. He proceeded to make his first two underwater films, *Par dix-huit mètres de fond* in 1942 and *Èpaves* in 1945. In English the first title means *Under Eighteen Meters of Water* and the second *Wrecks*. It is interesting that the occupying Germans allowed him to proceed. They regarded him as a harmless eccentric.

By 1956 Jacques Cousteau resigned from the French navy with the rank of *Capitaine de Corvette*. He devoted full time thenceforth to underwater explorations, expeditions, writing books, making films, developing underwater equipment, starting skin diving companies and pursuing his love of oceanography. His first book published in the United States and France, *The Silent World*, sold over five million copies. He obtained backing from the National Geographic Society, bought *Calypso* (his specially outfitted ship) and made a documentary film of the same name. It won the Grand Prize at the Cannes Film Festival of 1956 and an Academy award in 1957. The rest is history. He was eventually awarded six medals in both the United States and France, two honorary Doctor of Science degrees (Brandeis and Berkeley), the position of foreign associate of the National Academy of Sciences, and he became part owner of skin diving companies all over the world. This is what a person with Virgo rising can accomplish when pursuing detailed information.

I. The horoscope illustrated in Figure 18 and Table XVI is the bucket type with Uranus the handle planet in the fourth house. It also rules the fifth. The focus in Capricorn is upon technology and new inventions that will result in advancement of science. Neptune and Mars opposite are in the water sign Cancer and that is where the adventure was to be found. With a Gemini Sun close to the zenith providing communication skills, recognition and a love of books, this thin six-footer with Virgo rising became a dedicated man with a mission. It is stated that he weighs 154 pounds. His Gallic nose is of the type belonging to Virgo—long, sharp and down-pointing. His daily regimen of exercises to maintain a trim body and good health are exactly according to specifications. His intercepted fifth and eleventh houses attest to his ultimate goals of creating books and films to entertain.

II. The planetary positions reinforce these earlier conclusions. The ruler of both the first and tenth houses is Mercury in the ninth house of travel and publications. In Taurus, travel is performed for highly practical reasons. His Sun is also there, in the sign Gemini, and it results in documentations performed at a distance from his birth place. Jupiter in the first house, and in the air sign Libra, seeks expansion. It is intriguing that air is the principal need associated with the Aqua-Lung, submarines and under-water habitation. Jacques Cousteau's antipathy in youth toward

JUN 11 1910 00:25 PM GMT
SAINT ANDRE DE CUBZAC, FRANCE
44 N 59 59 000 W 27 20
00:23:01 PM TLT 00:24:51 GMT
Tropical *Placidus* *True Node*

Naibod Secondary
JUN 23 1969
00:24:51 GMT

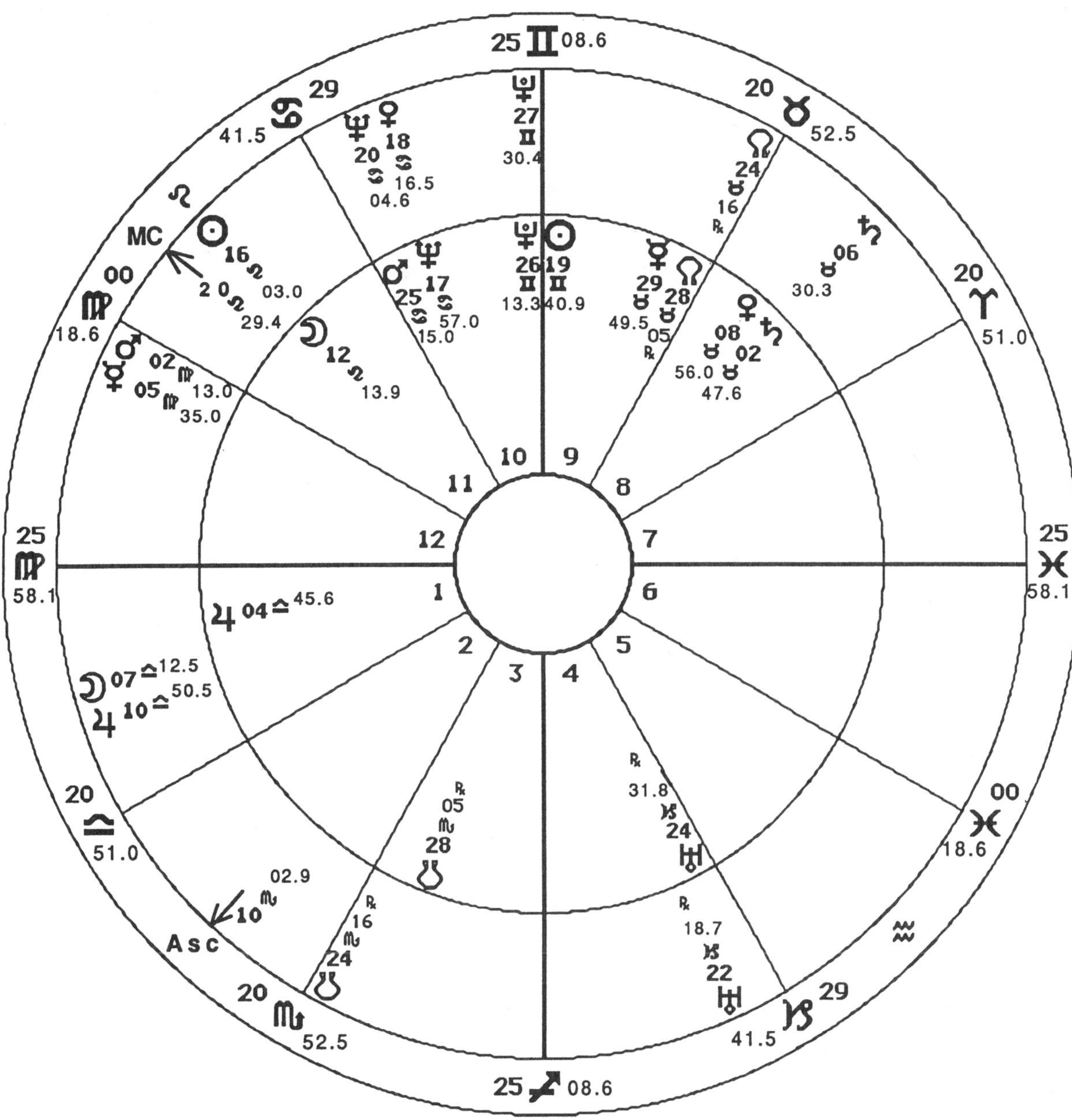

Figure 18. **Horoscope of world-famous oceanographer Jacques Cousteau. Progressions are to the date of his filming *The Tragedy of the Red Salmon.***

constantly changing schools, and his misdemeanors are shown by Neptune, co-ruler of the fourth house, contraparallel Uranus (a rebellious miscreant having a form of fun) and conjunct damaging Mars, the ruler of the third house of primary schooling. Venus, the ruler of the second house in his eighth conjunct Saturn, builds a fortune carefully and pragmatically with other people. Both planets are in Taurus, and that could hardly be better for stability. Pluto, Neptune and Mars in the tenth house provide recognition for his work, which include films of dangerous sharks and large octopi wrapping tentacles around the diver's arm. He faced dangers while under water and a number of accidents did occur. Deaths occurred. In spite of these tragedies, Moon in his eleventh house indicates that the fulfillment of his dreams was thoroughly enjoyed and exploited. His Moon was in Leo. He became an authority because of his unique knowledge which is so typical for the

Table XVI. Natal and Progressed Declinations of Jacues Yves Cousteau

Planet	Natal Decln.	06 23 1969 Salmon Film
♃	00 S 36.9	03 S 12.7
Asc	01 N 36.3	14 S 50.3
♄	10 N 16.4	11 N 18.3
♀	12 N 20.7	21 N 57.3
☿	16 N 05.7	10 N 14.2
♇	16 N 45.0	16 N 46.6
♆	21 N 36.5	21 S 19.4
♅	21 S 43.8	22 S 07.0
☽	21 N 58.2	00 N 31.5
♂	22 N 22.0'	11 N 42.1
☉	23 N 03.1	16 N 02.1
MC	23 N 21.8	14 N 40.1

Moon's placement in that sign. Mars and Pluto in the tenth house and Sun parallel his Midheaven show his military involvements and his leadership roles. In fact, his ego was supreme, and he was number one in all of his activities for public consumption. Uranus contraparallel the Moon suggests that a number of controversial issues became frenzied while being discussed, although

Neptune is also parallel and providing support. For example, it has been written that Jacques wanted to include a chapter on sex in one of his books, but his publisher objected strenuously. He eventually gave in on that argument. Mercury parallel Pluto provides much energy to write books and scripts for films. If any planet in this horoscope did not fit the real person it was not found.

III. The biographies reviewed for this citizen of the world were weak on dates. One author was charitable in giving a month and year now and then for occurrences noted. However, the progression of a successful event is worthy of being highlighted, and after reviewing still other biographies, such a date was found. June 23, 1969, was the date a film was made in Kodiak, Alaska, about the tragedy of the red salmon. This particular film received exceptional reviews and later received awards. On that day progressed Sun was parallel Mercury within 3.6 minutes, progressed Venus was parallel Moon within 0.9 minutes and progressed Mercury was parallel Saturn within 2.2 minutes. His direction of this documentary film at a remote location went well and was tastefully done. It resulted in considerable attention and monetary payoffs.

Five events were eventually progressed, including his marriage, the date his ship, *Calypso,* was officially signed over to the Jacques Cousteau Society, an arrival and demonstration in New York, etc. All were characterized by his flair for showboating. Either his progressed Midheaven or his progressed Sun or both were combined with other planets in close angles for these events. Each one had aspects that met the 4 minute accuracy requirement. This is one Virgo who dramatized his activities, including his marriage.

Mohandas Karamchand Gandhi is still another individual whose physical birth time horoscope has been cast with Libra on the Ascendant, while the natal horoscope that agrees with his life has 05 Virgo 07.2 on the Ascendant. That he should exhibit some Libra characteristics is perfectly natural, because his Sun was in the sign of the unbalanced scales. Picture Gandhi for the moment with his pear-shaped head (another term often used to describe the appearance of Virgo), his long straight downpointing nose and his relatively thin body. His head appeared to be even more triangular in youth. Remember also that as a lawyer he was conversant with a multitude of facts, and he used those facts in exercising passive opposition. His biographer, Geoffrey Ashe said, "...his life and work have usually come veiled in a spiritual cloak that is foreign in every sense of the word. We only assume that behind the image of the demigod there must have been a man who ate food (and how occupied he was with the problems of what to eat for most of his life); who made love (or tried so hard to abstain from carnality); who was sometimes insufferable in his quest for victory through suffering; who experienced countless humiliations and defeats; who, moved by the seeming impracticalities of Tolstoy and Thoreau and others less well known to us, shaped the second largest nation in the world." Such was the power of one individual who combined a cardinal Sun sign with the passive Virgo rising sign as shown in Figure 19 and Table XVII. That horoscope is full of contradictions, as one might expect. But first, a small portion of his life will be reviewed, sufficient to establish his personal characteristics.

Mohandas Karamchand Gandhi was born in Parandar, a village on the West Coast of India that lies on the peninsula North of Bombay in the state of Gujarat. His name was picked after his father and mother consulted an astrologer. The Gandhi family belonged to the *Vaisyas Caste* (that is mid-ranked, as it includes farmers and merchants) and to the *Modh Bania* sub-caste, theoretically a sort of bourgeoisie. His father, who was named Karamchand, or Kaba, was a premier of Porbandar, and subsequently premiers of Rajkot and Wankaner. He had no formal education and was quick tempered, but managed to compete through his ministerial offices. This was his fourth wife, Putlibai, who gave birth to Mohandas on October 2, 1869.

After a few years the typical Hindu education was administered. Mohandas was an average student. He was guided by the strong religious and moral principles instilled by his mother and experienced some conflicts between honesty and maintaining friendships. By the age of thirteen he was married, in typical Hindu fashion, to Kasturbai, the daughter of a local merchant. To quote a little more from his biography, "They settled down in the family home at Rajkot. Mohandas read pamphlets giving advice on happy marriage and applied the bits that appealed to him. Full of ideals, he expected Kasturbai to be as faithful to him as he was to her. No doubt she was. But his perfectionism, at this point, took the form of infantile jealousy. He resented her going anywhere without him, even to the temple or on visits to friends. She was indignant, and their life jerked along through a series of tiffs and sulks." The gist of that quotation could fit thousands of immature young married men with Virgo rising.

At this youthful stage there were still no signs of saintliness in the young Mohandas. It was the custom for young married men not to work and for their education to be continued if the family could afford it. "His struggle against his own mental road-blocks extended his perfectionism to school. He became over-sensitive and could not relax. His best loved exercise was solitary walking. Games and gym, which he was to think highly of later, had no charms for him now." Thus his life continued in the ways of Virgo. Ultimately, his mother pawned jewels to send him to England for more advanced study. He left his wife and son behind, received objections from other members of his sub-caste and was required by a Jain monk to solemnly swear that he would abstain from touching meat, wine or women while abroad. The meatless diet proved to be his biggest hurdle, and he virtually starved until finding two vegetarian restaurants in London. Perhaps that set the stage for his later fasts. Meanwhile, it was in London that he studied law, languages and philosophy.

This brief sketch of his youth is sufficient to reveal strong Virgo characteristics that are not to be found in a Libra rising horoscope. The rest of his life is history. It is therefore appropriate that his horoscope now be tested.

I. At first glance the only remarkable thing about the horoscope of Mohandas K. Gandhi appears to be his strongly aspected Moon tucked away in the twelfth house. It is when the declinations are reviewed in Table XVII that subtleties emerge. First and foremost, Saturn is within 13.7 minutes of a contraparallel with his Midheaven. That coincides with his notorious struggles and frequent setbacks. Uranus is also close enough to his Midheaven to have its revolutionary effect. Venus and Mars are parallel within 11.5 minutes. Harmony and combat are conjoined in a way that resulted in his method of passive resistance. Moon and Jupiter are parallel within 0.9 minutes, and Jupiter is the most elevated planet in the ninth house. These two planets are square in longitude. It is little wonder that moral conflicts existed in profusion and his struggles with the British on behalf of his people became matters of public record. The Virgo rising sign has already been affirmed. Thus, the connection between this horoscope, the man and what he accomplished are beginning to emerge.

II. Sun in the second house might at first seem like a detraction. But no, it is not. First of all, Sun is in the sign Libra, where actions (in this case related to possessions and talents) are taken that are far left or right of center. Sun is widely in opposition to Neptune, which causes his attitude toward worldly possessions to be dreamlike or disdainful. The co-ruler of the second house, Venus, is conjunct and parallel Mars. This is where his conflicts between having and not having frequently consumed his mind. Still, his needs were provided by a doting public, since Sun is trine his Midheaven. The three planets in Scorpio and the third house fill his life with momentous events, including his assassination—Mars is co-ruler of the eighth. Mercury, one of those three planets is ruler of both his first and tenth houses, which is in keeping with his use of words and personalized events to sway nations and people. He wrote and he gave speeches that caused him to be a Frankenstein in the eyes of the British. Saturn in the fourth house correlates with his philosophical passion for austerity. Neptune in the eighth house indicates dramatization of his country's economic problems. Jupiter and Pluto in the ninth house are strong indicators of his legal studies, and their opposition to the third house planets is strongly indicative of the way he applied his training. Uranus in the eleventh house develops revolutionary plans for all of the peoples of India. Now we come around to the Leo Moon in the twelfth house. This Moon is what made him a demigod. It is the handle planet of a dual T-square. It is also in a grand trine with Neptune and Saturn. Any doubts about this horoscope that might have arisen at first are fading fast.

III. The final confirmation was obtained with lots of progressions. All provided positive support. As appropriate as any perhaps for illustrative purposes was the day when he appeared

OCT 2 1869
PARBANDAR
21 N 38 43
3:28:14 AM TLT

3:51 AM IST
INDIA
069 E 40 19
10:49:33 PM GMT

Naibod Secondary
MAR 18 1922
10:49:33 PM GMT

Tropical *Placidus* *True Node*

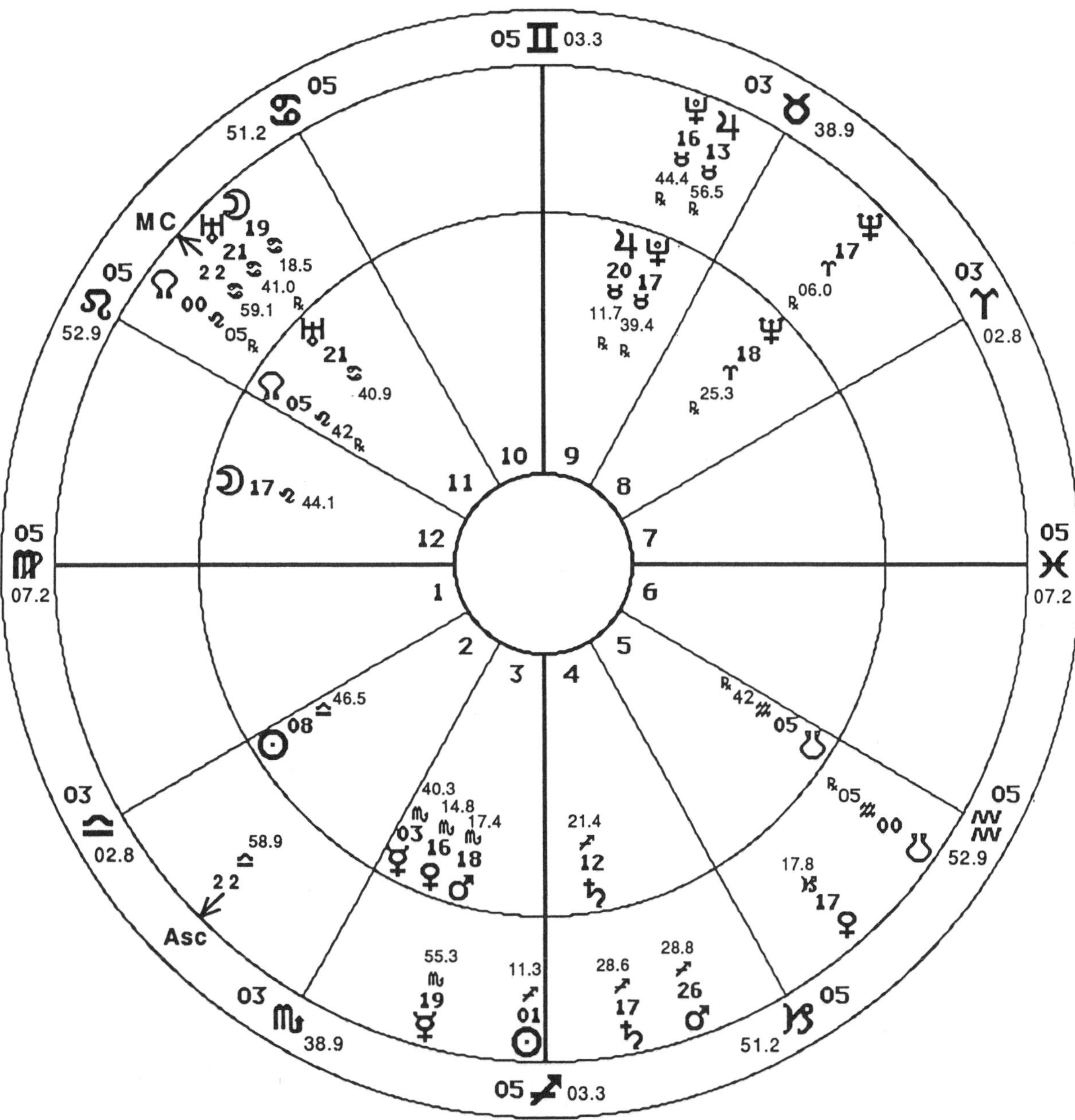

Figure 19. Horoscope of Mohandas Ghandi, leader of the Indian Revolution. The progressions shown are for the date he was first sentenced to jail.

Table XVII. Natal and Progressed Declinations of Mohandas K. Gandhi

Planet	Natal Decln.	03 18 1922 Sentenced
♇	02 N 15.7	01 N 59.2
☉	03 S 28.9	20 S 24.7
♆	05 N 38.9	05 N 09.4
Asc	09 N 38.5	08 S 56.4
☿	10 S 14.5	16 S 51.9
☽	16 N 32.1	21 N 07.4
♃	16 N 33.0	14 N 49.0
♀	17 S 37.5	25 S 06.3
♂	17 S 49.0	24 S 22.1
♄	20 S 55.7	21 S 36.9
MC	21 N 09.4	21 N 29.8
♅	22 N 08.6	22 N 10.3

in court and was sentenced to jail. "Gandhi was tried in a small, heavily guarded courthouse in Ahmedabad on 18 March 1922, before Mr. Justice Broomfield. The charge was sedition, on the basis of three of his more challenging articles in *Young India*. The publisher Shankarlal Banker was tried with him. At the preliminary hearing Gandhi pleaded guilty, and gave his occupation as farmer and weaver, a gesture of identification with the masses which he had first made when giving testimony in another case two years before. Technically he was a barrister still. But he had not practiced for a decade, and he was soon to be disbarred."

On that day Mohandas K. Gandhi's progressed Midheaven was square his progressed Ascendant within 0.2 minutes. The conflict had been building for some time. His progressed Moon was also parallel his Midheaven within 2.0 minutes. This trial was well attended by supporters and was well publicized. His exceedingly strong Moon attests to their presence. These aspects are profound, and he was incarcerated.

Of the examples presented to this point both Jacques Cousteau and Mohandas Gandhi are very typical of males with Virgo rising. Yet, it is important to see variations on the female side. A female with Virgo rising is Shirley Maclain—singer, dancer, actress. She is 5 foot 6 inches tall and weighs 118 pounds. This is slightly short for females of this sign. The shortness is due to a skeleton established by her Taurus Sun sign. Taurus also causes her triangular head to be somewhat broader than average. However, the most unique influence of this horoscope, illustrated in Figure 20 and Table XVIII, is the Moon sitting on her Ascendant and Neptune close by. No wonder she has been called a hoofer, singer, dramatic actress, comedienne, political activist, feminist, author, world traveler and devotee of the occult. She was the elfin beauty who became a member of the clan—the one including the likes of Frank Sinatra, Dean Martin and Sammy Davis Junior. In this "rat pack" she sounded off, was into fashion, became a political supporter (of George McGovern, for one), queen of rocks, a ring-a-ding girl and new-style star.

Shirley Maclain was born in Richmond, Virginia. She was given dancing lessons early in life and took them about as seriously as a comical girl with Virgo on her Ascendant could. By the age of sixteen she was dancing in a revival of *Oklahoma* given at the City Center in New York City. Then she was in the chorus of *Kiss Me Kate*. She eventually graduated from Washington and Lee High School in Arlington, Virginia at the age of nineteen. This was 1953 and she soon turned up in the chorus of Rodgers and Hammerstein's Broadway musical *Me and Juliet*. One of those performances was seen by Hal B. Wallis, who signed her to a long term film contract. Her movie debut in 1955 was in *The Trouble with Harry*. Others followed in rapid succession. This movietown clown princess rose swiftly. By 1964 she found it necessary to renegotiate her contract with Wallis and started making $800,000 per film. Then followed TV guest appearances, more

Table XVIII. Natal and Progressed Declinations of Shirley Maclain

Planet	Natal Decln.	09 17 1954 Marriage
☿	03 N 50.8	19 N 44.3
♃	04 S 58.7	04 S 15.2
♀	05 S 08.0	02 N 15.3
☽	07 N 42.4	26 N 41.2
♆	08 N 44.9	08 N 48.6
Asc	09 N 04.3	02 N 45.6
♅	10 N 11.1	10 N 35.3
♂	11 N 42.1	16 N 41.5
☉	12 N 49.5	18 N 41.8
♄	13 S 43.6	13 S 24.1
MC	20 N 51.1	23 N 13.3
♇	22 N 56.1	22 N 54.6

APR 24 1934 2:05 PM EST
RICHMOND VIRGINIA
37 N 30 37 077 W 19 53
1:57:30 PM TLT 7:06:49 PM GMT
Tropical *Placidus* *True Node*

Naibod Secondary
SEP 17 1954
7:06:49 PM GMT

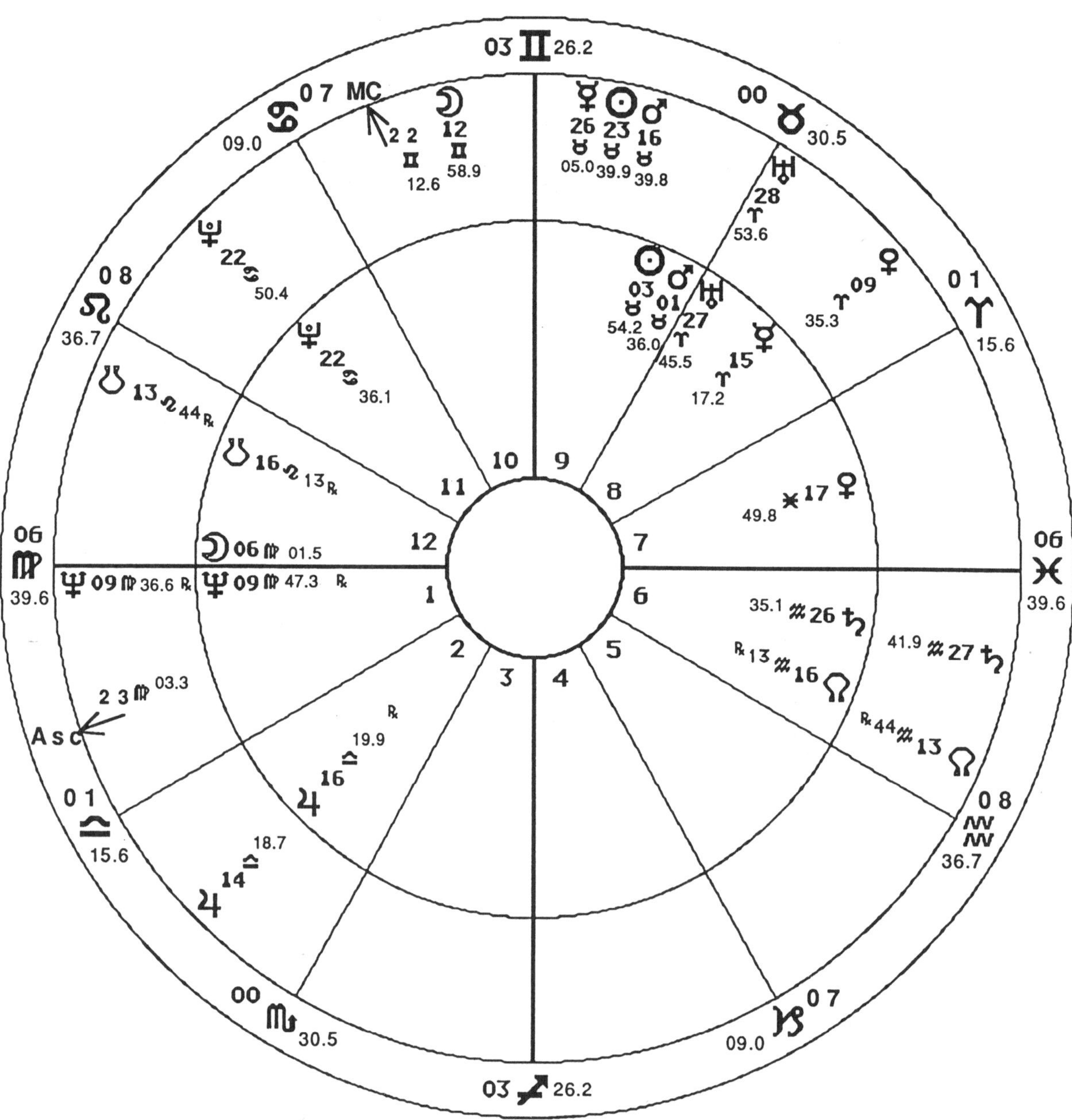

Figure 20. Horoscope of singer-dancer-actress Shirley Maclain with progressions to date of her marriage to Steve Parker.

award winning performances, activism and her book, *You Can Get Their From Here.* She led twelve American women into the People's Republic of China and participated in making *The Other Half of the Sky: A China Memoir.* During the nineteen-eighties she startled everyone by openly declaring her belief in occultism and played herself in films concerning the supernatural that were aired on television. This is one legendary doll.

I. Does the 6 Virgo 39.6 minutes rising chart equate to this bundle of energy, or does someone want to try and make a case for 29 Virgo 11 minutes that was computed from her reported birth time? Both are in the same sign, Virgo, but that is little consolation. The planets causing all of this commotion, Moon and Neptune, are nowhere close to her Ascendant in the later one. They are back in the twelfth house where the purpose would be much more serious, such as in the case of Gandhi. Also, Pluto would no longer be in the eleventh house, and an entertainer must have an eleventh house outlet. No interceptions are present, mind you. But, Pluto and the other ruler of the eleventh house, the Moon, are strong. The earlier chart is clearly the better fit.

II. A dancer must have rhythm and a body with the kind of muscles that respond. Both Mars and the Sun in the artful sign Taurus are trine Moon and Ascendant (with the mystique of Neptune added). Both are in the ninth house which is appropriate for viewing audiences. Mercury, the ruler of the first and tenth houses, is conjunct Uranus in the Arian sign of exploration. Well, that is appropriate for a person who is concerned with life in the hereafter. Those two outer planets Neptune and Uranus are placed in positions to cause both mystical and radical viewpoints. One should remember that the eighth house is considered to be the domain where departing souls go (and from which they return) in addition to being related to the possessions of partners. Mercury and Uranus are square Pluto, which cultivates the controversies.

As we look closer, each of the planets adds to what we know about this woman with Renaissance charm. She has clearly made a lot of money. Jupiter in a sign that he likes very well would not deny that. Sure it is opposite Mercury, which required that the original long term contract with Hal B. Wallis, at a modest pay scale, would need to be scrapped. Oppositions do that kind of thing. Saturn in Aquarius indicates a very hard worker. Saturn is in the sign of the Aquarian Age. Her actions and accomplishments are definitely of that nature. Seventh house Venus, also in a sign she is most compatible with, trines Pluto and provides the harmony with others that helps any production This time the declinations do not add a great deal, except for Neptune being closely parallel to her Ascendant. This reinforces the conjunction and gives the Eastern sector a unique character. It is a strong indicator that the body, the memory and a dramatic flare are combined. Bolstered by two major sources of energy, Mars and the Sun, you have none other than Shirley Maclain.

III. If the date when her contract was terminated and payed off were known, that would have been a perfect event to use for illustrative purposes. However, the biography only implied that it was around late 1963 or early 1964. We do know that Mercury progressed to a sextile with its own position about that time, and shortly afterwards her progressed Sun came into a parallel with her Midheaven. Those would be appropriate aspects. However, the date of her marriage to Steve Parker is given instead, because it was dated. The proper confirmations were produced. Progressed Venus was inconjunct Neptune within 1.3 minutes on September 17, 1954. Both Venus and Neptune indicate seventh house activity. Also, progressed Saturn was sextile Uranus within 3.6 minutes. These two aspects meet our accuracy criterion, and they are appropriate for the event.

All three of these Virgo rising individuals accomplished much in life. They overcame obstacles, especially Gandhi. Among them are three different races and two sexes, yet a certain similarity exists in their physical appearances. None, it might be added, looked anything at all like President George Bush, or Sadam Hussein or former President Dwight D. Eisenhower. The other significant point is that each Virgo rising horoscope agrees with the person represented.

CHAPTER 7. LIBRA

Physical Attributes

Libra is represented by the scales, and it is a cardinal air sign. Balance is the strong central thrust, although that condition may be elusive and unachieved. The dominant characteristic of taking contrary sides to seek equilibrium can sometimes be sensed in the body and demeanor. The shape of the head is compressed ovate. That is, the length of the head from top to bottom is less than average, while the structure is basically oval. This often conveys an impression that the head is small in proportion to the rest of the body. However, especially the women can be comely. Dimples may be present and sometimes a cleft in the chin. On average the hair is straight and smooth. Bright eyes and a nicely shaped mouth are typical. In males the voice is often resonant or pleasant in tone and in females the voice is often sweet. Their bodies are normally well formed and slender, especially in youth. They remain slender if a good diet is maintained later in life, but tend toward plumpness if not. The stature ranges from short to medium tall, depending upon the Sun sign and planets conjunct or parallel the Ascendant. Also, the complexion is ordinarily very good. The disposition is mostly amiable, contented and polite. It seems as though they should be lovers and the pursuits of cupid often start young.

Libra rising contrasts sharply with the adjoining signs. Scorpio's hair is more wavy and the face is fuller. Virgo's head is triangular or pear shaped. Neither shape resembles Libra, which is more oval. From a personality standpoint, Libra is usually quicker with responses and taking sides than either of these other two signs.

Mental Attributes

With a Venus ruler, Libra rising seeks beauty, peace and harmony. The opinions of others will always be sought, but not necessarily shared. Thus, they are normally sociable, genial and sympathetic, although not necessarily warm. The intelligent Libra rising individual is well equiped to play the role of mediator in disputes and to seek concordance of positions. Seeing the viewpoints of both sides is quite easy for them. Seeing a compromise solution is also relatively easy. Yet, in their personal lives they can be changeable, quick to anger and quick to be appeased. The scales become easily unbalanced from small disturbances as the pointer oscillates back and forth seeking a null. So Libra rising people often take extreme positions on either side of a consensus in attempts to correct a perceived unbalanced scale pan and bring the pointer to zero. In such cases others may consider them to be radicals. Yet they try to nudge the collective consciousness toward their viewpoint with propriety and in good taste. Sometimes this gives the appearance of vacillation. At other times they may take the less popular position in a debate, at which they are very good.

Libra is a mental air sign, while Scorpio is emotional water and Virgo is exacting earth. It is true that Virgo is ruled by Mercury, which is a mental planet. But, in Virgo the mentality is super-critical, whereas in Libra the mentality is manifest in a far more pleasure-seeking or cool, unemotional way. In fact, ideas flow more freely than physical actions. Libra is usually faster to respond or choose sides than the two adjoining signs and enjoys the use of forceful opposing thoughts, as long as they can be kept amicable.

Among individuals who are not well developed, Libra on the Ascendant often gives the impression of indecision, indifference or laziness. They are dabblers in life and fickle. It is easy for them to ridicule others or to make them look silly. Some of this class consider themselves to be the thinkers of the world and leave finer details to others. They look upon people, who are cruder, slower or less sophisticated than themselves, as being colorless, vapid, callous and uncongenial in ways that prevent them from appreciating the many factors that must be considered in order to redress balances that have been upset. Yet they themselves, can be unemotionally cruel in dealings with the opposite sex or with associates. While appearing outwardly to be polite and friendly, they can undercut and discard long-standing friends if they think it is to their own advantage. Love affairs are natural, but engagements or marriage vows can be broken when the next good looking person comes along who fascinates. Their hearts are not broken as they trifle. They have a craving for the lovely in life, are incapable of saying no, live for the present and can be perfectly guileless.

The advanced soul who is born with Libra on the Ascendant is highly cultured, loves justice, neatness and order, has superlative tastes and loves beauty in all forms. Nature, art, music, literature, sculpture, poetry, love—these are their joys and pleasures. Harsh notes or discordant elements of life are avoided, and they are less prone to hurt other people's feelings than those who are not as well developed. Modesty and refinement are admired. They are ambitious and make good professionals, especially in pursuits that permit them to exercise their innate sense of acceptability to the widest audiences. This causes them to be good at advertising. They often have a way of converting the writings of others into more acceptable forms. They like to go places and do things. Being with sophisticated and amusing people is one of their chief pleasures. It is within their realm to be inspirational, impartial, even-handed and delightful. They mainly need to be true to themselves and guard against playing some part, deemed to be beautiful or important, that could not be said or done with the same conviction on the following day.

With this picture in mind, let us put our knowledge into practice. Among famous women Elizabeth Montgomery, Debbie Reynolds and Barbara Walters are alleged to have Libra on their Ascendants, according to reported birth times given for their horoscopes. But what a difference there is in physical appearances, at least between the likes of Debbie Reynolds and Barbara Walters. Therefore, one has a right to be extremely skeptical that all members of this group have a Libra rising sign. Similar comments might be made among men in this category. The group includes Lew Alcindor (Kareem Abdul-Jabar), who was the former outstanding center of the Los Angeles Lakers basketball team, Arthur Ashe, the tennis great, and Lew Ayres, the actor. One published horoscope even shows Sir Winston Churchill with a Libra Ascendant. Now the differences in body structures, say between our basketball playing friend Kareem Abdul-Jabar and Sir Winston Churchill, are absurd. To believe both have Libra Ascendants is to believe that rising signs in astrology have no effect on appearance or personality. Yet these kinds of mismatched horoscopes persist in the astrological press, often accompanied by authoritative-sounding words that shake confidence. An apology is due for being so blunt, but if astrology is to come out of its haze the truth must be told. For thinking individuals it is very good practice to review the lives of the celebrities just mentioned to determine which of them truly have Libra on their Ascendants.

Example Horoscopes

It is now appropriate to examine the lives of people with Libra on the Eastern horizon of their charts. What better place to start than with the man who has emceed the longest running night time television show in history, Johnny Carson. While unauthorized biographies describe his foibles, his unfaithfulness, his harsh treatment of fellow workers, his drunkenness, his few real friends and his many marriages (all in conformance with the Libra style), the facts are that he also developed a show that was very entertaining, and he did help many unknowns get their start. Several reasons why his *Tonight* show lasted so long are that it was enjoyed by a majority of viewers and he had a sense of understanding about what could be said that would be accepted by the public. Only occasionally were there slipups over too much sex, too much lampooning, too much character-assassination or too much raunchiness. After all, night time emcees often test the limits of tolerable social behavior and what might be said on the air. Johnny Carson seemed to know where to draw the line and get a laugh out of it. He has practiced since his grammar school days.

Kit Carson, Johnny's father, was a manager of Iowa Nebraska Light and Power. His mother was a proper, strong-willed woman who "henpecked" her husband and dominated the household. His later attitude toward women was no doubt molded by his mother. The family, which included an older sister and brother, was in Corning, Iowa, when Johnny was born. Every few years Kit Carson was shifted to another location in his work for the power company, which kept the family reasonably affluent. So Johnny attended a number of schools. Friendships with fellow students were left behind on each of these moves, and none appeared to be long lasting. For amusement he learned magic, practiced card tricks, bought books on how to become a ventriloquist, developed comedy routines and played pranks. He tried everything for laughs, wearing out anyone who would listen or watch, and called himself "the Great Carsoni." Throughout this period he seized every opportunity to show his card tricks, project his voice and tell jokes. He perfected his acts diligently and landed a few jobs, including being emcee at various clubs and ceremonies. These routines continued throughout high school, the war years in the U. S. Navy and later at the University of Nebraska. In his college thesis he dissected gags, punch lines and jokes, getting to the very core of what made comedians on radio successful. Television was still an unreal dream for the future.

After graduation from Nebraska, Johnny Carson got his first steady job at station WOW. On August 1, 1949, *The Johnny Carson Show* commenced. It was aired each morning, from 8:15 to 9:00, and consisted of recorded music, news, weather reports and sports, interspersed with his patter. He worked very hard during the evenings to perfect these routines. Two months later, on October 1, 1949, he married Jody Wolcott, a girl he had met in school. They eventually had three sons, but this was his rollercoaster start in show business and marriage.

By October 4, 1952, having left WOW, Johnny Carson made his West Coast television debut on KNXT-TV. His show was called *Carson's Cellar*, and it was not an overwhelming success. However, it did provide opportunities to meet lots of people, especially women and promoters. He also earned extra money by writing for Red Skelton. By June 30, 1955, *The Johnny Carson Show* began on CBS. He had made it to the networks. This also was a time of other women and other wives. Number two was Joanne Copeland who had a career of her own. Afterwards there were dates with movie stars. Later, after shutting Joanne out of their apartment and divorcing her, he married a girl with a similar first name, Joanna (Ulrich) Holland. This one lasted two years, with more to come.

The Tonight Show already existed with Jack Parr at the helm. Finally, it came time for him to step down. Johnny Carson had already substituted with considerable success. By this time his techniques were well honed. The day finally came on October 1, 1962, when Johnny Carson took over. It lasted 29 years, until 1991 when his retirement was publicized. Perhaps the best rationale for his show's longevity came from Johnny himself, "If you make your guests look good, you look good." He indeed has looked good, and some lesser known visitors eventually became stars themselves.

Perhaps one of the most revealing episodes occurred in May, 1976, when Johnny Carson returned to Norfolk, Nebraska, where he had attended high school. The purpose of this visit was to be the commencement speaker. Quoting from *King of the Night,* his biography by Laurence Leamer:

> "You don't know how terribly proud I am to be here today," Johnny told the graduating seniors and their families. "It means a great deal to me." He made a few obligatory jokes, but fifty-year-old Johnny was in a reflective mood. He told the graduates, "... to keep a certain child-like attitude of curiosity and sense of discovery of how everything works. Adults don't ask questions as a child does. When you stop

wondering, you might as well put your rocker on the front porch and call it a day.........Stay loose to keep from going bananas. Don't become rigid in your ideas or close the door from learning anything new. It is better to have doubts and go ahead."

After his address he received questions from the students. "Did you have any idea when you were here that you would reach the heights of success that you have?" one graduating senior asked.

"Success is a relative measure, " Johnny said. "I feel fortunate in doing what I want to do. When you are starting you want to move on to higher levels. By good luck I was able to move on to college, then into radio and finally into national television. However, this commencement address has made me prouder than anything I've done."

Another student stood up. "Do you find that you are happy with what you did in life, and would you change part of your life if you could?"

"I've found that there is more unhappiness than happiness in life," Johnny said firmly. "I always have doubts and concerns, with ups and downs. Then I have to sit down and examine myself. Hindsight is wonderful, but I've been relatively happy and think if I had it to do over I'd stumble along as I did."

Table XIX. Natal and Progressed Declinations of Johnny Carson

Planet	Natal Decln.	10 01 1962 *Tonight Show*
Asc	02 S 16.4	12 S 59.6
♅	03 S 50.5	04 S 03.5
♂	05 S 36.8	14 S 31.3
☉	11 S 18.2	21 S 25.6
♆	13 N 42.9	13 N 36.8
♄	14 S 20.0	15 S 34.5
☿	15 S 24.2	25 S 12.8
♇	20 N 49.4	20 N 52.6
☽	21 S 21.0	14 N 45.0
♃	22 S 53.6	22 S 04.4
MC	23 N 17.0	17 N 25.9
♀	24 S 55.0	24 S 12.3

OCT 23 1925 04:42 AM CST
CORNING IOWA
40 N 59 10 094 W 42 08
4:22:16 AM TLT 10:41:04 AM GMT
Tropical *Placidus* *True Node*

Naibod Secondary
OCT 1 1962
10:41:04 AM GMT

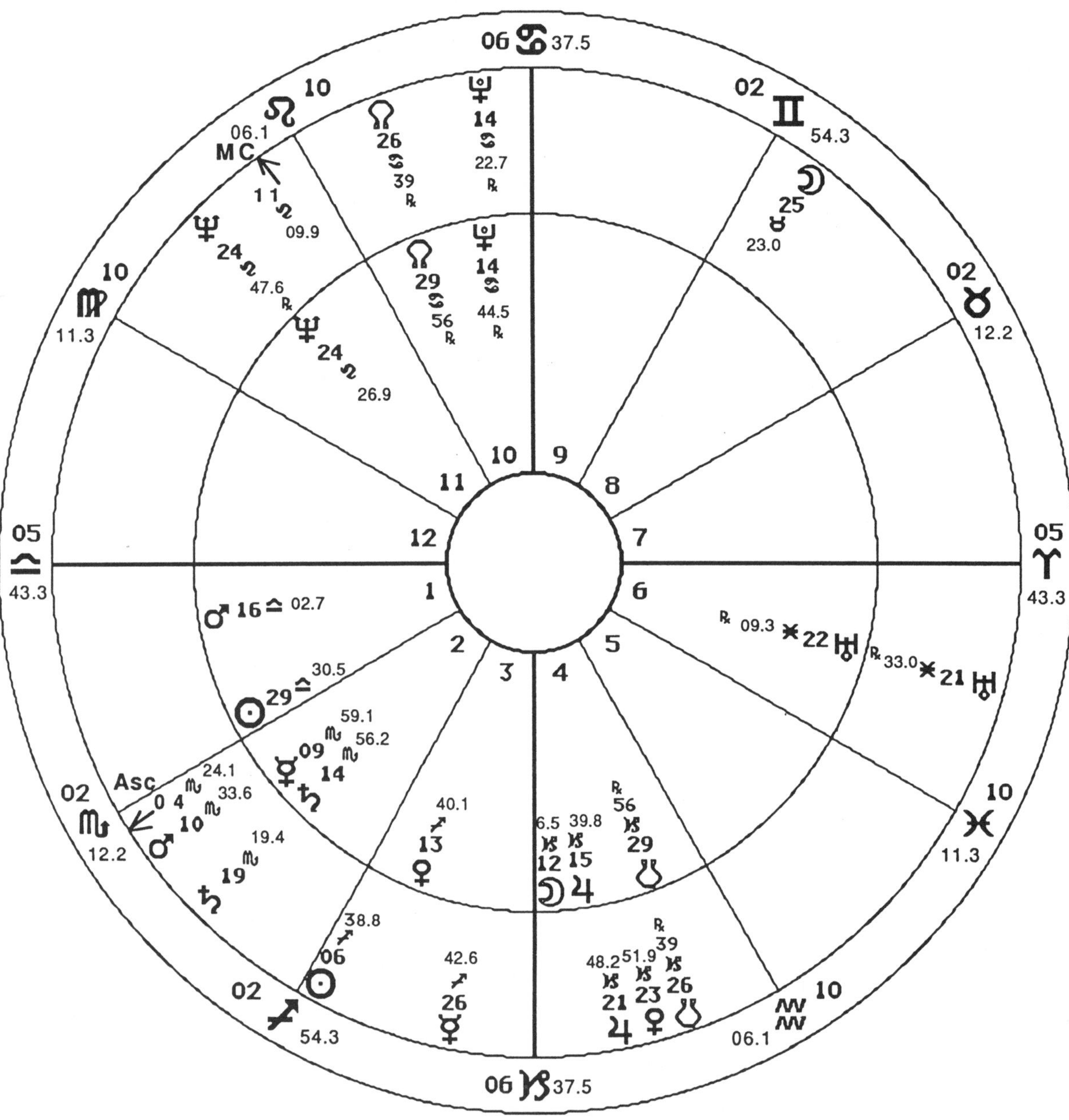

Figure 21. **Horoscope of Johnny Carson, emcee of the long-running *Tonight Show*. Progressions are to the date when he took over from Jack Paar.**

So, "He-e-e-e-ere's Johnny," with his Libra Ascendant, the guy who, when told to have a few teeth fixed before appearing in front of the cameras, had all of his teeth ground down and capped in one week.

I. The above incident is pure Libra. Our question is, does the horoscope of Figure 21 and Table XIX match the man? The review does grow on one as the many conflicts are observed and resolved. There has to be a strong eleventh house for a comic. Leo is on the cusp, the sign of emcees. Neptune is there, agreeing with his slight of hand card tricks, ventriloquism and magic acts that got him started. Neptune is sextile his Sun, the eleventh house co-ruler in the first house, and that makes it very strong. All that first house energy conveyed by the Sun and Mars demands personalized efforts—featuring himself. Venus, the ruler of the Ascendant sign is in the third in Sagittarius. Again, it is his material, his jokes, his lifted eyebrow, his art, that are center stage. The possibilities are strong.

II. We need to look at the other planets. First, Mars is the focal point of a strong T-Square. Mars squares Moon and Jupiter in the fourth house and Pluto, the most elevated planet, in the tenth. Pluto has a way of getting recognition in such a position. Moon and Jupiter agree with his frequent moves and new homes. Neither Moon or Jupiter are particularly happy in the sign Capricorn, but they aspire to more and better. They conform with his answers to student's questions at the high school commemoration exercises. Meanwhile, Mars is his downfall with wives, but not necessarily with women in general, because of its sextile to Venus. Mercury and Saturn in the second house receive considerable remuneration over time for communications and wit. Uranus in the sixth provides work for a person on radio or television, especially clever work. Also, it is the focal point of a yod from Sun and Neptune which increases these opportunities enormously. Most of the declinations are spread apart, except for the contraparallel between Jupiter and his Midheaven. Jupiter is conjunct Moon, however, holding on to his popularity, although there were many moments of controversy.

III. This is one individual whose biographer gave many dates. Therefore it was easy to check all kinds of progressed events. The one chosen for illustration purposes was for his takeover of *The Tonight Show* from Jack Parr. That first show began on the evening of October 1, 1962. On that day progressed Sun was inconjunct his Midheaven within 1.3 minutes. He gained an opportunity to make something of this show. Jack Parr had been quite popular himself, and that made the task more difficult. But Johnny Carson was successful, and he has held on all of these years, renegotiating bigger and better contracts. On the date of that first show his progressed Sun can be observed as having just passed a parallel with his Moon. This aspect was exact at the time of a previous substitution for Jack Parr. The audience responses he got probably convinced NBC management to go ahead with their choice of a successor.

If a black man can be said to look like a white man, then a reasonable similarity exists between Johnny Carson and Jesse Jackson. Being a Reverend, the black man has not been as free with women since he was married, although that profession was not a guarantee. But Libra rising similarities do exist. Jesse Jackson might even give the impression of having Virgo rising from his physical appearance, but that is mainly due to his coiffure. His hair is often cut much wider than his face, making his jaw look narrow. If you see photographs of him during his youth or without as much hair, the compressed ovate look of his head can be observed. Add the personality traits, and Libra rising is unmistakable (see Figure 22 and Table XX).

Jesse freely and openly acknowledges that he was a bastard. His father, Noah Louis Robinson, lived at 22 Haynie Street in Greenville, South Carolina. Noah wanted a man-child. His wife wasn't producing one, so he solved the problem by going next door to 20 Haynie Street, where Helen Burns lived, and she did. Jesse was born through the help of a midwife, Minnie Munson, who describe him as "the cutest youngun you ever seen in your life. It seemed the child was in a hurry to get here. By the time the doctor arrived I had wrapped him in a blanket and laid him in bed with his mother." After this excitement the time of 9:00 a.m. was recorded. That recondite sentence has been written without further comment.

Jesse's mother, Helen Burns, had some Irish and Cherokee blood in her veins. Two years after the birth Helen married an athlete by the name of Charles Henry Jackson, and that is where Jesse got his last name. The two families eventually got together when Jesse had pneumonia twice, but it was an unusual relationship. Jesse knew that he had a mother in one house and a father in the one next door, which left him out of things he wanted to participate in at times. Segregation was another matter to contend with. He had every opportunity to wind up like some of his chums did, but there were those who were praying for him. His grandmother, Aunt Tibbie on the Jackson side, was the one person who always believed in him and to whom he could always turn. Aunt Tibbie was the one who prodded him on to make something of himself.

His biographer, Barbara A. Reynolds, said, "Every teacher Jesse came in contact with took note of his insecurities, masked by a stoic sense of superiority. They never perceived him as brilliant, but rather each saw him as a charmer, a spirited, fierce competitor with an almost uncanny drive to prove himself by always winning, always being number one in everything." One of his teachers, Mrs. Sarah Shelton, said, "he was a leader of devilment. If I could calm him down the whole class would settle down." However, his leadership abilities were beginning to emerge. He was elected president of his class, president of the honor society and member of the student council. He won a state office in the *Future Farmers of America.* During this period Jesse wore suits and ties to class while other were wearing blue jeans. This affectation received the kind of small talk one might imagine, but it made him stand out, and that is what he wanted.

Jesse Jackson was also a very good quarterback on his football team. That led to his first encounters with prejudice in the North, which if anything was worse than in South Carolina, because it was hidden behind a facade. The then New York Giant professional football team had just won a bidding war. Two quarterbacks were offered contracts. Dickie Dietz was white, and he was offered $95,000. Jesse was black, and he was offered $6,000 plus a chance to go to college during the off season. It is doubtful that a 13-to-1 difference in their capabilities existed, and a reasonable question is whether they were even equal. Jesse turned this magnanimous offer down and opted for a scholarship at the University of Illinois instead. It was there that he encountered prejudice again and was told by an assistant coach that blacks could not be quarterbacks. With that input he delayed for a year and then transferred to Agricultural and Technical College of North Carolina where he was heralded as a pretty good college quarterback. It was there too, that he met Jacqueline Lavinia Davis, a 5 foot 1 inch beauty from Fort Pierce, Florida, and promptly announced, "Hey Jackie, you're going to marry me." She didn't believe him at first, but she did.

At A & T Jesse Jackson first became involved with the civil rights movement by participating in sit-ins. By 1963 he was leading many demonstrations. On June 6, 1963, he was arrested for inciting a riot in downtown Greensboro where he had led a column of students in a sit-down in the middle of a busy thoroughfare in front of the municipal building. The inspirational message he gave his followers was, "I know I am going to jail. I 'm going without fear. It's a principle that I have for which I'll go to jail, and I'll go to the chain gang if necessary." That last clause was melodramatic rather than factual since there were no chain gangs in North Carolina in 1963. However it was highly representative of his mission and behavior. By his senior year he became leader of CORE. This put him into contact with James Farmer, Floyd McKissick and indirectly with Dr. Martin Luther King Jr. The key roles ministers were playing in this movement accelerated a youthful desire to be one too. He entered the Chicago Theological Seminary and after completing his studies received the title. Meanwhile, his civil rights activities continued in Chicago, and he eventually met Dr. Martin Luther King, who became a father figure. Later, in Memphis, Tennessee, he was present when King was shot.

Jesse Jackson has been called one of the most influential moderates among the younger generation of black leaders, and a protegee of Dr. Martin Luther King. He responds to the urgency and impatience of the black movement with a militant but non-violent call for black power based on black economic and political organization. While still a seminary student he was chosen, by King in 1966, to organize an alliance of black businessmen and clergymen in Chicago. He was extremely successful and became National head of Operation Breadbasket. Upon King's assassination, Jesse Jackson met with political opposition from within the black movement, perhaps be-

OCT 08 1941 | 6:21 AM EST
GREENVILLE | S.C.
34 N 51 13 | 082 W 31 04
5:49:38 AM TLT | 11:19:42 AM GMT

Tropical *Placidus* *True Node*

Naibod Secondary
OCT 06 1973
11:19:42 AM GMT

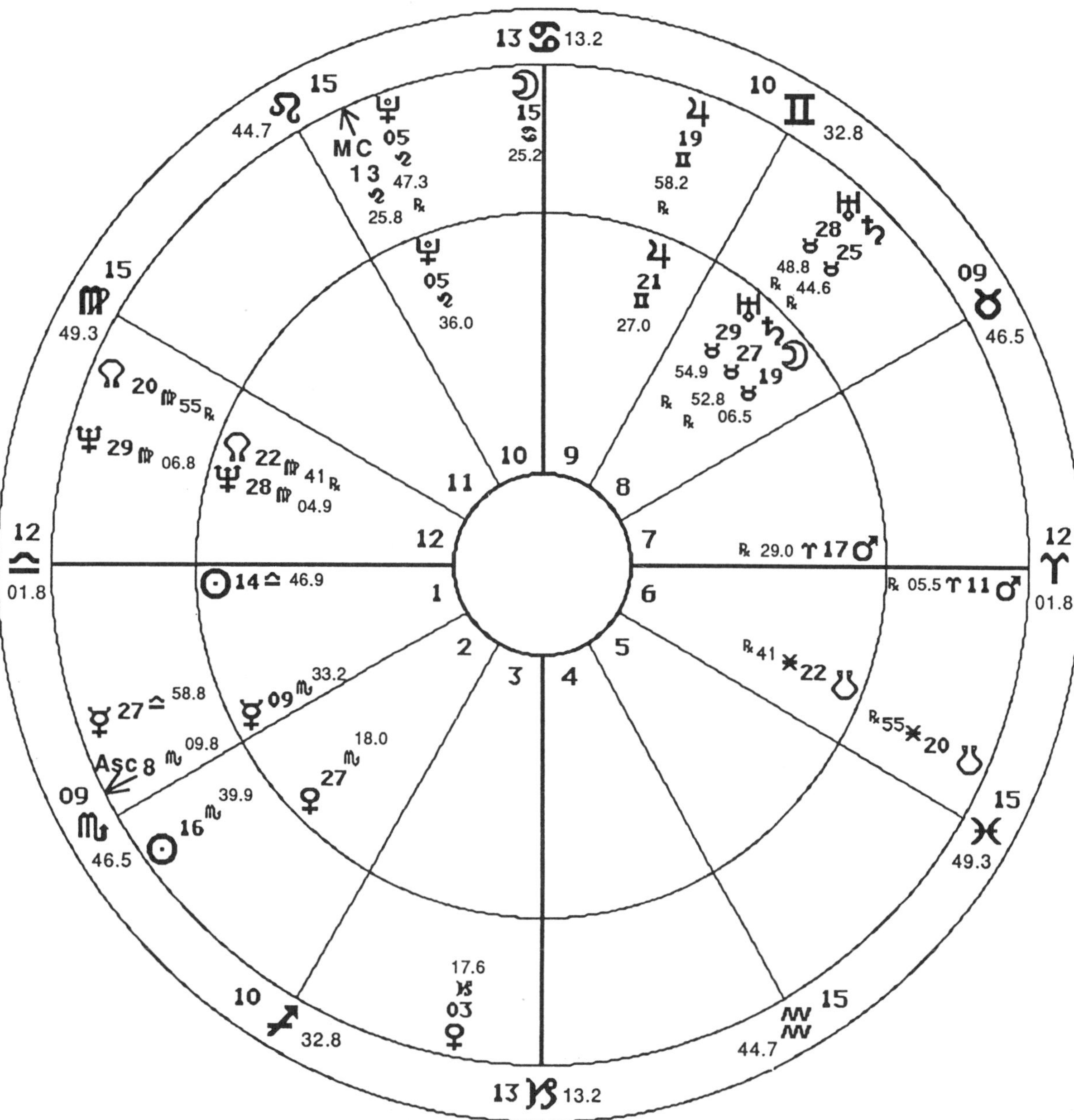

Figure 22. **Horoscope of Jesse Jackson, civil rights leader, with progressions to the day declared by the city fathers of Greenville, South Carolina in his honor.**

Table XX. Natal and Progressed Declinations of Jesse Jackson

Planet	Natal Decln.	10 06 1973 Honored
♆	01 N 54.4	01 N 30.7
♂	03 N 37.9	03 N 12.1
Asc	04 S 45.4	14 S 13.9
☉	05 S 49.6	16 S 49.3
☽	13 N 18.3	17 N 55.9
♄	17 N 25.0	16 N 53.8
☿	17 S 45.0	08 S 40.0
♅	19 N 55.3	19 N 41.1
♀	21 S 22.2	26 S 33.1
♃	22 N 28.3	22 N 22.5
MC	22 N 47.3	16 N 47.7
♇	23 N 10.1	23 N 13.1

cause of his youth, drive, ego and success. However, he has continued his efforts as a strong force to be reckoned with. In his own words, "If I thought we were just developing some more black capitalists with the same value system as white capitalists I'd drop the whole campaign. The only thing dangerous about black power is that it might become like white power—compassionate toward machines, not people. What we need is white folks' technology and black folks' love." The Chicago Theological Seminary awarded him an honorary Doctorate.

Jesse Jackson is 6 foot 2 inches tall and his normal weight is 215 pounds. He is afflicted with sickle cell anemia, a disease peculiar to his race, and that lowers his resistance to virus infections. The clues to this disease might be observable in his validated horoscope (Figure 22 and Table XX).

I. The very first thing that can be observed in Jesse Jackson's horoscope is Sun conjunct his Ascendant. No wonder he wants to be first in everything. It is opposite Mars in the seventh house—no wonder he is a militant leader, even when the Venus of his Libra Ascendant sign calls for non-violence. It is entirely possible that sickle cell anemia could be related to such a debilitating opposition. Evenso, it gave him strength to lead.

II. The placement and aspects of every planet seem to confirm the biographical accounts of Jesse Jackson. Mercury, also in the first house and contraparallel Saturn, provides the ability to communicate his power struggle and to center it upon economics. Venus, the ruler of his first house is in the second. That conforms with his dressed up attire in high school. It also conforms with later criticisms he received from fellow blacks for flaunting his affluence and riding around in luxury automobiles. The concentration of planets in his eighth house opposite Venus emphasizes the economic weapons he uses. They have been very effective. The ninth house Jupiter in Gemini agrees with his desire to become a minister. It might be argued that he is a minister for talking purposes more than he is a minister for leading a flock in a small church. That is a correct conclusion, but Jupiter in Gemini takes the broader view. Anyone with Pluto in the tenth house has special abilities to persuade other people. Moreover, Pluto is parallel his Midheaven and that contact brought him worldwide prominence. Neptune in Virgo in the twelfth house causes him to continue his efforts for his people along idealistic but pragmatic lines. Neptune is trine that strong group of eighth house planets. Success results from this configuration.

If it makes any difference to anyone, the standard approach, using 9:00 AM to cast his horoscope would have put 15 Scorpio 58 on Jesse Jackson's Ascendant. Now Scorpio is a formidable sign of power, but it doesn't look like him. In that chart there are no planets in the tenth house pointing the way to prominence. Venus would have been in the first opposite the three planets that have now moved from the eighth to the seventh. Nothing really indicates the economic methods he used. It would be strange that he has had only one wife with such a line up. So please, let us forget the chart not worth casting from a very approximate time.

III. On October 6, 1973, Jesse Jackson was honored in his home town of Greenville, South Carolina. The event was complete with police escort, chauffeured limousine, eating with the mayor and all the trappings of being a celebrity. This was Greenville, a small Southern town honoring a black son who had become famous. On that date it is interesting to note the lineup of planets in declination. The Midheaven would have to be making some kind of aspect and it was. His progressed Midheaven was contraparallel his progressed Sun. That is most appropriate. Also, his progressed Sun was parallel his progressed Saturn. The one aspect was within 1.6 minutes, and the other was within 4.5 minutes. The three-way contact adds subtlety. Contraparallels are like oppositions, and the irony was there. Parallels are like conjunctions, and his recognition did come without doubt. Incidentally, when three planets are enmeshed very close to the same numerical degree all should be considered together even though one aspect is weaker than the other. The Sun-Saturn parallel is outside our 4.0 minute limit, but barely, and it has that extra kick. It is interesting that no longitudinal aspects were sufficiently strong to be counted. Progressed Mercury was already past an inconjunct with Saturn by 6.0 minutes, and it could be felt, but was not the main aspect. It probably occurred when the event was first planned.

Two Libra rising individuals have been shown with radical tendencies. The next one is a female actress who is less of a radical, but very pretty and very talented. In fact gorgeous might be a better term. This is Sally Field, who started out in youth not even wanting to be an actress. Her mother, being a Paramount starlet herself, was the one who pushed her forward. Thus, upon her graduation from high school in Pasadena, California, she enrolled in Columbia Pictures Workshop. This was 1964. By 1965 she was selected for a role in the television comedy *Gidget.* That show lasted through 1966. From 1967 through 1970 she became the perky, airborne Sister Bertrillo in *The Flying Nun.* Then she starred in the television movie *Sybil,* and the new roles continued to arrive. Her motion picture debut was in *The Way West.* Like Shirley Maclain she became sufficiently political to support George S. McGovern in his 1972 campaign. Otherwise, we have simply a very good actress in the 5 foot 2 inch Sally Field, whose horoscope is given in Figure 23 and Table XXI.

I. Neptune on her Ascendant is where the drama is. No planets reside in the eleventh or fifth houses. This agrees with the fact that she is more of a dramatic actress on display than a comic or entertainer. Yet Sun, ruler of the eleventh, is conjunct Jupiter and semi-sextile Neptune and her Ascendant. It is square Saturn and Pluto, trine her Midheaven and inconjunct her Moon. Those are rather strong aspects, and the Sun is also in the group of planets residing in her second house. Still, one might consider this to be a bit weak for an actress, although the filled second house points to an enormous variety of personal talents in addition to personal possessions. It should be remember that acting was not an all-consuming desire, at least in the beginning. She was

NOV 06 1946 03:43 AM PST
Pasadena California
34 N 09 54 118 W 08 25
03:50: 26 AM TLT 11:43:00 AM GMT
Tropical *Placidus* *True Node*

Naibod Secondary
SEP 11 1977
11:43:00 AM GMT

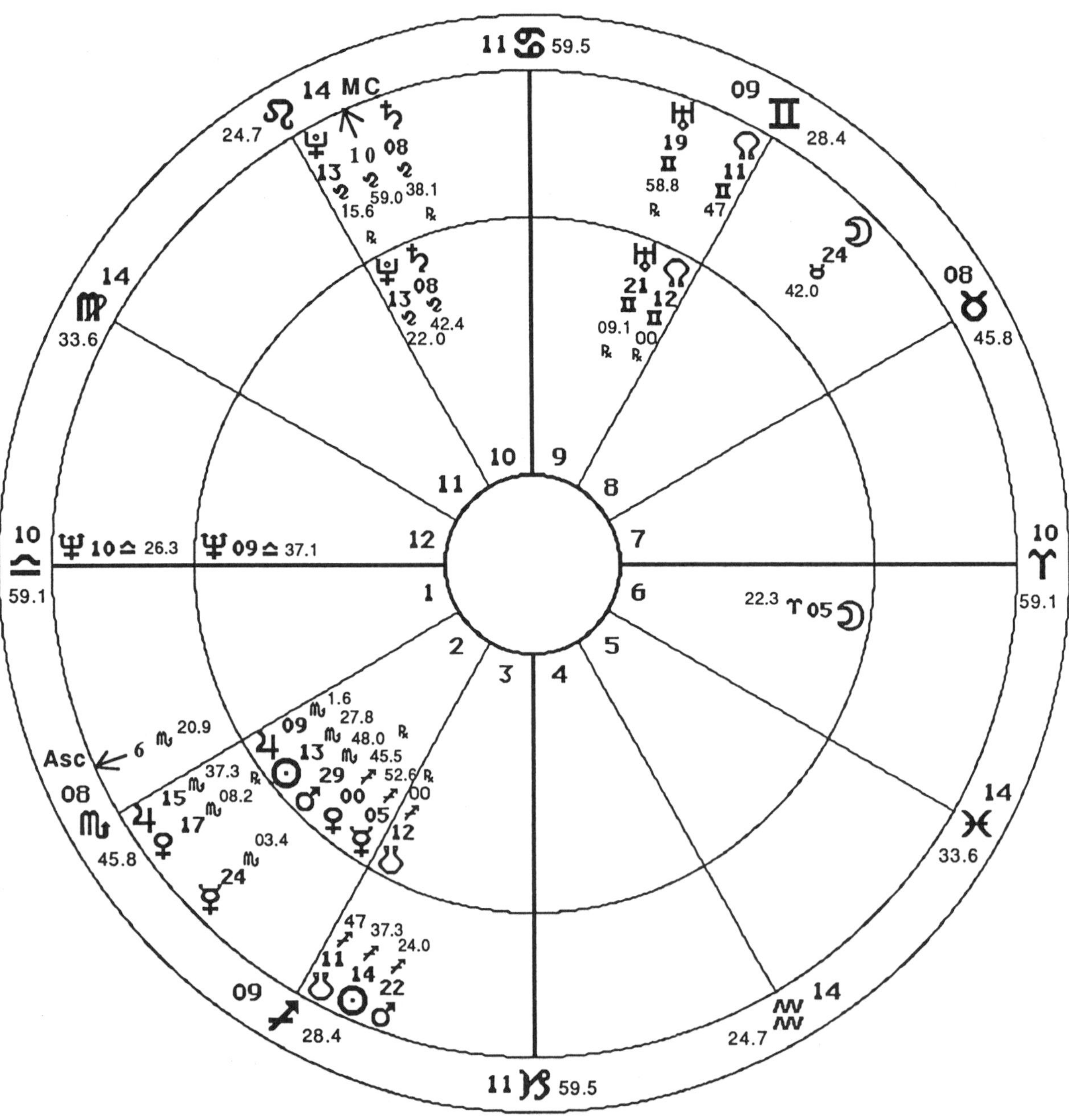

Figure 23. Horoscope of Sally Field with progressions to the night of her Emmy award.

pushed into this career.

II. One set of aspects reinforces the picture. That is the very strong parallel of Midheaven, Pluto and Uranus. Now we have found the widespread recognition. Supporting the drama of Neptune, which in itself indicates activities in motion pictures, Uranus now urges television appearances from his ninth house position. Here is Pluto, again performing his miracles of publicity. Not to be overlooked is that powerful parallel between Moon and Neptune. The opposition might have caused more of an emotional tussle over her career, but with that strong parallel her memory is enhanced and the pair work more like a conjunction. Moon is trine Saturn-Pluto in her tenth house, and that shows popularity, which she certainly has. It is the declinations that bring out the strength of this horoscope, because the aspects and locations in longitude by themselves provide less assurance of a good match with the real person.

Table XXI. Natal and Progressed Declinations of Sally Field

Planet	Natal Decln.	09 11 1977 Emmy Award
☽	02 S 15.7	17 N 26.1
♆	02 S 28.4	02 S 46.5
Asc	04 S 20.9	13 S 38.5
♃	13 S 35.3	15 S 35.5
☉	15 S 53.1	22 S 33.6
♄	18 N 29.0	18 N 34.5
♂	20 S 31.3	23 S 55.2
MC	22 N 54.4	17 N 28.9
♇	23 N 09.2	23 N 20.2
♅	23 N 13.8	23 N 09.1
☿	24 S 01.3	16 N 23.2
♀	25 S 38.6	15 S 39.1

III. A very good candidate event for illustration purposes was the evening Sally Field received an Emmy award from the Academy of Television Arts and Sciences. This was September 11, 1977. If there were any previous reservations about her horoscope the progressions for that date should eliminate any doubts. First, her progressed Midheaven is sextile her Ascendant within 0.1 minutes. Since this progression was routinely calculated for her birth time (not the event time), it was probably exact by evening when her award was presented. Progressed Midheaven is also parallel her progressed Moon within 2.8 minutes, and her progressed Ascendant was parallel her Jupiter within 3.2 minutes. Additionally, progressed Uranus was parallel her Pluto within 0.1 minutes. That is one bunch of close aspects agreeing with the event. Her reported birthtime horoscope, which has Libra rising in the nineteenth degree, would have missed the event with the lone exception of the slow moving Uranus progression to Pluto. By itself that aspect does not award an Emmy. With the others the combined forces did.

CHAPTER 8. SCORPIO

Physical Attributes

Scorpio on the Ascendant of a person's horoscope yields a rectangular head. It is about as broad at the jaws as at the temples. The eyes are sharp and may be penetrating, especially noticeable in one-on-one conversations or when presentations are being made. These eyes look right at you and through you. The nose is straight to aquiline, or hooked. Males of this sign typically have hairy arms and legs. Hairy chests predominate as well. The beard will typically be heavy with a tender skin to match that can easily be nicked. The complexion is fair to dusky. Among both sexes the hair on top of their heads is normally thick or luxuriant, and curling or wavy, especially in youth. Eyebrows are prominent. The height is short to medium and the body has strength and virility. Another characteristic of the body is that it is often high-waisted. Whether thin or weighty it is usually, but not always, square built like the head. Much depends upon the underlying Sun sign in this regard. A Gemini Sun sign, for example, can cause the body to be taller and thinner, but the high waist and distinctive head of Scorpio is there. Lips are normally full, and this is a sensuous sign. Scorpio is fixed water, and the saying goes that "still water runs deep." Hence there is a seriousness and depth of character that stands out. It is just as fascinating in women as in men, if not more so. In youth especially they are passionate and sensitive, yet the majority are quiet mannered and reserved. Much is hidden behind the expressions on their faces and their controlled features. They rarely give themselves away. Scorpio rising makes strong impressions on other people.

Scorpio cannot be mistaken for Libra or Sagittarius on the Ascendant. There is Libra, with the small compressed ovate head for earlier births, the quick mannerisms, seemingly biased positions and straight hair. There is Sagittarius, with the elongated head for later births, the jovial nature and tall bodies. Scorpio is between with the more rectangular build, the short proportioned body as compared with the length of the legs, the more distinctive nose, the sharper eyes, the wavier hair, the fuller lips and all that personal magnetism.

Mental Attributes

Scorpio rising provides quiet earnestness and great powers of observation. The characters of strangers are sensed right away. The willpower is strong and can be applied with great intensity. Most are occupied in productive work, and they tend to make good use of time. Efficiency is important, and they may be experts at it. Wasting time is an abomination. The powers of concentration are enormous and this sign is willing to devote many more hours than most to furthering objectives. Yet a shield is up which few can get behind. Often secretive or untalkative about their personal activities, they are not prone to discuss their innermost feelings. Inscrutable in nature, they may even be casual about holding back on minor details others are dying to know. A part of the fun is in the mystery and intrigue. They have a reserve and hidden resources that are not for public consumption. Yet the speechmakers among those with Scorpio rising can spellbind an audience. It is as though an invisible force connects them to their listeners. This combination of traits makes it difficult for them to be imposed upon by others, although it can happen with people they like. They are extremely interested in life's secrets, death, the arcane and esoteric and they make staunch friends. Stinging sarcasm can be heard coming from their lips when the mood strikes, and they can be blunt or brusque with other people who appear foolish or waste their time. In matters of negotiation or handling day-to-day problems they are normally shrewd and make advantageous decisions. Most have penetrating minds.

Scorpio rising natives who are not well developed can be contemptible, vindictive, fiendish or wicked. There are no half-way measures. Two symbols have been used to describe the sign Scorpio--one the scorpion and the other the eagle. Thus, the range of social behavior is much wider than average. These people can sink to the lowest levels of a scorpion with a tail that stings, or soar to the greatest heights of an eagle with eyes that survey all below, before carefully choosing their quarry. A low level trait is getting even with anyone who in their minds causes harm. This can be a lover who cheats, an associate who does not live up to the terms of a contract or a person who takes offensive action. Then you had better watch out. Scorpio rising can get even in more ways than most people can imagine, and they are not above using trickery. The timing of the sting can also be long delayed, like the antagonized elephant who can wait years to catch an offender napping. They may also be overly aggressive and have intense faults, such as anger, rebellion or jealousy in the most forceful forms. They can be critical of weaknesses in others and it is sometimes difficult for them to say only kind words about associates, or nothing at all. The tendency is to say what is on their minds without omission of flaws. They are highly sexed but dislike gush and sentimentality. Fortunately, even the less sophisticated spend most of their time at productive pursuits, and they can set their sights on incredible objectives which they meet. They are adept at keeping more than one ball in the air at a time.

The eagles among Scorpio rising types have absolute self-mastery, or come very close to it. They are extremely resourceful, which is the overriding characteristic of the ruling planet Pluto. They understand when to apply force characterized by the other ruling planet Mars. Therefore, they excel in their work. The main ambitions include control over the will, the intellect, the passions, the emotions, the desires, the bodily functions, the psychic faculties and the ego. The enlightened Scorpio rising native gives freely of his perfections and of his moral, mental and physical vitality. They can be fabulous healers, great doctors, superior engineers, legendary organizers, charismatic ministers and unrelenting detectives. Whatever their pursuits, hobbies as well as work, their aim is to do exceptionally well and not just middling, moderate or passable. Whatever it takes to be successful, Scorpio will do it. They may have to guard against overwork because nothing is going to stand in their way.

The above traits apply to the females of this sign, as well as to the males. Of course it is one thing to read these words and another to match them to real people. It has been claimed that Bette Davis the movie actress, Sylvia Porter the financial columnist, Grace Kelly the former actress and princess of Monaco and Dianne von Furstenberg the fashion world entrepreneur, have Scorpio rising. That is a potent group of women. Among men Daniel Berrigan pacifist, Hugo Black jurist, Vida Blue baseball pitcher, Lawrence Taylor football defensive specialist, Glen Campbell singer-guitarist and Ronald Reagan past President have Scorpio rising according to previous publications. Here the bag is a little more mixed. For those not having Scorpio rising, the likelihood is that the Ascendant slipped back into Libra.

Example Horoscopes

To illustrate this sign a female athlete was selected first. Her reported birth time gave late Scorpio (the 24th degree) on her Ascendant. Considering her accomplishments and rise to prominence, Scorpio appears to be correct, but an earlier degree is far more appropriate. The shift backward is only eight degrees for the Ascendant of Chris Evert, whose horoscope is given in Figure 24 and Table XXII. Now the Ascendant is conjunct Moon and Saturn, with Venus close by. She was called America's Sweetheart and Miss Charisma. With the correction in time those word descriptors have a place in her horoscope. Without the correction the match is not as apparent.

DEC 21 1954 3:55 AM EST
FT LAUNDERDALE FLORIDA
26 N 06 20 080 W 08 34
3:31:38 AM TLT 8:52:12 AM GMT
Tropical Placidus True Node

Naibod Secondary
FEB 07 1972
8:52:12 AM GMT

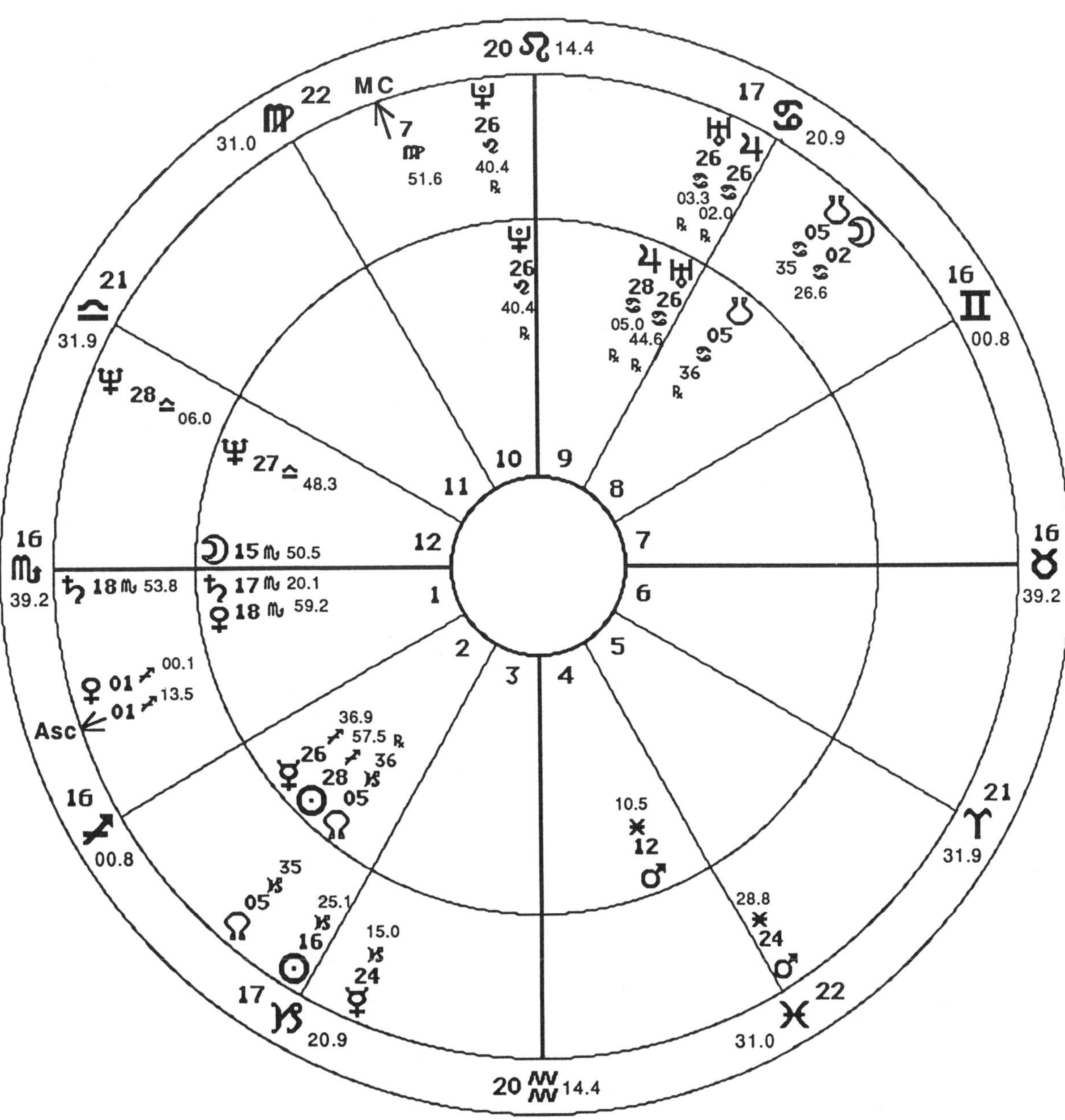

Figure 24. Horoscope of "America's Sweetheart" Chris Evert, now retired tennis player extraordinaire. Progressions are to the day she trounced Billie Jean King.

Chris Evert was born the second of five children in Fort Lauderdale, Florida. Her father, James Evert, was both a manager and teaching professional of Fort Lauderdale's Holiday Park Tennis Center, the largest in Florida. He had attended Notre Dame on an athletic scholarship. Chris's mother, Collete, was from Westchester, New York, a town whose average residence is regarded as opulent. The Evert family was immersed in tennis as a sport and partly as a living. Two of the boys, taught by their father, gained state rankings in each of their age groups. Jeanne, a sister, was runnerup before reaching the age of sixteen. But Chris became the real star. She devoted two-and-a-half hours to tennis each day after school and eight hours on weekends. Twenty-and-a-half hours per week concentrating on tennis, plus all of the hours in school and studying too, are typical of the devotion and determination applied by a person with Scorpio on their Ascendant. No question remains about her being prodded, although the claim is that she was not pushed. Chris Evert put in those long hours of practice because to this sign it was the way to success.

Table XXII. Natal and Progressed Declinations of Chris Evert

Planet	Natal Decln.	02 07 1972 Trouncing
♂	07 S 46.4	02 S 38.0
♆	09 S 07.2	09 S 12.6
♀	14 S 15.7	16 S 25.0
MC	14 N 44.6	08 N 37.5
♄	14 S 55.4	15 S 18.9
Asc	16 S 49.1	20 S 24.7
☽	20 S 26.9	23 N 42.7
♃	20 N 53.5	21 N 20.0
♅	21 N 20.4	21 N 28.5
♇	22 N 18.5	22 N 28.6
☉	23 S 26.5	22 S 26.1
☿	24 S 39.8	23 S 22.0

What really startled everyone, was this sixteen year old girl who arrived in early September 1971 at the West Side Tennis Club in Forrest Hills to play in the U. S. Open. She proceeded to beat Edda Ruding of Germany 6-1, 6-0. Then she took on Mary Ann Eisel of the United States and the scores were 4-6, 7-6, 6-1. She beat Francois Durr of France 2-6, 6-2, 6-3 and Leslie Hunt of Australia 4-6, 6-2, 6-3. By the tenth of September, in the final match against Billie Jean King, on the grass courts of Westchester, she finally lost 6-3, 6-2. Billie Jean King was the reigning tennis queen of that period. But that was a typical Scorpio rising accomplishment at Chris Evert's first national outing. She hadn't even graduated from high school yet. That was still two years in the future. Four months before the occasion of that ceremony she trounced Billie Jean King 6-1, 6-0 on her own turf which featured clay courts.

Chris Evert was ranked number one among female tennis players for many years. By 1974 she had won 96 of 103 matches. By 1976, her fourth year as a professional, she earned more than one million dollars. Sports writers penned many accolades during her supremacy and among other sobriquets called her Little Miss Cool and Little Miss Sunshine. It was mainly hard work and a fierce determination to win that was responsible for her achievements, but she also had backing from a very proud family.

I. Mars is expected to be prominent in the figure of an athlete. It is in Chris Evert's horoscope. With Moon, Saturn and Venus positioned on her Ascendant, Mars trines the entire group from the fourth house. That planet looks like her athletic father in a most favorable and harmonious aspect. Her Sagittarius Sun sign is athletic, and she is 5 feet 6 inches tall with a playing weight of 115 pounds. She might have grown a little taller, except for Saturn sitting within a degree of her Ascendant. Sagittarius usually produces large hands and feet. Scorpio produces small hands and feet. The combination resulted in hands large enough to grip a tennis racket well and feet that got her to the ball as needed. The sizes worked out between the two signs were what she had to work with. It is interesting that Chris Evert became famous for her two-handed backstroke. The Scorpio rising sign and the imprints of an athlete are confirmed in the horoscope presented.

II. The small backward shift in time from Chris Evert's reported birth time horoscope caused only four planets to change houses. Otherwise the interpretations are the same for those that stayed put. The main transitions are Saturn and Venus from the twelfth house to the first, Pluto from the ninth to the tenth and Neptune from the eleventh to the twelfth. If Saturn had remained in the twelfth house, Chris Evert probably would have been several inches taller because of her Sagittarius Sun sign. Saturn in the twelfth house might have wanted to perform pragmatic, slow-developing services for others. On her Ascendant, Saturn takes personal time, increases physical commitment and hardens muscles in the manner of the sign it is in. Venus in the twelfth house would have urged more activities of an artistic nature, such as decorating for others. In the first it is more concerned with having a tasteful personal appearance. Pluto, added to Uranus and Jupiter in the ninth house, but nearly conjunct her Midheaven, would not have caused a strongly altered picture from the one given by the two planets in the ninth house and Pluto in the tenth. Pluto elevated always attracts attention. Neptune in the eleventh house would probably have caused a more dramatic flare while entertaining spectators. She might even have worn fancy pants like one of her peers, or gone into the movies. In the twelfth house the illusory nature of Neptune leaves records to posterity in a more subtle way.

What really seals the fate of the later chart is the interception of fourth and tenth houses. A person with such interceptions would have been far more likely to enter politics or a military branch and go out of her way to command others. That she concentrated on her sport, without insistent notoriety or the need to direct other people, argues for the earlier horoscope. For that matter, every factor reviewed has favored the earlier horoscope.

III. Nothing could be more appropriate for a progression to use for illustration purposes than the day Chris Evert won a tennis match against the only person she did not beat at Forrest Hills. The match was with Billie Jean King, but this time it took place near her home. Wimbledon courts are grass and Chris Evert excelled on clay courts. The trouncing was so one-sided one could hardly believe that Billie Jean King had been rated Number One. The scores were 6-1, 6-0. On that date Chris Evert's progressed Ascendant was parallel Moon within 2.2 minutes, her progressed Sun was parallel progressed Pluto within 2.5 minutes, her progressed Jupiter was conjunct progressed Uranus within 1.0 minute and progressed Neptune was square Jupiter within 1.0 minute. She had soared over the tallest mountain.

So, it is evident from this first example that a typical Scorpio rising person is serious, reserved, dedicated and willing to put in long hours of work to succeed. As committed as they are, no one can say they are colorless. Chris Evert was definitely colorful in her prime, and she is both attractive and talented. At times these people may be controversial, but they normally produce well and often get strong reactions. Most of them are outstanding, or near the top, at whatever they undertake.

A similar male example is Alan Greenspan, the economist. No birth time was available from the records reviewed of this responsible individual, and no previously published horoscope has been found. Thus there is nothing to compare the horoscope of Figure 25 and Table XXIII against, although it is a good example of Scorpio rising. This horoscope was simply computed and selected because it fits.

Alan Greenspan was born in Washington Heights, New York, and he attended George Washington High School. It just so happens that he was two classes behind Henry Kissinger. Upon graduation, his main interests were not with economics, but with music instead. He enrolled at Julliard School of Music and became a good enough clarinettist to play in professional dance bands for several years. The ability to excel at different occupations is a hallmark of Scorpio rising. But Alan Greenspan began to tire of the routine of his life and its limitations. He decided to return to college and this time it was New York University. The major he picked was economics. He received his bachelor's degree in 1948 graduating *summa cum laude*. His Master of Arts degree was received in 1950. Then he proceeded to Columbia University for his doctorate, where he studied under Arthur Burns.

For fifteen years Alan Greenspan was president of the New York consulting firm of Townsend-Greenspan. By August 21, 1974, he received national recognition when he was confirmed as chairman of President Nixon's Council of Economic Advisors, where he succeeded Herbert Stein. This position continued under President Gerald Ford. During President George Bush's tenure in office Alan Greenspan was appointed head of the Central Bank with responsibility for the nation's economic affairs. He has his critics, but the country's inflation rate, one of his chief concerns, is now in his hands and he has been reappointed for a second term.

Today (1991) he is considered by many to be the high priest of the old-time religion regarding traditional Republican economic policy. This policy features balanced budgets and fiscal constraints. Neither a liberal Keynesian economist, nor a conservative monatarist, he calls himself a free enterpriser. He believes in as little government intervention as possible in the free market system. In common with economic theorists Milton Friedman and John Kenneth Galbraith, he considers inflation to be the chief menace. The combination of skyrocketing prices and sluggish business activity that currently plagues the United States constitutes his main concern. He is generally opposed to wage and price controls and an advocate of continuing the fight for economic health through tight credit controls, reduced government spending and balanced budgets.

An interesting sidelight is that for several decades Alan Greenspan has been a friend of Ayn Rand, the philosopher-author of *The Fountainhead* and *Atlas Shrugge*d. She labels her philosophy objectivism. He has credited her with weaning him away from an early liberalism in favor of a higher morality, the ultimate desirability of complete *laissez-faire* capitalism and what she calls rational selfishness. So perhaps there is a touch of Ayn Rand in today's interest rate policies. It is hoped that the approach will continue to be successful. Meanwhile, our subject is the Scorpio Ascending sign and the correctness of the referenced horoscope.

I. In Allen Greenspan we have a former musician, an intellectual and a world class economist. What one sees first in his horoscope is a second/eighth house interception. The economic interests are obvious. With Pluto, the ruler of his Ascendant in the eighth house as well, the main calling is sealed. Venus conjunct Jupiter and contraparallel Moon is sufficient for musicianship, especially when aspects of diligence are present. Strong third and ninth houses show the intellectual bent. Overall we have a match.

MAR 26 1926 10:33 PM EST
WASHINGTON HTS NEW YORK
40 N 59 39 073 W 51 52
10:38:41 AM TLT 3:34:09 PM GMT
Tropical Placidus True Node

Naibod Secondary
JUN 02 1987
3:34:09 PM GMT

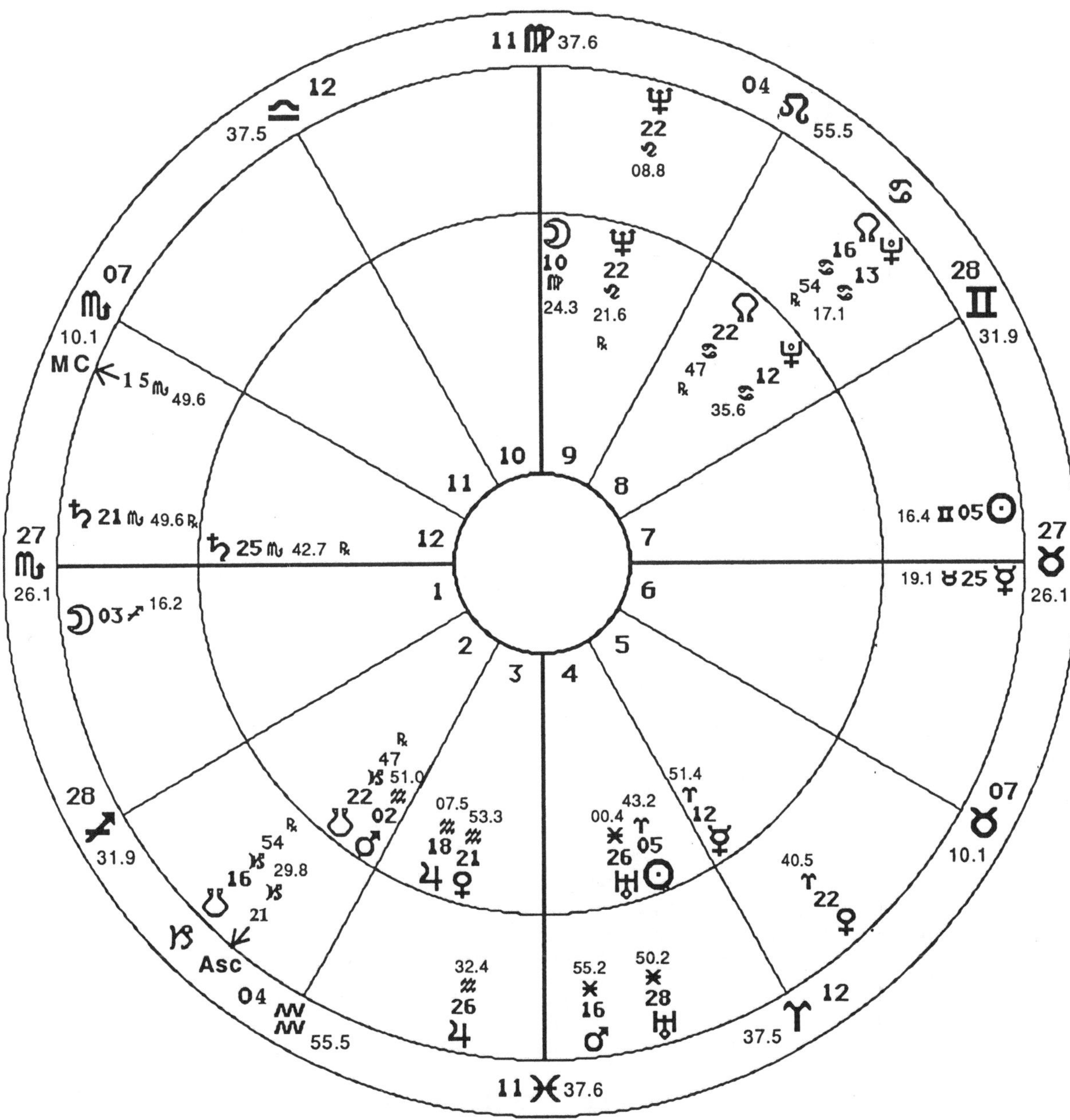

Figure 25. Horoscope of economist Allen Greenspan with progressions to the day he was nominated head of the central bank of the United States.

Table XXIII. Natal and Progressed Declinations of Alan Greenspan

Planet	Natal Decln.	06 02 1987 Nomination
♅	02 S 14.9	01 S 08.5
☉	02 N 16.4	21 N 11.3
MC	07 N 12.4	16 S 35.0
☿	08 N 12.3	18 N 22.6
☽	11 N 06.0	17 S 18.6
♀	11 S 13.8	06 N 53.8
♆	14 N 26.6	14 N 30.6
♃	15 S 57.6	13 S 25.4
♄	16 S 54.6	15 S 55.3
Asc	19 S 35.7	21 S 43.9
♂	20 S 29.8	07 S 04.7
♇	21 N 11.9	21 N 13.6

II. While discussing Chris Evert's horoscope the question of Saturn being in the twelfth house or the first was briefly reviewed. With Chris, her Saturn was essentially on the Ascendant, affecting the first house. She was not especially tall. It so happens that Alan Greenspan has Saturn close to the Ascendant (less than two degrees away), but clearly in the twelfth house. The influence on height is far less, as Alan is an even six-footer and weighs 180 pounds. But the desire to make a solid contribution to the nation, one that may be a long time in coming, is found in his chart rather than hers. Saturn is also the handle planet of a T-square with Neptune on one side and Jupiter-Venus on the other. The interests in music and literature are emphasized. A yod, formed by Mars in the second house and Sun in the fourth with Mercury in the fifth, focuses energy onto the elevated Moon. This Moon, which is also conjunct his Midheaven, is one important reason for public recognition.

Sun in Aries contraparallel Uranus has had a somewhat abrupt impact upon Alan Greenspan's home environment, which has seen many changes. His Arian Sun inspired the formation of a consulting business. Its contact with Uranus causes the need for sudden departures, such as the times when he is called to Washington. The close trine between Uranus and Saturn has been a steadying influence. Yet the square between Sun (as well as Mercury) and Pluto from time to time breeds uncertainties shown by the repeated discussions in the press about whether he would be reappointed, and the demands for faster actions. Moon contraparallel Venus has led to aborted incidents regarding marriage in which emotions erupted. Thus we have a brilliant economist in the hot seat, with a very trying and difficult job, whose reputation fluctuates due to articles from the press that range from the complimentary to the ludicrous. Understanding Scorpio on the Ascendant, and the layout of his horoscope, show that he works with an even hand, does the best possible job he can and leaves no stones unturned. Pluto sextile both his Moon and Midheaven provide support from his ultimate boss and some good fortune, including good fortune in a popular sense. It is extremely doubtful that the president could find a better man to fulfill this important economic mission.

III. An appropriate event was the date Alan Greenspan was first nominated to head the Central Bank by President Bush on June 2, 1987. On that day his progressed Sun was parallel Pluto within 0.6 minutes. Progressed Saturn was parallel Jupiter within 2.3 minutes. He was being offered a position that would further his aims to do something worthwhile for his country. The position is described by the eighth house. It would call for a change in location, in accommodations, in local actions and in income. These close aspects show natal astrology working the way it is supposed to work. Incidentally, looking at progressions in longitude alone would not have provided a clue about the important event that was taking place. This fact must be emphasized every time it is encountered to call attention to the progressions that do not appear in most astrological publications. Unless the authors provide the tables of declinations, along with the longitudes, and are insistent about their being printed, it does not happen. Very few do.

Of course this event was not the only one checked for Alan Greenspan. Others were the dates of his earlier appointments to advisory posts, his confirmation dates, graduation dates, etc. The aspects for those occasions met the 4 minute criterion and told the correct stories.

One observes that Scorpio rising people are sober and businesslike in their occupations. Little or no nonsense is tolerated by them, and they go all out. In picking another example political fairness has been exercised. Greenspan is a Republican, so it is appropriate to show a Democrat next. One individual that fits the mold perfectly is Senator Sam Nunn from Georgia, the distinguished head of the Armed Services Committee. See Figure 26 and Table XXIV. He has been described as a somewhat owlish looking man with horn-rimmed glasses and a receding hairline. He controls his weight by jogging and playing golf, but devotes most of his time to his responsibilities. An alleged fun weekend for him is to take a satchel full of weapons manuals home for light reading. A senate aide said that he lives by the old fashioned virtue of hard work. Those words come up time and time again for Scorpios. He has been a pivotal figure in the debates over ratification of arms limitation agreements with the Soviet Union.

Sam Nunn was born on September 8, 1938, in the little town South of Atlanta called Perry. This date gives him a Virgo Sun, which is responsible for his slightly owlish look. But the shape of his body, his outlook on life, dealings with the nation's security and responses to reporters' questions are in the mold of Scorpio. He was the son of Samuel Augustus and Elizabeth (Cannon) Nunn, and spent his youth, like many other Georgia boys, growing up on the farm. He attended his home town high school, where he was an all-state basketball player, and graduated in 1956. It is interesting that his first thoughts about a profession leaned toward engineering, and he promptly enrolled at the Georgia Institute of Technology, much the same way Jimmy Carter had done earlier. Sam survived longer than Jimmy—for three years versus one—at this very difficult and intense school of engineering. Then he enlisted in the United States Coast Guard, had one year of active duty, and was discharged in 1958. Sam decided to resume his studies at Emory University in Atlanta, but this time to pursue a degree in law. He took his AB degree in 1960 and his LLB degree with honors in 1962. Shortly afterward he was admitted to the Georgia state bar.

One of his next decisions was to move to Washington, D.C., where he became legal counsel to the House Armed Services Committee, which was then chaired by his great uncle, Representative Carl Vinson. Returning to Perry in 1964 he became a member of the law firm Nunn, Geiger and Rampy. He also raised soy beans, pecans and peanuts on the family farm that is traditional for South Georgia sons. He was active in community affairs, was elected President of the Perry Chamber of Commerce in 1964 and Director of the Georgia Planning Association in

1966. He also sat on the administrative board of the Perry United Methodist Church. On September 9, 1965, he married the former Colleen Ann O'Brien. By 1966 he was elected delegate from Houston County to the Georgia House of Representatives, where he served two terms. The Georgia Junior Chamber of Commerce selected him as one of five outstanding young men of the state in 1971. In 1972 the Georgia District Attorney's Association pronounced him the most effective legislator in the field of law enforcement. These honors were the result of—one more time—hard work typical of a Scorpio rising individual.

On August 8, 1972, Sam Nunn ran in the primary election to fill Richard B. Russell's Senate seat. This was a man he deeply admired. Sam was one of fifteen candidates, but he came in second to David H. Gambrell. He won this runoff election a few days later, taking 53.8 percent to 46.2 percent of the vote. The general election campaign against his Republican opponent, Fletcher S. Thompson, was a nastier affair. Thompson was already a two-term Atlanta congressman. Both leaned right of center, but it became marred by ugly racial overtones. Also, Sam Nunn took a bold step by repudiating the candidacy of Senator George S. McGovern, the liberal Democratic presidential nominee. Sam overcame the disadvantages of a weak national ticket and won 635,970 votes to 542,371. This gave him a six-year term plus the two months remaining on Richard Russell's term. He was sworn in on November 7, 1972.

As a junior senator Sam Nunn immediately found himself in a contest with Senator Mike Mansfield, who wanted to reduce the number of troops to conserve money. Sam went on an investigative tour and came back with a studied report. He was for, "a long range NATO stance that we are willing to live with politically, economically and militarily." He recommended, "strengthening conventional forces and devising a more equitable cost-sharing arrangement, a quantum jump in NATO's conventional firepower and Eastward repositioning of combat units." By demonstrating this remarkable interest in military affairs Nunn won a place on the Senate Armed Services Committee and quickly won the respect of his colleagues. Today he is the senate's premier defense analyst, an expert on NATO, nuclear weapons and manpower. He has been called a self-styled common sense conservative. Nunn has also tackled domestic problems with the same vigor and determination—especially in rural and urban redevelopment, education and social welfare.

This was another example where no prior published horoscope was found (unless one wishes to count a solar chart) and no time of birth was available. Accordingly, our validation criteria cannot make use of comparisons between planetary positions in a reported birth time horoscope and the one computed for soul entry. The criteria will simply be applied in customary fashion, and you can be the judge of applicability.

I. Legendary Scorpio rising qualities have already been described in giving his brief biography. The Mars-Mercury conjunction in the tenth house stands out in his horoscope. This pair, and Pluto in the ninth house, are the three most elevated planets. Mars gave Sam Nunn his interest in both engineering and the military. Mars is in the detailed sign Virgo, conjunct Mercury in Leo, and they are strongly indicative of his thorough and persuasive reports. Pluto, the ruler of his Ascendant in the ninth house, is highly appropriate for eventually gravitating to law. Prominence of the sign Leo for Pluto, Mercury and his Midheaven, increases his influence and rejects underling roles. No promotion during his short stay in the U. S. Coast Guard is about the only nonconfirmative situation—but then one needs to understand the promotion policies of the Coast Guard, and the short service time.

II. A wide Jupiter-Moon conjunction opposes Senator Sam Nunn's tenth house Mercury-Mars. Being uprooted and having to move for the sake of position is shown. Yet, increases in prosperity are also shown. If Scorpio is the sign of hard work, Saturn in the sixth house doubles that trait at a minimum. Saturn in Aries works in a pioneering way and it probably relates to his slightly receding hair line, that is not usual for Scorpio rising. Seventh house Uranus in the down-to-earth sign Taurus has its strongest longitudinal aspects with Sun and Neptune in the eleventh house. His wife and close associates help him meet objectives, though the square between Pluto and Venus (the seventh house co-ruler) causes some problems with travel

SEP 08 1938	10:18 AM EST	Naibod Secondary
PERRY	GEORGIA	AUG 30 1972
32 N 27 21	083 W 44 08	
09:42:53 AM TLT	03:17:49 PM GMT	03:17:49 PM GMT
Tropical	*Placidus*	*True Node*

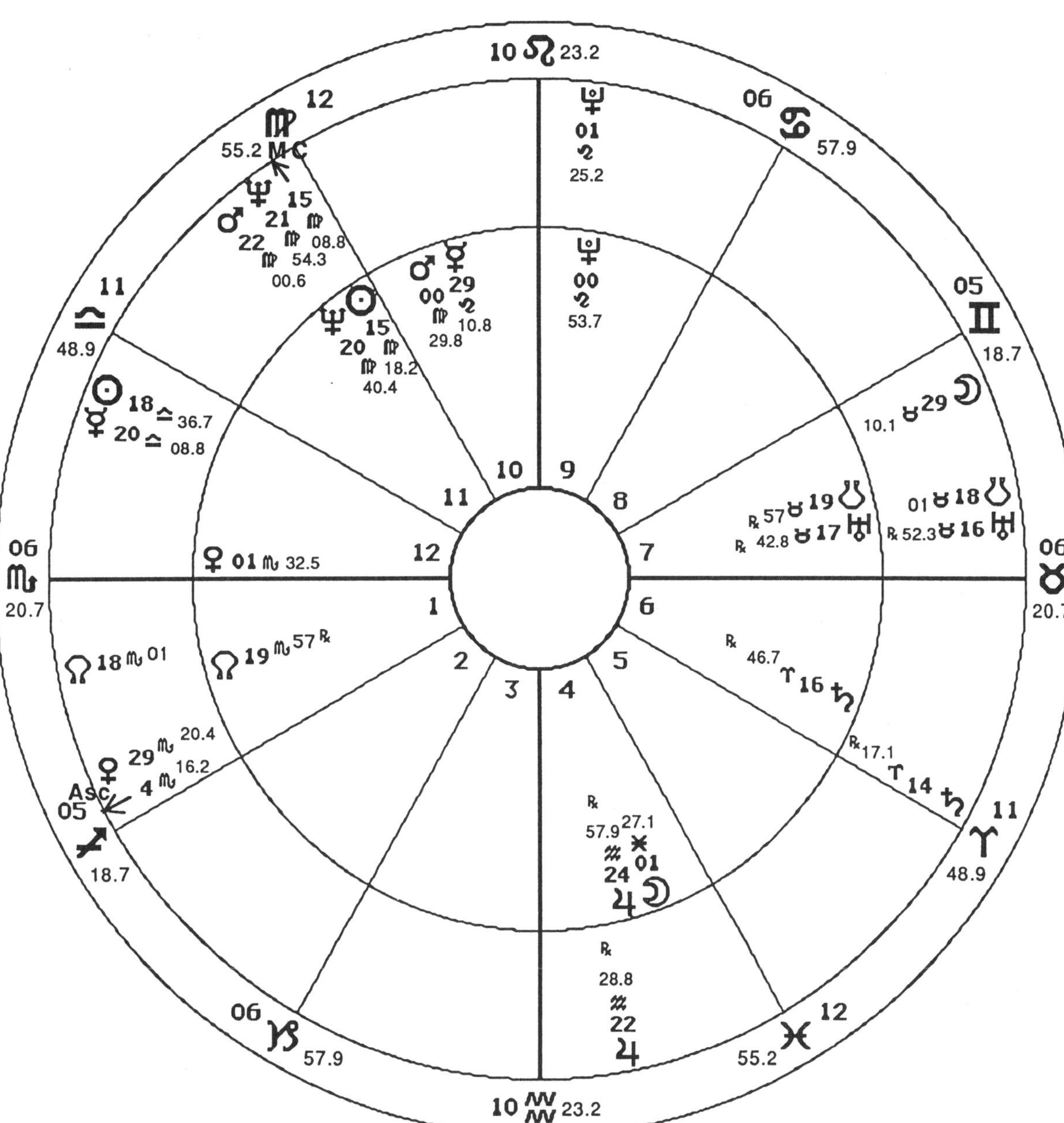

Figure 26. Horoscope of Senator Sam Nunn, Chairman of the Armed Services Committee. Progressions are given for the date he won his first runoff election.

and legal affairs. Venus applies to females and that probably goes for secretaries as well as his wife. The support is bolstered by a close Venus-Jupiter parallel however, and that is a fortunate aspect for home life. Another close declination aspect is Saturn to Neptune. Saturn is in an inconjunct aspect with both Sun and Neptune, offering carefully reviewed opportunities for advancing ideas. The parallel improves his presentations and causes them to be more readable and more noteworthy than some of his dry subjects might indicate. The Sun and Neptune in his eleventh house make his pronouncements noteworthy news items, and they are accepted as carefully thought out words of wisdom.

Table XXIV. Natal and Progressed Declinations of Senator Sam Nunn

Planet	Natal Decln.	08 30 1972 Won Runoff
♄	04 N 05.8	03 N 05.8
♆	04 N 42.4	04 N 13.8
☉	05 N 47.6	07 S 17.7
☽	06 S 20.9	18 N 58.7
☿	10 N 52.3	07 S 05.6
♂	12 N 23.9	04 N 15.2
Asc	13 S 38.4	21 S 00.3
♃	14 S 21.3	15 S 08.3
♀	14 S 23.7	25 S 26.8
♅	16 N 45.2	16 N 30.8
MC	17 S 38.6	05 N 51.3
♇	23 N 00.8	22 N 58.3

III. Numerous dates were available for testing confirmative progressions. It was very encouraging, especially when a birth time was not given, to find so many aspects that agree with each of these events. The one selected for illustration was the date he won the runoff election, August 30, 1972. That had to be a pivotal date. If he had lost that election we might not even know who Sam Nunn was. Another truthful aphorism comes to mind: "One cannot hope to become a great statesman without first winning the election." So it happens that on the appointed date, Sam Nunn had his progressed Midheaven parallel his Sun within 3.7 minutes. The progressed Midheaven in longitude was approaching a conjunction with his Sun, and it came within range during the general election. So Sam Nunn is now a senator and most of us have heard about him. Of course it did not hurt that progressed Mars was parallel progressed Neptune within 1.4 minutes. And the stresses in speechmaking and campaign particulars were shown by progressed Moon square Mercury within 0.9 minutes. Also, progressed Pluto was inconjunct Moon within 1.9 minutes. This was indeed a momentous occasion, and the aspects did not fail to portray the scene of that moment.

It should not be assumed from the examples given that all people with Scorpio rising forever have their noses to the grindstone. They can be just as intense at love making or pleasure as in their professions. It is not uncommon to learn about Scorpio rising males who have been called *bon vivants* or Scorpio rising females who are exotic and intriguing. In fact that is what life is all about for these natives. They live all aspects of life to the fullest.

CHAPTER 9. SAGITTARIUS

Physical Attributes

The most distinctive characteristic of Sagittarius rising is the elongated head. The distance from the top of the head to the chin is proportionately longer than the width, and much longer than for any other sign. The head is also characterized by a pronounced ridge at the eyebrows, and either a full convex forehead, or a back sloping forehead. In either case it is deep, which may not always be the case for other signs that can range to the tall side such as the Aries-Libra pair or Gemini. Any tendency toward baldness in later years may result in an apparent increase in the depth of the forehead. The ears are relative large and the ear lobes are relatively long. This is generally the tallest sign in the zodiac, but anomalies appear with a few people who are extra short, including midgets. Weight also can cause their faces to fill out. Feet and hands generally run to the larger sizes even when the body is short. They are usually congenial and easy to get along with. Their eyes will twinkle when having fun and the happy ones can be demonstrative. Sagittarius, being a mutable-fire sign, also tends to be restless. In youth especially some may twitch, fidget or blink when asked to sit still. They have a constant wish to know, for which they may be reprimanded. Stammering or stuttering has resulted among a few young people of this sign, which in later years often leads to controlled responses, or speech that has a clear separation between words. Again, the underlying Sun sign makes a difference. If the Sun is in a fire sign such as Sagittarius, Leo or Aries, the speech is more vigorous, will flow and have more intonations. With more sedate Sun signs the Sagittarius rising native usually appears to be more philosophical, intellectual and kindly. However, with the emphasis on size and speed in professional sports, many find superb remuneration in such occupations, where they excel at techniques that require concentration and teamwork. Good hunters and marksmen are found among them. They also find themselves frequently in leadership positions where their size, innate consciousness of human relations and friendliness toward others have a psychological effect causing them to be looked up to and respected.

Scorpio is the sign before Sagittarius, and Capricorn is the sign after. When the time is known to be in the quadrant of the day that causes one of these signs to appear in the East, selection becomes relatively easy with practice. Scorpio has the proportionately shorter, broader, rectangular head with curly or wavy hair. Capricorn has the more ovate head with a noticeable difference in the shape of the ears. Sagittarians are the long-heads with deep foreheads and longer feet and hands regardless of height.

Mental Attributes

The symbol for Sagittarius is the centaur bearing a drawn bow with an arrow. When the arrow is released it hits its mark. Thus, the most noticeable trait of people with this sign on the Ascendant is a passion for finding the central truth, the heart of the matter, in all debates and controversies. This sign ascending has the tendency to ask questions constantly at all ages. They are not easily hoodwinked and can cut through snow jobs with ease. Their vision is typically keen and their attention will be absorbed in the conversation at hand. They have a thirst for more knowledge and for greater understanding. That knowledge must be shared. Sagittarius on the Ascendant is noted for being frank, just, charitable and cheerful—or perhaps a better term would be jovial, because Jupiter is one of the ruling signs, Neptune is the other. It would be rare if they did not like travel, intellectual pursuits and outdoor sports. Yet they can be deeply humiliated by being forced into a sudden betrayal of emotion or display of temper.

The more primitive people with Sagittarius on the Ascendant are too independent and don't want to be tied down while searching new fields for expansion, excitement or change. Members of both sexes can be casual, careless, free-and-easy, discourteous, unfeeling and inconsiderate in spite of a certain kindliness of manner. They may lack loyaltyand be so detached from their kindred that family is not a high priority. It has been said that their sins are pardonable, but perhaps that is meant to be in contrast to truly wicked individuals. Another way to understand this idea is to realize that some have a peculiar, child-like transparency—probably due to the lack of complex emotions, jealousies or vindictiveness—which makes them vulnerable to easy detection for their misdeeds. These types do not lie or cheat successfully. They can also be sloppy or lazy about preparations for upcoming events. Those that are hurt by others can develop a limit to pleasant friendships and gain the reputation for being shallow-hearted.

The evolved person with Sagittarius on the Ascendant brings reason to bear upon every observation. Their mental energy never flags and their curiosity is insatiable. Discoveries of causes and effects are natural processes that lead to the education of others. Powers of association are strong. This person is helpful and illuminating, in the manner of Socrates, making him or her a very good teacher to those who are seeking more knowledge. They do not do as well with uninterested juveniles or those who would get the subject off track. In welfare, they often show much practical common sense in suggesting remedies for ills. Their conclusions are based not only upon book learning, but also upon prior experiences and reality. They will fraternize with all sorts of people to gain clear-headed knowledge and are devoid of snobbery. Once an expertise or bank of knowledge is acquired they consider it the duty of fathers and elders to enlighten the young and uneducated. All revelations are delivered logically, factually and openly. They have a penchant for conveying every significant aspect of a subject, the good as well as the bad. Such frankness can be misconstrued, or it can be jolting to more emotional types. For example, very few with Sagittarius rising would be engaged or married with a lie on their lips. They would tell all and rub the slate clean for a fresh start in life. But the kindliness of this sign is real to those who experience it and mankind benefits from their disclosures of the truth.

According to published horoscopes Marlon Brando, James Dean, Elvis Presley and Micky Rooney have Sagittarian Ascendants. Reviewing the physical and personality characteristics of these men in comparison with the above descriptions is good mental exercise. Progress is being made if one finds that the bag is mixed. Likewise, Shirley Temple Black, Maria Calas, Eartha Kitt, Linda Rondstadt and Ethel Waters have published horoscopes with Sagittarian Ascendants. That certainly is a mixed bag. The obvious differences virtually guarantee that not all of them have the same Ascendant sign. Could this problem with rising signs be any plainer?

Example Horoscopes

It is time to look at certain other celebrities, and Sagittarius does have its share, whose horoscopes can be verified. The first one selected to provide an excellent example is Leontyne Price, the lyric soprano with the fabulous voice (Figure 27 and Table XXV). On the stages of both light opera and grand opera, she has been there. Acclaimed in both the United States and Europe, she is acknowledged as being one of the better female opera stars available.

Leontyne Price literally went from the bottom to the top. Born to James Anthony Price and Kate (Baker) Price in Laurel, Mississippi, the family was not exactly impoverished, but it was not well off either. Her father was a carpenter who worked at the local saw mill. Her mother was a nurse and on call midwife. It is interesting that both grandfathers were Methodist ministers. So, Leontyne grew up in an old fashioned, God-fearing environment. At Saint Paul's Methodist

Church in Laurel, Leontyne sang in the choir and played the piano. She graduated from Oak Park High School in 1944 and applied to the College of Education and Industrial Arts (now Central State College) in Wilberforce, Ohio. Her intent was to become a teacher. It has been reported that she wrote on her application, "I am worried about the future, because I want so much to be a success." Before her graduation in 1948 she had decided that she wanted to sing professionally, but was afraid she might have to get one of those slick dresses and try to hoof it at night clubs. She was the recipient of a scholarship at the Julliard School of Music in New York, but neither her father or mother had sufficient money to pay the other expenses.

That was when a very fine lady in Laurel came to her rescue. A teacher who had always had faith in her vocal talents decided to help. Her name was Mrs. Elisabeth Chisholm. She offered and paid for all of Leontyne's living expenses while at Julliard, starting in January of 1941. Mrs. Chisholm was her other family, and she later attended Leontyne's major debuts.

While at Julliard, Leontyne studied under Florence Page Kimball who was her vocal coach for four years. She was not only her teacher, but also her advisor and friend. Leontyne, under her direction, sang the part of Mistress Ford in the student production of Verdi's *Falstaff*. Composer Virgil Thomson heard her sing and selected her to sing the role of Saint Cecelia in his production called *Four Saints in Three Acts*. That was in April of 1952. By June she was given the feminine lead in *Porgy and Bess,* and it played for two years. *Summertime* was the piece she sang so well while laying the groundwork for grand opera. She had a Towne Hall recital on November 14, 1954. However it was not until September 20, 1957, that she made her debut in grand opera, singing the part of Madam Lidoine in the American Premier of Poulenc's *Dialogues of the Carmalites*. This was at the San Francisco Opera House. Although at first progress was slow, she gradually obtained more singing roles. A major triumph was in 1961. After singing in Verdi's *Il Trovatore* at the Metropolitan Opera House, Leontyne Price received a rare forty-two minute ovation. That came as a surprise, and it was accompanied by sincere humility. On September 16, 1966, at the opening of *Anthony and Cleopatra,* she sang the leading role at the New York Opera House in Lincoln Center. This is where her acclaim broadened, and from then on she was the *prima donna* in many operas at many famous opera houses throughout the world. Besides having critics call her, "the perfect *Aïda* at last," notable honors have been the receipt of a Presidential Medal of Freedom in 1964 and the Spingarn Medal to a Negro American providing the greatest distinguished service in June 1965.

I. One might ask, what kind of horoscope does an opera singer have? Look at Figure 27 and Table XXV, and you will see one. You will definitely not see an opera singer in the horoscope having Aquarius on the Ascendant that was once published for her. The only attachment to Aquarius comes from her Sun sign, but there any resemblance ends. Her long head is a very good example of Sagittarius rising. The Aquarius head is so perfectly square that you would think it had been squashed. The effects of these two signs on the Ascendant are entirely different. Another major difference between the two horoscopes is that most of the planets have moved two full houses. The move is from the horoscope of an introvert who could not possibly go on stage in front of all those people to one of a performer of the highest order. The strength of this opera singer's horoscope is in the intercepted third and ninth houses. No houses were intercepted in the other one.

In previous chapters comments were made about strong fifth/eleventh houses being present for entertainers. The emphasis is on the word entertainment. Jokes, laughs, comedy and fun are entertaining and creative. By contrast, those people with strong third/ninth houses may be in some form of show business also, but then they are presenters, exhibitors or demonstrators who provide happenings or showings. These events can be in the form of written or spoken words, singing or the utilization of any media that conveys information from the past. Staged shows fall into this category, as well as education, law, publications, travels and dramatic acting. While elements of entertainment are present, arias are from the past. Thus, opera singers would be expected to have strong third/ninth houses. Leontyne Price does.

FEB 10 1927 2:55 AM CST
LAUREL MISSISSIPPI
31 N 41 00 089 W 09 11
2:56:57 AM TLT 8:53:34 AM GMT
Tropical *Placidus* *True Node*

Naibod Secondary
JAN 27 1961
8:53:34 AM GMT

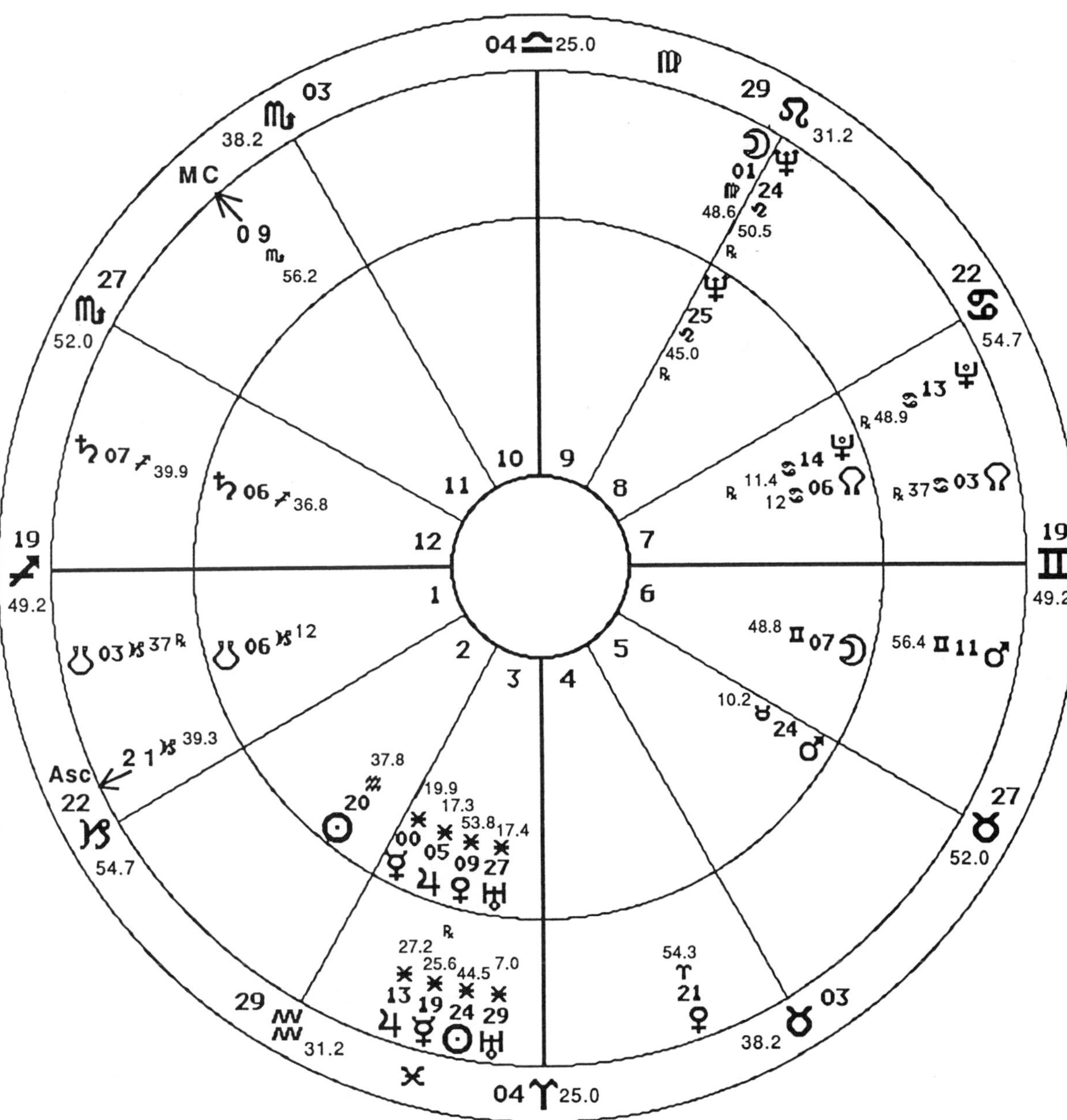

Figure 27. Horoscope of *prima donna* Leontyne Price with progressions to date of her debut in Verdi's *La Traviata* at the Metropolitan Opera.

Table XXV. Natal and Progressed Declinations of Leontyne Price

Planet	Natal Decln.	01 27 1961 Debut
♅	01 S 44.2	02 S 05.4
MC	01 S 45.4	14 S 48.0
♀	09 S 12.8	08 N 07.7
♃	10 S 26.8	19 S 37.7
☿	12 S 43.9	01 S 16.2
♆	13 N 22.6	13 N 41.2
☉	14 S 37.2	02 S 05.4
☽	19 N 10.4	14 N 47.9
♄	19 S 32.2	19 S 37.7
♂	20 N 29.4	23 N 55.5
♇	21 N 20.2	22 S 26.1
Asc	23 S 03.5	21 N 25.5

II. In the Aquarius rising horoscope a concentration of planets show up in the personal and indwelling first house. In the horoscope presented those same planets fall into the third house. The third house is where a singer spends hours and hours practicing. The Sun is a benefactor. Sun is in her second house providing financial support from Mrs. Chisholm when it was needed. The Sun is in a T-square with Neptune and Mars, the handle planet. The strife over monetary matters was there. Mars is in steadfast Taurus, which shows the hardship on parents. Another T-Square with extra power has the opposition between Moon and Saturn with three handle planets—Mercury, Jupiter and Venus. Jupiter is ruler of her Ascendant sign and Venus is the ruler of her Midheaven. The entire life's focus is upon third house practicing, learning and individual performances. Uranus parallel Midheaven causes her successes to be sudden surprises. Moon is contraparallel Saturn, just as they are also opposite each other. This indicates a perpetual pulling between desires for personal accomplishments and making solid contributions to opera and her people, between earnings kept and the amounts felt owed or obligated.

III. Many events could have been chosen for illustrating the accuracy of progressions based upon the given horoscope, but there is a kind of sameness to many of them—an opening here, an outstanding performance there. In the final analysis a debut has to be important, and it might even be accompanied by some fears. Thus, her debut at the Metropolitan Opera House in New York was selected. Progressed Midheaven was contraparallel her progressed Moon within

0.1 minutes, and that accounts for her butterflies at this career milestone. But the progressed Midheaven was also trine Venus within 2.4 minutes, so the practice payed off and the performance was beautiful. *Il Trovatore* is one of the great, melodious Verdi operas, and a superb Leonora is an experience that stays with the audience for years. As for all validated horoscopes, the progressions were accurate.

When an opera star or person who demonstrates skills of memory or dispaly does not have interceptions, the ninth house must be strong. Partly for this reason, partly for illustrating a variety of professions and partly to show differences between physical and vocal skills, Peggy Fleming was selected for the next example. She too, has the elongated head of Sagittarius rising. It is interesting that her reported birth time produced a horoscope very close to the one shown in Figure 28 and Table XXVI. The few minutes difference would have caused her Ascendant to be in Scorpio rather than Sagittarius. But the length of her head is positive confirmation. The two charts are so close that all the planets remain in their same houses. It is also noteworthy that her birth is not given to the nearest hour or half hour, but it appears to have actually been clocked at 3:39 PM PDST. For a change we obtain a validated natal horoscope that does not differ much from the one for the reported birth time. There are no guarantees that a carefully measured time will cause the validated horoscope to be much closer than one that is approximated. But, here it did.

Table XXVI. Natal and Progressed Declinations of Peggy Fleming

Planet	Natal Decln.	02 10 1968 Gold Medal
♂	02 S 17.8	07 S 13.9
♆	02 S 46.5	02 S 57.8
MC	05 N 18.1	02 S 59.2
☽	06 N 13.8	26 S 55.5
♄	14 N 52.7	14 N 04.3
♀	17 N 59.5	18 N 53.2
☉	19 N 04.7	13 N 41.5
Asc	20 S 46.0	23 S 00.1
☿	22 N 07.0	13 N 39.9
♃	22 S 43.1	22 S 43.8
♇	23 N 26.5	23 N 17.1
♅	23 N 36.4	23 N 37.1

JUL 27 1948	3:57 PM PDT	Naibod Secondary
SAN JOSE	CALIFORNIA	FEB 10 1968
37 N 20 09	121 W 54 31	
2:48:57 PM LST	10:56:35 PM GMT	10:56:35 PM GMT
Tropical	*Placidus*	*True Node*

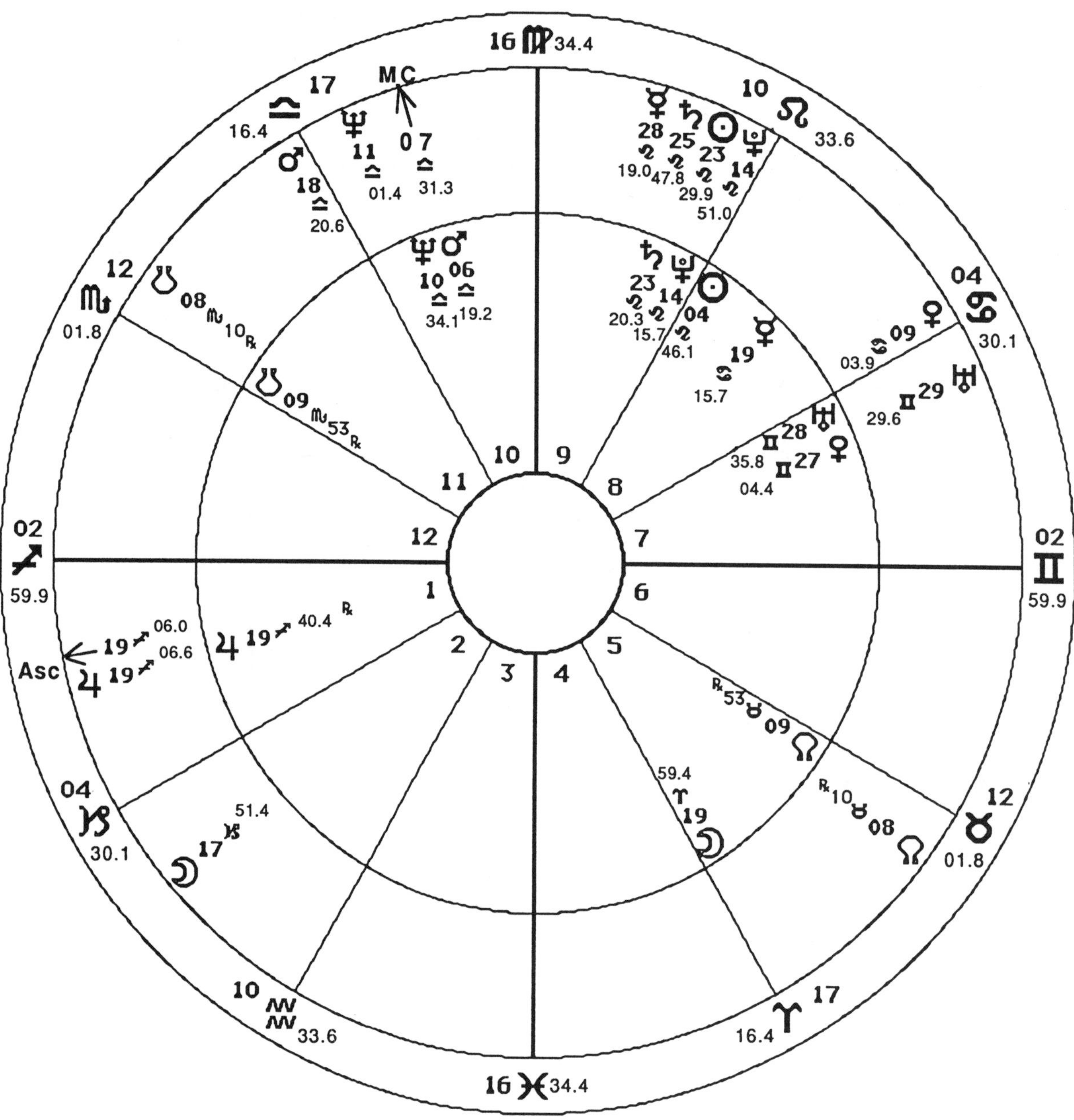

Figure 28. Horoscope of Peggy Fleming, who was a champion ice skater. Progressions are to the date she first won an Olympic gold medal.

Peggy Fleming was born in San Jose, California on July 27, 1948. This gives her a Leo Sun and the sunny disposition to go with it. Her father was Albert Eugene Fleming, a rotogravure pressman. Her mother was Doris Elizabeth (Deal) Fleming. Peggy has an older sister and two younger ones. She began skating at the age of 9. Shortly afterward the family moved to Cleveland, Ohio, where she continued skating. Her father recognized her potential for becoming a world champion and began to plan around her continued high-quality lessons. He moved the family back to California, and searched for better coaching. She won her first title at the age of twelve. That was the Pacific Coast Juvenile Figure Skating Championship. The next year, 1961, she moved up in class and won the Pacific Coast Novice Ladies Figure Skating Championship. In 1962 it was the Pacific Coast Senior Ladies Figure Skating Championship, and she came in second nationally in the Novice Class. The meet happened to have been held in Cleveland. In 1964, at the advanced age of fifteen, she entered the Olympics and came in sixth at her first outing in Innsbruck, Austria.

The family was in Southern California at this time, and Peggy entered Pasadena High School. However, she soon transferred to Hollywood Professional School which had flexible schedules for young people with professional careers or unusual extracurricular activities. Next her father got himself a job in Colorado Springs, Colorado, so that Peggy could be coached by Carlo Fassi, a former European champion, supplemented by Dick Button, a U.S. gold medal winner. It was Dick Button who said she was, "too much starch and too little protein." At another interview he said, "She is a delicate lady on ice. She is not a fiery skater, and she shouldn't be made to be one. With some skaters there is a lot of fuss and feathers, but nothing is happening. With Peggy there is no fuss and feathers, and a great deal is happening...."

At the 1988 Winter Olympics Peggy Fleming had a 77.2 point lead over her nearest competitor in the compulsories. In the free skating routine she increased the lead to 88.2 points. She stunned everyone present with a "spread eagle, double axle, spreadeagle." Please don't ask what that is, but it had never been tried before in competition. While the United States did not fare well that year in other competitions, Peggy Fleming came away with the gold.

It has been said that her tastes are modest and simple. She likes music, swimming, golf, tennis and cooking, with a special weakness for macaroni. She is only 5 feet 3.5 inches tall and when skating actively weighed 109 pounds. She turned professional on April 3, 1968. Her latest ventures have been to provide color on television during subsequent Olympic broadcasts of skating events.

I. It is interesting to note the contrasts with Leontyne Price. Third house planets denoted practice for the singer. Peggy's first house ruler, Jupiter, is in the first house where her physical body was used to perfect her routines, not to remember lines. The co-ruler of the first house, Neptune, is in the tenth house conjunct Mars. Mars, the athletic planet of daring, with Neptune, the planet of drama, are in the highly visible house of recognition. Those two planets are elevated, conjunct and parallel, making them unusually strong. As an exhibitionist (not an entertainer) her ninth house is very active. Doubts are fading fast. If the Ascendant had been Scorpio, more than likely its ruler, Pluto, would have indicated a major direction in life related to law, acting or the education of others. Mars, the other co-ruler, would still be in the tenth house, but the need to use her body in a physical way would not be as strongly emphasized.

II. Leontyne Price's family and a benefactor provided her financial support. Peggy Fleming's father provided moral support and beneficial physical relocations so that she could be near good coaches. Finances may have come up as a topic of discussion, but they were not the main issue. The fourth house represents parents in the confines of the home, and its ruler is Jupiter, which is in her first house. Jupiter is expansive, sees bigger things in life and in this case caused movement to other places. That Peggy Fleming enjoyed the adventure provided by figure skating, and being first with a new and dangerous routine, is written into her Aries Moon in its fifth house location. It is trine the ninth house Saturn-Pluto pair where she can travel and show her abilities. Saturn's placement also shows her ultimate source of earnings. Uranus is closely conjunct Venus and closely parallel Pluto. The willingness of professionals and other associates to help her perfect attractive routines is supported. Sun and Mercury in the eight house, the latter being contraparallel Jupiter, shows a certain amount of generosity with respect to others, but also concern over repayment of debts, her heritage and obligations. Nothing but her small size seems out of line, and this is an anomaly of Sagittarius rising that occurs now and then. Mickey Rooney is another example.

III. There is no better date to illustrate a validating progression than February 10, 1968, when Peggy Fleming won her gold medal for the United States team during the Winter Olympics. Progressed Midheaven was parallel Neptune progressed within 1.4 minutes. Her Progressed Ascendant was conjunct Jupiter within 0.6 minutes, and progressed Sun was parallel Mercury progressed within 1.6 minutes. The fast-moving nodes, Midheaven and Ascendant, were accurate in denoting this event, and they are the best validating yardsticks. The contacting planets agreed with the nature of the activities and the jubilation from the outcome. Peggy turned professional less than two months later, and that incident was marked by her progressed Ascendant coming to an inconjunct with Mercury while her progressed Moon was in a semi-sextile aspect with her Jupiter. Every other noteworthy event that was checked had appropriate progressed aspects.

Figure skating is considered an athletic sport. Like most people in sports Peggy had her Mars located in a strong house, the tenth. An observation is that most professionals in sports have Mars in either the first, fourth, seventh or tenth houses, because prominence is gained through those locations. Also, as stated earlier, many people in sports have Sagittarius rising. But one who did not have Mars in any of those dominant house was the legendary Willie Mays. See Figure 29 and Table XXVII. Willie's Mars gained prominence in another way. His Mars aspects every other planet in his horoscope, plus his Midheaven. Granted that three of those aspects are eight to ten degrees from exact, but all the rest are close. His Mars is also elevated in the ninth house with one co-ruler of his Sagittarian Ascendant, Neptune. His athletic feats were exhibitions of Martian batting and Neptunian circus catches. He was a money player, and his other co-ruler of the Ascendant, Jupiter, is in his eighth house.

Willie Mays was born May 6, 1937, in Fairfield, Alabama, a suburb of Birmingham. That puts his Sun in Taurus and gave him his determination. His father worked in one of Birmingham's steel mills in a tool room. His mother died when he was eleven, and he was taken care of by his father's sister-in-law, Sarah Mays, during the remainder of his school days. Willie always liked to play baseball, and before completing high school he managed to get hired by the Birmingham Black Barons as a utility outfielder. He signed for $200, which wasn't bad money for a kid at that time, black or white. The manager of the team was Lorenzo (Piper) Davis, and some techniques must have rubbed off during that period. Willie proceeded to have batting averages in successive years of .300, .316 and by 1950, .350. Scouts do attend minor league baseball games on occasion. Two from the then New York Giants, Bill Harris and Ed Montague, discovered him. They paid the Birmingham Black Barrons $10,000 to buy out his contract. Then, on June 20, 1950, he was given a contract for $6,000 plus bonuses, and farmed out to a Giant Class B team in Trenton, New Jersey. Willie hit .353 in 81 games. They sent him to the AAA Minnesota Millers in the American Association. The competition must have been easier for him, or he received better coaching, because he raised his batting average to .477 and hit 8 home runs. He was acknowledged the outstanding player of the Minnesota club, and scout Hank DeBerry said, "It was a banner day for the Giants when this boy was signed."

Willie Mays lacked some confidence in taking the next step to the majors. He argued with Leo Durocher about not wanting to go up there and hit them major league pitchers. The savvy Durocher evidently knew what he was doing and insisted. Even so his debut in Philadelphia on May 25, 1951, wasn't especially auspicious. In twenty-six times at bat he hit only one home run. But the Giants were thirteen-and-a-half games back at the time and Willie wanted to win. By the end of the season they were in first place. Then came a stretch in the army where he also played baseball. Afterwards he came back to the Giants, where his batting averages continued to improve. In fact it improved so much that the Giants won the 1954 pennant. Willie hit 41 home runs, had 110 runs batted in and an average of .345. He was voted by the Baseball Writer's Association

MAY 06 1931	7:41 PM CST	Naibod Secondary
FAIRFIELD	ALABAMA	FEB 11 1966
33 N 28 54	086 W 58 23	
7:54:33 PM TLT	1:42:26 AM GMT	1:42:26 AM GMT
Tropical	*Placidus*	*True Node*

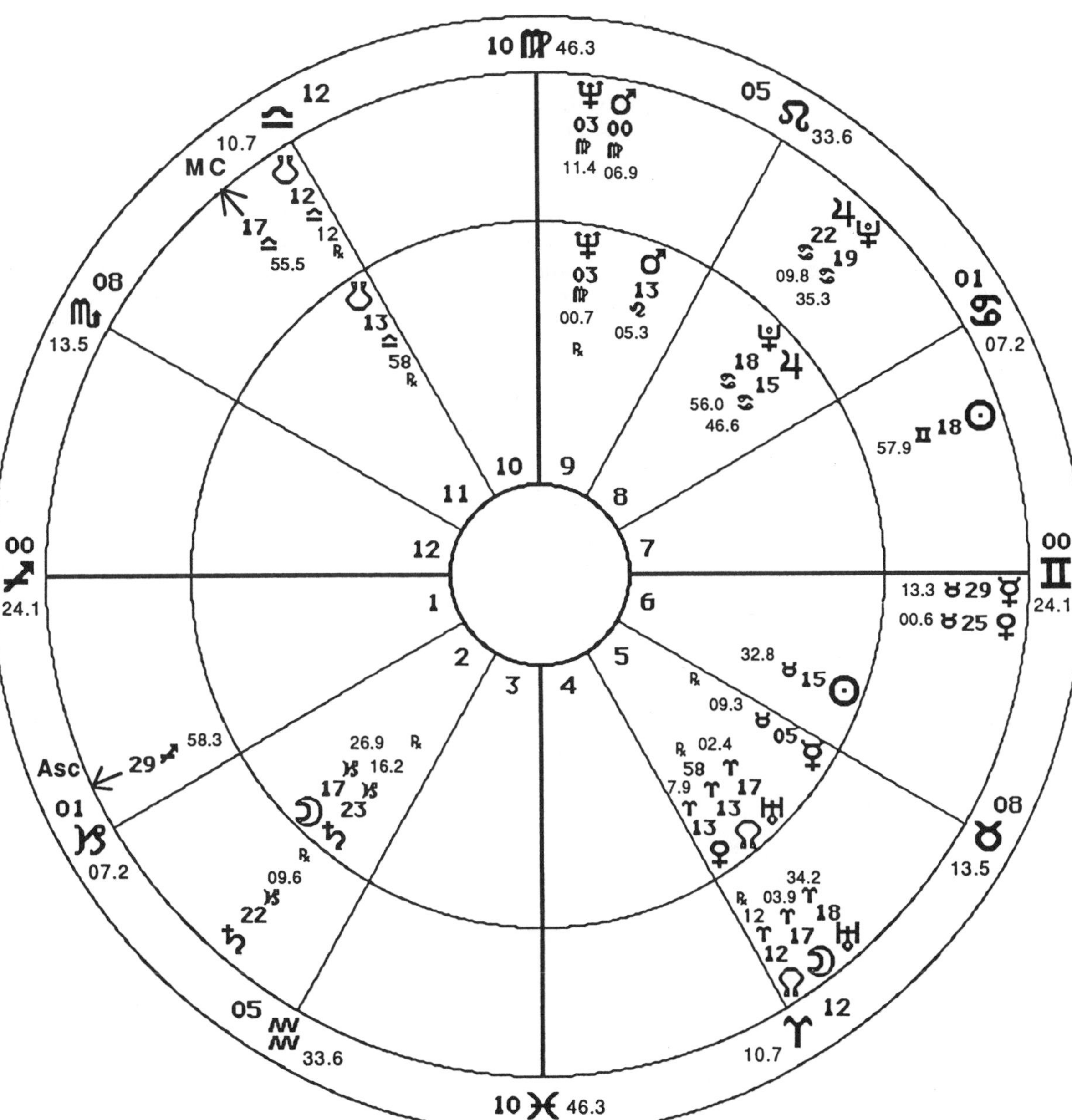

Figure 29. Horoscope of baseball great Willie Mays. Progressions are shown for the day he negotiated the highest salary in baseball history up to that time.

as the Most Valuable Player of 1954.

Willie Mays did not like the Giants move to San Francisco, and at first felt rejected by the fans. They already had a favorite son in Joe Dimaggio. It took a few years before he really began to feel at home. Meanwhile, he continued to do wonders for his team, and his accomplishments, measured and deciphered as they are in this game, could not be ignored. On February 11, 1966, Willie Mays set another record. He became the highest paid baseball player in the history of the game by signing a two-year contract with the San Francisco Giants for $130,000 per year. On May 5, 1966, he broke Mel Ott's old record with his 512th homer. He continued to be one of the Giant's key players for many years.

"Say hey, Willie Mays" has led a life devoted to fun. Baseball, a game, paid his way. It is said that he has few vices other than tormenting pitchers. "He likes western movies, action-filled television shows, pinball machines, gin rummy and Ella Fitzgerald records," according to Arnold Hano. What a life, some would say. Now our problem is astrological verification of his horoscope and his Sagittarian Ascendant. He is 5 foot 11 inches tall, about right for first house Sagittarius with a Taurus Sun. His playing weight was listed as 180 pounds.

I. This horoscope has two main features. One is the double T-square with handle planets in the fifth house of personal pleasure. The other is the trine aspects between fifth and ninth house planets, recognizing that those in the fifth house are the focal points of the T-squares. These ninth

Table XXVII. Natal and Progressed Declinations of Willie Mays

Planet	Natal Decln.	02 11 1966 Hi Contract
♀	03 N 36.0	17 N 43.9
♅	06 N 07.0	06 N 41.5
MC	07 N 31.9	07 S 02.1
♆	11 N 04.8	11 N 00.5
☿	12 N 13.8	18 N 01.2
☉	16 N 30.2	22 N 59.5
♂	18 N 44.3	12 N 36.4
Asc	20 S 14.7	23 S 27.1
♄	21 S 13.0	21 S 26.3
♇	22 N 21.5	22 N 17.9
♃	22 N 50.5	21 N 58.8
☽	27 S 27.7	07 N 06.5

house planets have already been alluded to in the context of his being on display in playing his sport. About the only planet left is the sixth house Sun, and it is making extremely harmonious aspects with the money planets, plus a trine with his Midheaven. The T-square planets concentrate energy in the second, eighth and fifth houses. It took a lot of effort, and much had to be overcome, to make a game pay off for a Southern black kid. While he accomplished that goal spectators saw many good sporting events.

It is almost annoying to have to bring it up, but the 10:30 PM recorded birth time horoscope for Willie Mays shows 7 Capricorn 30 on his Ascendant. On the following pages Capricorn rising will be discussed at length, but fun-loving "Say hey, Willie Mays" does not fit that description at all. His interests are in games and money, which Sagittarius rising in the illustrated horoscope can support. The Capricorn rising horoscope places the T-square handle planets in the third house, where some kind of memory activity like Leontyne Price's would be more likely to occur. Mars does make it over to the seventh house in this later chart, but there is no evidence of his having many wives and abrupt relationships with other people. Also, the ninth house in that fictitious horoscope is void. The even half-hour reported time of birth brands this horoscope as fictitious .

II. Half the planets are within three-and-a-half degrees of being in exact aspects with each other. Two more are within seven degrees. This array includes Mars, the sporting planet, at the top. Mars may be weak by house, but it is not weak by aspects. Both the Sun and the Moon are included in the group, which increases energy and prominence.

Moon and Saturn in the second house says that Willie found a good way to make money. His income increased with time, a Capricorn stamp, and it was emotionally satisfying. Venus, Uranus and Mercury in his fifth house show artistry, originality and speed in his games. Sun in the sixth house emphasizes his job. In Taurus it has a conscientious emphasis with steadiness and a desire to build competence. Jupiter and Pluto in the eighth house motivated him to do much for his family after he came into money. They also caused him to be an extraordinary negotiator. Mars and Neptune are, of course, out at the ball park.

III. A perfectly natural date to show as verification of Willie May's horoscope is February 11, 1966, when he signed the landmark contract making him the highest paid baseball player in history up to that time. As shown in the chart and table of declinations, his progressed Sun was semi-sextile Pluto within 1.1 minutes. His work (Sun) was in a mildly favorable relationship to the agreement for a new salary (Pluto) with management. His progressed Jupiter was opposite progressed Saturn within 0.2 minutes. These second and eighth house planets are contesting each other, as expected in a contract negotiation. The progressed Midheaven came into an exact contraparallel with his progressed Moon later when the news got out. Some jealousies and carping were aimed at him, and he felt they tarnished his image in the public's eyes. That hurt. But these are progressed planets aspecting other progressed planets, so the results were not long lasting. Willie Mays would have to be included among the handful of super baseball players who played the game. He often was the spark that carried his team to victory.

All three examples of Sagittarius rising could be called long heads, an old term recalled from fables. Each has risen to the top in their respective fields of endeavor. All are likable people, and they have enjoyed popularity and acclaim. One might have to know them better to discover their ability to probe for the kernels of truth they seek, and their biographers were not especially adept at portraying this side of their personalities. On the other hand, there is no reason to doubt their common rising sign.

CHAPTER 10. CAPRICORN

Physical Attributes

The most prominent feature of people with Capricorn rising is an elfin look. This is caused by their ears. If you ever see a person with no ear lobes at all, the outer edges of their ears angled into the sides of their head from above, Capricorn is almost certain to be rising. Some Capricorn rising people do have ear lobes, but they are then small and close to the face. With a typical ovate head those ears tend to be conspicuous unless covered by long hair. The ovateness produces a narrow chin. The sides of the face come up on either side of the chin at angles that appear to continue into their ears, which are wider above. It is unusual for the upper parts of the ears not to stick out, although once in a while they will be flattened against the head. Frequently the first impression is of a pixie, if a woman, or an imp, if a male. By contrast to their sometimes droll or devilish outward appearances, the majority are serious in their behavior unless comedy is their game. Then their wit is often dry or based on human foibles. The seriousness is fostered by a great love of work and ambition. As always, the Sun may cause the structure of the head to be modified to a more rectangular form, but the ears have it every time.

Most people with Capricorn on their Ascendants are short to average in height and have thin or bony bodies with long necks. The nose is usually long and thin. In men the beard is usually sparse. The body is normally active with sure-footed movements. It is amazing how many professional dancers have Capricorn rising. An air of formality is often observed among them. They usually aspire to continuous advancement, as the symbolic mountain goat climbs higher and higher, never wanting to take a downward step. Having made these remarks, it is important to add that variations can cause their bodies to be wider and taller, their attitudes more anxious or their movements less than rhythmic. However those are exceptions, not the rule.

Sagittarius is before Capricorn in time as the earth rotates. Aquarius is after. The long head of Sagittarius and the square head of Aquarius are distinctly different. Neither of these other sign's ears come close to resembling those of Capricorn.

Mental Attributes

Trust, respect and appreciation are greatly admired. Position, wealth and power are normally among their aspirations, accompanied by an ability to look out for themselves. Ambition is a key motivator, and if they are despondent it is usually because, for the moment, ambition has been thwarted. A meaningful adage to Capricorn is that rank has its privileges. Full advantage of rank is taken at every level. Their ideas are usually practical and prudent. One ruler of Capricorn, Saturn, normally causes them to be cautious, persevering and steady, rather than spasmodic. On average, they are not especially demonstrative in conversations, but will apply increasing forces, if necessary, to prevail. People of this sign have been known to endure long personal hardships rather than give up or abandon a commitment.

This is a cardinal sign and most individuals with Capricorn on their Ascendant rise in life to advanced positions. Among the more primitive types ambition can become a source of worry and torment, or gloom and discontent. Sometimes they will imagine higher rankings and tell others little white lies about their assumed positions. They may also show reverence for superiors and a lot less courtesy or sympathy to others, somewhat like a primitive Leo. Success may be a disproportionate aspiration in life, leading to a constant pitting of themselves against all comers, the competition. They may also have a tendency to order others about, whether called for or not. Capricorn rising wants to control, to influence, to direct and manage. By doing so they feel themselves to be at a higher level in the pecking order. On the other hand they are usually good hosts and hostesses, have good deportment and remember anniversaries, birthdays or other important dates with gifts and cards. They typically want to show themselves off well.

The more highly developed people with Capricorn rising take life seriously and uphold tradition and authority. Work is approached with industry. They develop a sense of diplomacy and often enjoy life. High standards are often set for themselves and their associates, and they expect everyone to live up to them. However the expectations are realistically less for others than for themselves. If anyone else does not toe the mark they will try to persuade them. They look up to the gurus and giants in their fields and have gratitude for any guidance imparted by them. They often make good managers or commanders of other people. In contrast to those who would be gushy toward others, in times of adversity, they will more likely take practical stances to effect remedies. Despite a constant drive for personal advancement, the social welfare of humanity is also one of their interests. Historical values appeal to them, and they often approve of rules and regulations to uphold such guidelines. They often win great praise and much esteem through their abilities, especially when confronted with crises that require the exercise of tact and finesse.

Testing one's skills against the above criteria is an important step toward gaining a better grasp of natal astrology. Three very good examples of the lack of understanding about rising signs are the published horoscopes for Goldie Hawn, Jayne Mansfield and Joanne Woodward showing Capricorn on the Ascendants. It should be extremely clear to perceptive individuals that major dissimilarities in physical appearances and personalities exist among this trio. If you were among those who came to this conclusion on your own, then progress is being made. If you did not perceive a match with Capricornian traits, then even better progress is being made. Looking at horoscopes in groups this way often provides better insights than looking at a single horoscope. Similar comments can be applied to Dustin Hoffman, Alan Alda and Rocky Marciano. They too, are reported to have Capricorn rising—every one of them, if you can believe it. To carry this critical review further, no one who thinks could really believe that the latter two well known celebrities are similar physically or mentally, either? So why shouldn't an intelligent public be skeptical about all of astrology until this kind of mistake is eliminated? To continue the mistake-reduction process, let us look at famous individuals who can be proven to have Capricorn rising.

Example Horoscopes

The first very important person chosen to illustrate Capricorn rising has been picked specifically because there has been so much confusion about his horoscope. Claims have been made by various writers that former President and General Dwight D. Eisenhower had a morning birth according to relatives, an early afternoon birth time according to Ike himself and an evening birth according to the man who went for a doctor. With such a solid foundation to start with, the procedure was to assume no birth time was available at all. Every potential incarnation time for the twenty-four hour period encompassed by the date October 14, 1890, had to be calculated. All had to be tested. The results favor Ike's remarks about his own birth time. Other published horoscopes displayed weak placements for Mars and not much else to back a leader of this magnitude.

For a change of pace the actual procedure used in finding and verifying the horoscope of Figure 30 and Table XXVIII will be disclosed. The *INCARN* algorithm, now embedded in a large computer program having that name, was used to calculate potential moments of incarnation. One of those moments of incarnation, when the soul is thought to enter the human body, has always corresponded with the correct natal horoscope and proven to be verifiable. This time is rarely the same as the recorded physical birth time—whatever the instant representing this transition period is claimed to be. Experience with the algorithm, over nearly half a century, has shown that the natal horoscope is correct for a time between three-and-a-half to four hours before the reported physical birth time, to ten or fifteen minutes afterwards.

INCARN, the software program, looks from five hours before to one hour ahead of whatever time is inserted as a starting point. This is to make sure the range is wider than the empirically observed limits reported above. The inserted time simply establishes a window. It is not used for rectification. To blanket one day it is only necessary to make four runs spaced six hours apart. The actual quantity of incarnation times computed by the algorithm for a given location and period is never known in advance. This quantity depends upon the signs of the Moon, Sun and Uranus. Screening four times as many potential horoscopes as for a single six-hour period, places a bigger burden on the person doing the screening. With practice and experience, however, it becomes an easier task. Successful screening is based upon the application of known astrological fundamentals and the standard for verification given in the first chapter. Screening by rising signs is the first effective step in this process. The Progressed Mode of *INCARN* makes the final verification steps fast and accurate.

Each *INCARN* run computes a complete horoscope for every potential incarnation time during a six hour span. Except for the planet Pluto, it uses the same formulas as those used to compile the American Ephemeris and Nautical Almanac. For Pluto, third order polynomials of short curve segments are incorporated. Output accuracies are governed by the internal machine word length, which is typically sixteen bits long in personal computers. The Nautical Almanac Offices of the United Kingdom and the United States of America use large mainframe computers with sixty-four bit words. They are seeking accuracies around 10^{-6} to 10^{-7} parts of a second of arc. However, even on a personal computer with the shorter word length, the results are very accurate indeed, especially since double precision arithmetic is used. With this assurance of accuracy, the selection process now commences.

After preliminary eliminations of horoscopes, on the basis of rising signs that do not fit the subject, confidence is gained in knowing that one of the remaining horoscopes will fit. One and only one always does. Another important principle is that even small changes in timing can cause certain planets to fall into one house or the other. As one narrows down the choices this becomes an important tool. A planet in an incorrect house is not acceptable, because it is downright misleading. For example, with Dwight D. Eisenhower the fit of the horoscope must be to a military man. It is certain that Mars must be prominent and possibly Pluto as well. A weak Mars would be unacceptable. He was also a commander-in-chief, an important leader. The locations of other planets must support these facts. Finally, major events must be upheld by close aspects.

The initial runs of *INCARN* in the Incarnation Mode produced four sets of possible soul entry times for Denison, Texas, on October 14, 1890. The tabulated natal horoscopes had the following rising signs: two in Libra, two in Virgo, three in Capricorn, two in Scorpio, one in Sagittarius, two in Aquarius, two in Aries, two in Pisces, one in Gemini, three in Cancer, two in Leo and two in Taurus. All were possible on that date. It should be revealing to some that morning horoscopes have counterparts twelve hours away, with corrections for the equation of time. At this point Virgo, Scorpio, Aquarius, Pisces, Aries, Taurus, Cancer and Gemini rising sign charts were ruled out on the basis of physical appearance. This swiftly taken step may come as a shock to some readers, and those of you in that category would of course like an explanation. Virgo cannot be Eisenhower's rising sign because he did not have triangular facial features, he was not known as an extremely detailed individual; he did not have a strong, overriding health complex and he did not have a thin-bridged nose, although it was down-pointing. Scorpio can be eliminated because he was not hairy; did not have the sharp, piercing eyes of the Scorpio rising native; and he did not have that sign's distinctive magnetic dynamism. Aquarius can be readily eliminated because his head was not square-shaped. Pisces is wrong because the special watery, translucent appearance of the skin was not evident. Aries does not fit, because he did not have a bony body structure, bushy eyebrows and noticeable high cheek bones. Taurus is wrong, because there was no fixedness in Eisenhower's manner the way Taurus is fixed, and no body with small hands and feet to match. A Gemini rising person would typically have an elongated head and be far more talkative. Cancer would have a narrowing at the top of the head, probably short arms and legs, not

OCT 14 1890	12:17 PM CST	Naibod Secondary
Denison	Texas	JAN 20 1953
33 N 41 20	096 W 33 17	18:16:15 GMT
11:50:02 AM TLT	18:16:15 GMT	

Tropical *Placidus* *True Node*

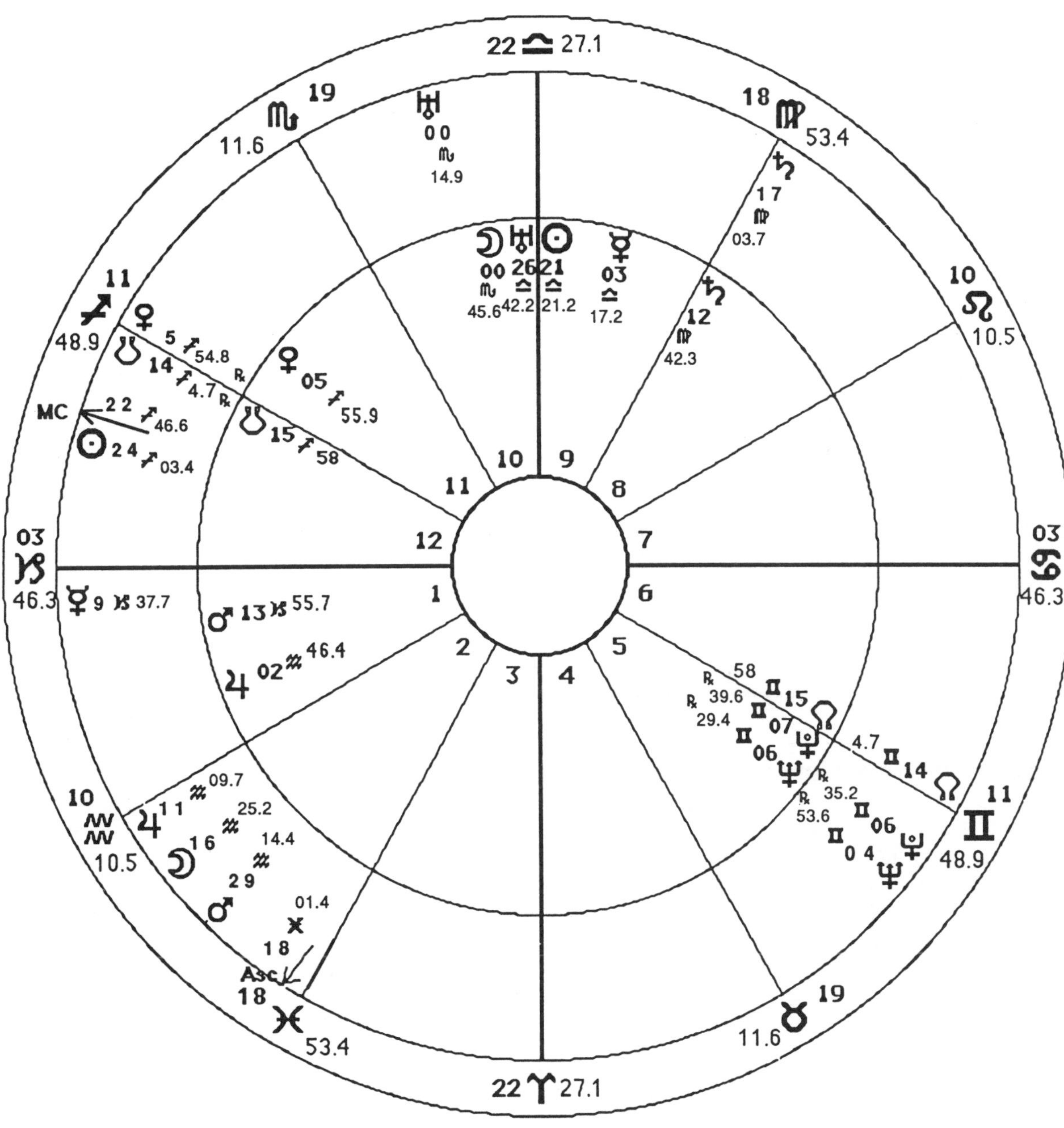

Figure 30. Horoscope of former Supreme Commander of Allied Forces and President of the United States Dwight D. Eisenhower. Progressions to the date of his inauguration are shown.

Table XXVIII. Natal and Progressed Declinations of Dwight D. Eisenhouer

Planet	Natal Decln.	01-20-1953 President
☿	00 N 14.5	25 S 21.5
♄	08 N 19.9	06 N 51.5
☉	08 S 20.0	23 S 19.2
☽	08 S 21.0	20 S 21.3
MC	08 S 44.7	23 S 15.5
♅	09 S 48.4	11 S 03.8
♇	09 N 54.1	09 N 42.6
♆	19 N 46.3	19 N 29.2
♃	20 S 19.2	18 S 09.5
Asc	23 S 24.1	04 S 44.3
♂	25 S 00.4	12 S 47.4
♀	25 S 58.3	19 S 03.2

hold ground when confronted and be content to rule from behind the scenes.

Now, if for any reason the remaining horoscopes do not produce good results we can come back to these rejected ones. It should not be necessary however. While the rising sign is not the only indicator of physical appearance, it is the strongest. Incidentally, if the physical birth time had actually been known, the first place to look would have been at the rising sign before the one given by the physical birth time, unless in a very late degree. It will usually be one or the other, and that makes the task of screening much, much easier.

For Eisenhower, the initial screening has left Libra, Sagittarius and Capricorn as potential rising signs, with Leo as a remote possibility. The Libra Sun sign is so strongly evident in this man that it would be very easy for his Ascendant to be the same, although the head shape did not appear to be right. Sagittarius is possible because of the full forehead. However, Sagittarius rising sign people usually have much more elongated heads, they have long feet and usually long ear lobes. So Sagittarius can be eliminated too. Capricorn is possible, because of Ike's somewhat puckish appearance and his clearcut ambition to rise toward greater heights of achievement throughout life. Capricorn rising natives usually have no ear lobes at all, or very tiny ones. The latter situation is the case with Eisenhower, which at first created some small doubts demanding further steps in verification. However, other considerations are that the individual with Capricorn rising generally has a dry sense of humor, and he or she is sure-footed and not extremely tall.

There was nothing in the personage of Eisenhower that would have denied those characteristics. Leo can be considered, because Leo's are often born rulers, and demand to be the center of attention.

Our next step was to look at these remaining charts to see if any of them fit. In this case the question is, does it fit a soldier, a commander, a president? Strong planetary placements caused the Libra rising horoscopes to be considered further, and certain of the Capricorn rising horoscopes, but not the one for Leo. In fact, the 3 Capricorn 46.3 rising chart looked almost too good to be true, because whoever places the Sun at the Midheaven without benefit of confirmation is immediately suspected of trying to force fit. This Capricorn rising horoscope not only has Sun with Uranus and the Moon on the Midheaven, but it also has Mars in the first house. This is a soldier-commander. The true local time was in the afternoon, as Eisenhower said it was. This afternoon time, it should be noted, is also in agreement with the story that a neighbor went for the doctor after dark. It gets dark very early in October in Denison, Texas, especially with an overcast sky, and more than likely street lights were on. Soul entry could easily have occurred three to four hours before physical birth, and that circumstance has been observed a number of times before.

The progressions are the clinchers. In the case of Dwight D. Eisenhower probably the most important event in his entire life was being appointed Supreme Commander of all Allied Forces during World War II. It was a very significant event. Another was his being elected president. We also have the date of his marriage, July 1, 1916. These three major occurrences, and others, were used for final verification.

At first the Progressed Mode was run for all of the remaining horoscopes on the list and for both Virgo rising horoscopes, because of previously published versions. That was a large number of computer runs, but it was accomplished in a matter of minutes. The Progressed Mode was run first for the date of December 5, 1943, when President Roosevelt picked Dwight D. Eisenhower to be the Supreme Commander. Only one of the horoscopes stood out. Again, it was that 3 Capricorn 46.3 rising chart. The progressed Sun and progressed Midheaven were in lock step, both in longitude and declination, a condition one might not have been too surprised to find considering his meteoric rise from obscurity. Second, his progressed Ascendant, a fast moving node that requires accurate timing, was within 1.3 minutes of being parallel his Uranus—suggesting a dynamic change in fortunes. But the real confirmation was from Progressed Mars coming to a trine with the Midheaven, within 1.9 minutes. Good heavens! What kind of an aspect would you expect for such an appointment? Could any other aspect be more fitting?

But it is not sufficient, in fact it can be dangerous, to rest on one's laurels on a single apparent correlation. Progressed runs had to be made for all of the candidate horoscopes and for all of the major event dates without bias. This thoroughness requires quite a bit of work, but it is regarded as essential. To make a long story short, only the same 3 Capricorn 46.3 rising horoscope supported those events with close aspects. On winning the presidential election, progressed Midheaven had been sextile its natal position. At the inauguration it was past that exact aspect, but not so far as to be ineffective. The progressed Moon was parallel his Jupiter earlier that day. The progressed Sun and Midheaven parallels of declinations, continuing their paths together, were now on his Ascendant. *Mon Dieu!* Those are aspects that would represent such an event—an event that comes only at four year intervals to one man in the entire nation.

Similarly, confirming the marriage chart, the slow-moving progressed Neptune was opposite Venus within 1.6 minutes. The progressed Moon was in opposition to Mercury. Then, progressed Pluto and Jupiter were parallel and contraparallel the Neptune involved with Venus respectively. These strong progressed Venus contacts relate to a female and to matters of the heart. There may have been something unexpected that did not go off quite right at that wedding because of the contraparallels, but the aspects are indicative of marriage in his horoscope. Most of the aspects came from slow-moving outer planets, and it did last. The indicators are not quite as close as usual, but they are again reasonable. No other prospective natal horoscope did as well at confirming this event.

Having determined that only one of the candidate times responded with close progressed aspects for every event tested, a final review is in order. Right away the first house Mars indicates either a military career or one in sports. That imposing Sun-Uranus conjunction with the Midheaven strongly suggests a dominant figure who is looked up to in contacts with his fellow man. He was commander-in-chief more than once in two different roles. Moon in the tenth house contributes popularity. The evidence is that Dwight D. Eisenhower found success comparatively easy to come by. That grand trine of Jupiter, Mercury and Neptune with Pluto support this reality. The Moon square Jupiter, and Mercury square Ascendant, aspects add tests in life to overcome, but not overwhelmingly. Mars trine Saturn shows the easy, for him, persistence in attaining his military objectives. Uranus is contraparallel Pluto, which could easily portend certain conflicts in trying to meet personal objectives, but with considerable resourcefulness. Then Mars and Venus are parallel, which doubtless reinforced his marriage and furnished considerable attraction to the females in his life. Mars does not get involved in such contacts without strife. But let us not overlook those fantastic alignments in declination. Saturn, Sun, Moon and Midheaven are all in parallel or contraparallel with each other. What an enormous amount of power that produces, and he was unquestionably a powerful man.

It is possible to go on and on about this horoscope. All placements of planets and aspects appear to be in line with what we know about this imposing individual and his life, including the criticisms he received for not creating dynamic national changes because of his ideal that the powers of congress should not be usurped by the President. The ninth house Mercury in Libra, and its grand trine position, shows clear thinking, an ability to communicate with others, his many journeys and an ability to apply logic easily. It also belies the fact that he was not regarded as an intellectual—such matters may have been too effortless on his part, and there is no strong aspect from Saturn to make his mental images endure. A Sagittarian Venus in the eleventh house corresponds to his philosophical desires for harmony in dealing with others that was sometimes thwarted by opposing forces. But that should be sufficient proof of the horoscope for this man with a Capricorn rising sign.

The confirmation of many progressed aspects in relation to events has to be, in the final analysis, a far more important criterion for verification than any other. This statement applies after a determination has been made that the horoscope appears to fit the person, and no configuration of planets or aspects leave doubts. A doubt is sufficient reason to check other times. If there are none, then close pertinent aspects for a quantity of events represents the final validation procedure. It might be pointed out that for Eisenhower many other events were progressed, and they also checked with close aspects. That includes his death, which took place when those formidable progressed Sun and Midheaven declinations returned to rest on his Capricorn Ascendant.

Another person who had a head shape and body, closely approaching the typical or ideal for Capricorn, was Dame Margot Fonteyn. Only a single *INCARN* run was needed, because a reported birth time of 2:15 AM on May 18, 1919, was available. This time yielded the 28 Capricorn 13.7 rising horoscope of Figure 31 and Table XXIX. Note that this horoscope is for the previous evening, over two-and-a-half hours earlier. Not as many earthshaking events were available for verification as for Eisenhower, but twenty-three curtain calls isn't bad for one of them, or her marriage for another, or an acknowledged, most outstanding performance, for still another.

Margot Fonteyn was her stage name. Dame was an honorable addition she was granted after becoming the leading ballerina in Great Britain and sustaining that position for decades. The full title is Dame Commander of the Most Excellent Order of the British Empire, which she received in 1960. Unfortunately the exact date was not printed in accessible biographies. But in the beginning, she was born Margaret Hookham of Reigate, Surrey. Her father was Felix John Hookham, who was an engineer working for the British-American Tobacco Company. Her mother was Hilda (Fontes) Hookham, a coffee heiress of Irish-Brazilian descent. Perhaps this unusual combination of bloodlines gave her that awe-inspiring capability to enchant an audience. At any rate she grew up with her brother Felix, traveling to many parts of the world. Stops after leaving England were Louisville, Kentucky, in the United States, China and then back to England. Primary education was either in private schools or by tutors.

MAY 17 1919	11:44 PM GMT	Naibod Secondary
REIGATE	ENGLAND	FEB 6 1955
51 N 14 03	000 W 12 16	
11:44:51 PM TLT	11:45:40 PM GMT	11:45:40 PM GMT

Tropical *Placidus* *True Node*

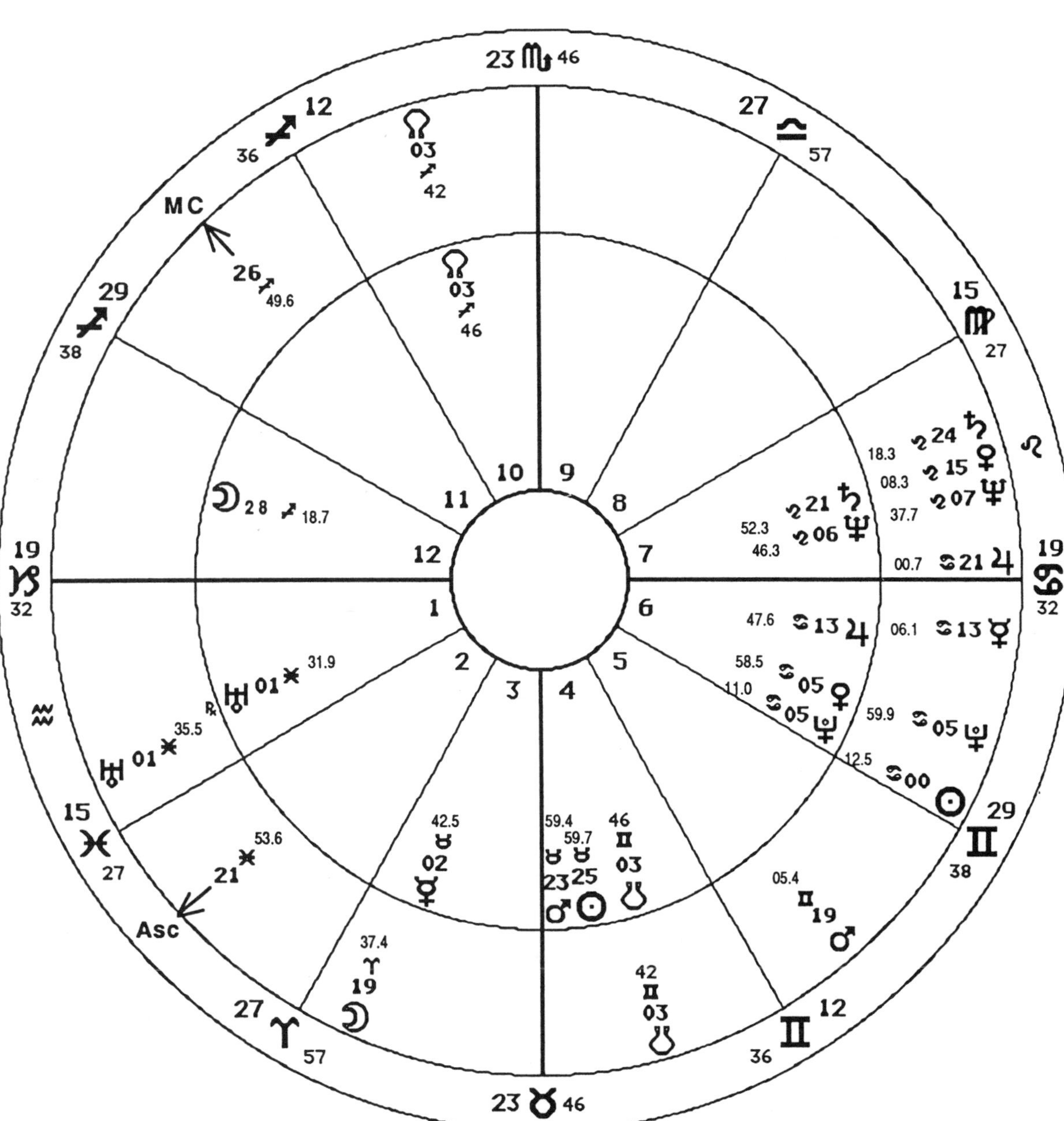

Figure 31. Horoscope of Dame Margot Fonteyn, *prima ballerina* of Great Britain for many years. Progressions are to the date of her marriage to Alberto Arias.

Table XXIX. Natal and Progressed Declinations of Dame Margot Fonteyn

Planet	Natal Decln.	02 06 1955 Marriage
☿	09 N 45.8	24 N 42.5
♅	11 S 37.7	11 S 37.7
♄	15 N 34.6	14 N 44.4
♆	18 N 31.1	18 N 18.5
MC	18 S 42.6	23 S 24.7
♂	18 N 50.8	23 N 26.1
☉	19 N 15.7	23 N 26.9
♇	19 N 23.5	19 N 24.7
☽	21 S 14.0	11 N 02.8
Asc	21 S 59.9	03 S 13.1
♃	22 N 59.0	22 N 05.8
♀	25 N 33.7	18 N 04.6

Margaret Hookham first began to dance seriously at the age of five, and she took lessons under Grace Bestulow in Ealing. Her lessons in the United States were not reported, but her father searched out George Gontcharov, a Russian of excellent reputation, while they were in Shanghai. By the age of twelve, when the family returned to England, she was tested at the Royal Academy of Dance. Results were encouraging, and at the age of fifteen she enrolled in the Vic-Wells Ballet School (a forerunner of Sadler-Wells). Gradually her professional career expanded until finally she became *prima ballerina* of Britain's Royal Ballet.

Years later David Blair said, "She was very, very easy to work with. She is completely professional, cooperative and so very, very musical. Her sense of phrasing is beautiful, and her sense of rubato, of being able to play with the music inside a phrase....She has matured, her art has become enriched, but in *Romeo and Juliet* or in *Sleeping Beauty* , where she played a sixteen year old, she actually convinces an audience that she is sixteen years old. She is youth itself." Dame Margot Fonteyn caused a sensation when she danced exquisitely with the much younger Russian expatriate, Rudolf Nureyev. At an even more advanced age she was called, "a living legend in contemporary ballet, active, seemingly ageless, a graceful paradigm of the pure classical style."

Others may not know that she was, in addition to being *prima ballerina* of the Royal

Ballet, an ambassadress from her country to Panama, that she married a Panamanian politician, Roberto Arias, who was shot in an assassination attempt, and that she took care of him, since he was confined to a wheel chair, for the rest of his life. This was one multi-talented person with far more to her credit than just being a dancer. She was an excellent example of Capricorn rising. All one needs to do is to look at her picture and see the nymph of Capricorn personified, especially enhanced by her ears. The grace of her body on the stage of a ballet theater was a perfect setting for this mountain climber.

Dame Margot Fonteyn's horoscope is very unusual. It has intercepted houses—the first and seventh. The pair corroborates the use of her own body in her art and her almost idealic relationships with other people—those she worked with, those she interfaced with as her country's representative and her husband, who was wealthy but who had to be taken care of. The third and ninth houses are stronger than might at first be suspected. The close conjunctions and parallels are responsible. There is Venus conjunct Pluto, which shows enormous depth of resourcefulness in her first occupation of artistry. Venus, being the ruler of the ninth house, shows that this artistry is on display. Sun parallels Pluto. This adds inherent energy. Mars parallels Neptune, but Mars is also contraparallel Midheaven and square Saturn. The story is engrained in her chart of a husband who is incapacitated by a bullet. Opposition to her marriage was also indicated. Moon is parallel Ascendant, and her main accomplishments in life were enormously popular.

The main progressed aspect at the time of her marriage was progressed Ascendant inconjunct Saturn. This seventh house planet in Leo represents a man in a high level position. The aspect was within 1.3 minutes of the 150 degree angle. The slow-moving progressed Pluto was conjunct Venus within 1.4 minutes. Her progressed Sun was also parallel progressed Mars within 0.8 minutes and contraparallel Midheaven within 2.2 minutes. This was an affair of state, since she represented England in Panama, and not simply another marriage. Those familiar with basic, fundamental natal astrology should be able to see the significance of these correlating aspects. When the horoscope time is correct, 100% correlation is achieved for all astrological elements. In fact, it is essential.

While this has been a lengthy approach to the illustration of Capricorn rising, at least one more needs to be given for equitable reasons. Another writer was chosen, one who has had much to tell the rest of the world. That man is Alexander Solzhenitsyn. Instantly, from our experiences of earlier chapters, the third/ninth house interception in his horoscope brands him as a potential writer. See Figure 32 and Table XXX. Also, if possible to observe his photograph, one will see the distinctive Capricornian features. Ovate face and ears that project upward and outward. But what is this—Mars in the first house? Of course. He was trained as an artillery officer. In 1941 he became commander of an artillery battery. He served at the Leningrad front until February of 1945. He was twice decorated for wounds received in battle. It was only after he had written a letter alluding to the conduct of the war by the whiskered one that insidious Russian counter-intelligence agents arrested and imprisoned him.

Imprisonment included enforced labor, transfers, Siberian camps, prison research and lack of freedom as we believe that we know it. It also included bouts with Cancer. In 1962 he wrote *One Day in the Life of Ivan Denisovich*. That book, clandestinely printed and slipped to the outside world, made him famous. He wrote more books, including *Nory Mir, Incident at Krechatovka Station* and *Matryona's House*. He wrote *We Never Make Mistakes*. He won a Nobel Prize for literature. By 1964 the situation had changed sufficiently within Russia that he was nominated for a Lenin Prize. The KGB confiscated his manuscripts and later, according to the political climate, found reasons to return them. So what we have is a Russian military officer and writer who was often oppressed, imprisoned for long periods of his life, suffered from the ravages of Cancer, which were apparently arrested, won literary prizes and survived into a new political era.

DEC 11 1918 08:50 AM EAT
KISLOVODSK RUSSIA
43 N 57 05 042 E 43 39
8:40:14 AM TLT 5:49:19 AM GMT
Tropical *Placidus* *True Node*

Naibod Secondary
AUG 15 1990
5:49:19 AM GMT

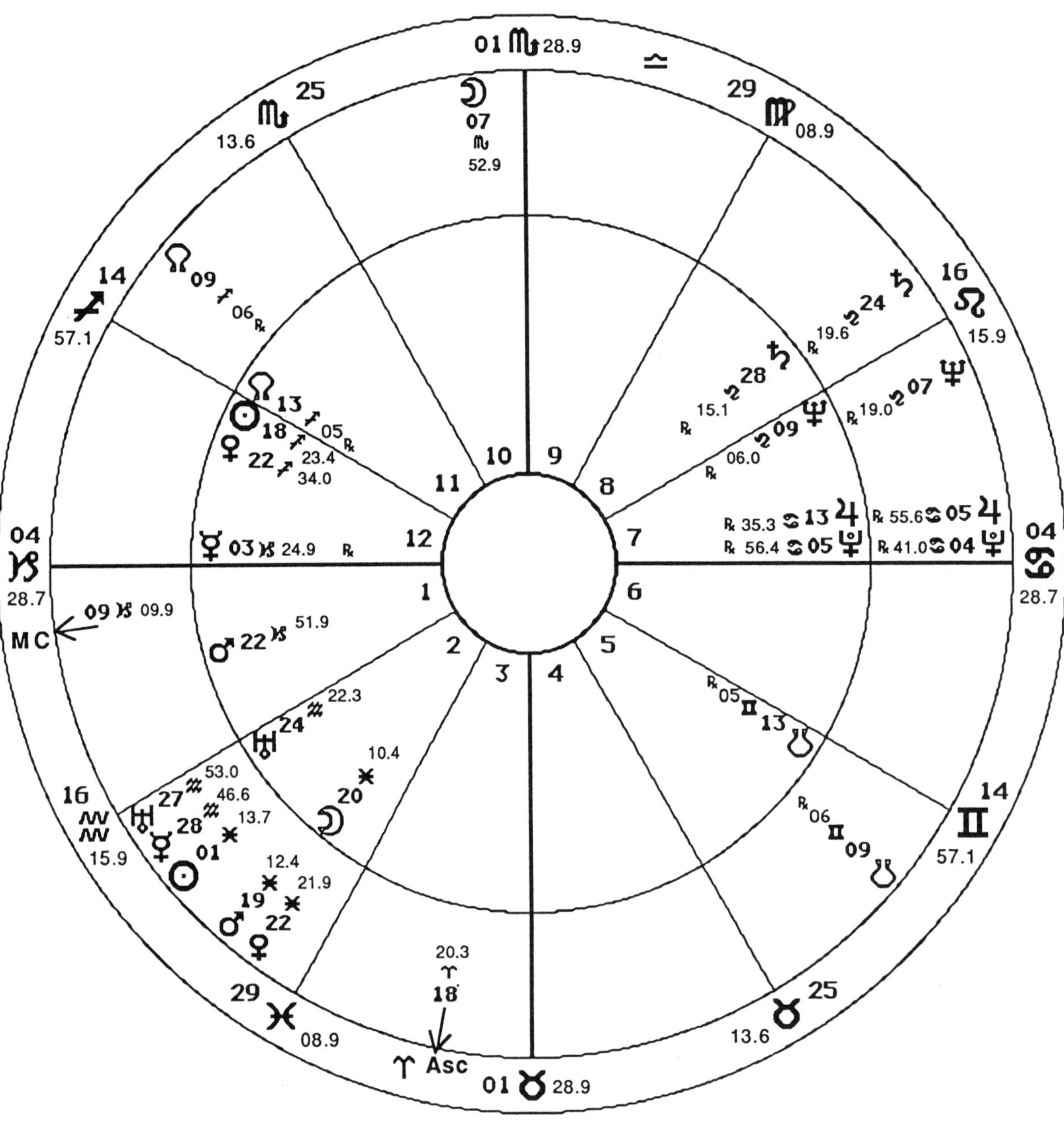

Figure 32. Horoscope of Alexander Solzhenitsyn with progressions to the date his citizenship was restored.

Table XXX. Natal and Progressed Declinations of Alexander Solzhenitzyn

Planet	Natal Decln.	08 15 1990 Citizenship
☽	00 N 55.4	16 S 36.9
MC	11 S 59.7	23 S 08.0
♄	13 N 17.2	14 N 48.8
♅	14 S 05.3	12 S 52.7
♆	17 N 53.3	18 N 21.8
♇	19 N 03.5	19 N 12.6
♂	22 S 43.5	05 S 01.7
♃	22 N 44.2	23 N 27.2
☉	22 S 56.5	11 S 02.5
Asc	23 S 22.4	07 N 11.6
♀	23 N 32.9	04 S 12.6
☿	23 S 47.0	13 S 48.1

Does this horoscope match the kind of life he faced? Certainly yes. Sun, Venus and Mercury are in the twelfth house, and its ruler, Jupiter, is conjunct Pluto. Both are opposite Mercury and the Ascendant. This set of aspects creates weaknesses making him susceptible to Cancer. He was most concerned, however, with letting the rest of the world know about the heinous oppression under Stalin. Mars and Sun contraparallel Jupiter in this alignment are circumstantial. He almost had to be arrested. Ascendant and Mercury contraparallel Venus simply add detail to the overwhelming forces present.

The progressed event used to illustrate the validation, was the day his citizenship was restored. His progressed Ascendant was trine Sun within 3.1 minutes. His progressed Jupiter was conjunct Pluto within 0.8 minutes. Numerous other dates are available and they produced appropriate aspects. Among them were his graduation in 1941 from the University of Rostov with a degree in Mathematics and Physics, his initial arrest in February of 1945, his release from prison on March 5, 1953, his letter opposing censorship of May 16, 1967, and the attacks against him in June of 1968 declaring him to be a "willing tool of anti-Soviet propaganda." Interested astrologers will find nearly exact progressions for these dates based upon the given horoscope.

So, Capricorn rising comes in many forms, as do all of the signs. But the physical and mental similarities are perceptible to those who make an effort to understand.

CHAPTER 11. AQUARIUS

Physical Attributes

The most prominent feature of any one of any race with Aquarius rising is a square shaped head. The width is approximately the same as the height, and the jaws are as wide as the forehead. One might think of a squashed rectangle. The stature of the body is medium to medium tall. Unless Venus is afflicted, the complexion is usually very good. The outward appearance is generally friendly, and their smiles may be especially delightful. Movements are leisurely on average, or serene. Unless the Moon is in an emotional sign, they will have dispassionate and platonic natures and they are usually gentle and helpful. Occasionally their friendly, cooperative, agreeable natures will suddenly appear to change to one that is more intense. Then they can be forceful and outspoken, as though a thought had to be expressed out of the blue. Such outspokenness can be startling or upsetting to others. It usually comes from a deep seated conviction or the violation of some behavioral pattern they detest, such as slyness, hypocrisy or double-dealing. Afterward, their stances will change back to one that is more engaging and humane, although humanity may have been at the core of the outburst.

Uranus is one of the rulers of Aquarius. Therefore certain tendencies may be unorthodox or different from those of other people. For example, an individual with Aquarius rising can have peculiar eating habits, or be eccentric in other ways, such as having nonconformist likes or dislikes. Their eccentricity may even show up in their bodies in one form or other, such as broader hips in a male or narrower ones in a female. However, these variations are not common. Saturn is the other ruler of Aquarius. Saturn crystallizes, waits and consolidates, so a great deal more patience is present in their mannerisms than might be the case for Uranus alone.

Pisces rising, further ahead, gives a fish-like appearance when looking straight on. Capricorn rising has just been desribed in the last chapter, and the head is ovate with ears that slope in toward the face. It really should become easier at this stage to notice the differences.

Mental Attributes

The sign Aquarius on a person's Ascendant is symbolized by the water bearer and by nature it is fixed air. The water bearer provides a life-sustaining liquid to others, even though it is an air sign, meaning that it is more mental than physical. Aquarius takes up for the underdog. In fact, they are conspicuous at being the first to help the less fortunate or those who are injured. The orientation of this fixed air sign is toward being original, and some viewpoints may be idiosyncratic. Self-will is expressed in strong likes and dislikes. In general, intercourse with others is easy, and their attitudes are positive. Their blithe dealings with others come as second nature, and they are rarely dejected.

People with Aquarius on the Ascendant have a special insight into human nature. They can take advantage of this faculty by manipulating other people, or by effortlessly ridiculing them, when so inclined, or to benefit themselves. With equal ease they can harbour a special kind of understanding, idealistic guidelines or new social orders, when the intent is to help other people or all mankind. They constantly seek clearer insights into life.

The undeveloped or rudimentary person with Aquarius rising often takes advantage of others under the mask of artless coolness and friendly interest. While having special insights into human nature, they may be inefficient at using them. Practical details are lost in a general haziness, and procrastination is the order of the day allowing them to fritter away much time and energy. Perhaps because of the tendency to ridicule others, they themselves are sometimes accused of moral and physical cowardice. This is the person who is more concerned with right and wrong than with practical solutions to everyday problems. After arguments, or sessions during which others have offered to help, one finds their viewpoints, no matter how impractical, will be unchanged. Rather, they will cling to a peculiar behavior or to an untenable idea contrary to public or private opinion. Sometimes they take delight in having thoughts that are different for the sake of being different, though appearing extreme or unbalanced to others.

The evolved person with Aquarius rising has that extraordinary breadth of vision that is without bias or prejudice. Tradition and authority must be regarded with the same level of intelligence as that which is new and unusual. Most are without vanity or conceit when it comes to knowledge, and if later findings upset an earlier position, then they are willing to take a new stand based on the evidence at hand. Unmoved by passions, and what are regarded as other frailties of human nature, they make perfect theoretical scientists. They can form their own hypotheses, marshall all of the facts, work long and patient hours, test opposing theories with levels of intensity equal to those applied to their own ideas, and come to rational conclusions based purely upon the evidence. The emphasis is on the theoretical, rather than the practical, however. An Aquarian makes a better mathematician, physicist or scientist on average than an engineer. They also do well as ministers (unless agnosticism is present) and in human relations. No one or no thing is taken wholly on trust, but words and actions are cooly separated for careful scrutiny, special abilities are identified along with shortcomings, motives and cravings are identified. Only the whole picture, with rose tinted glasses removed, is real to them.

The truly advanced person with Aquarius rising, liberally pours his waters into needy mouths of the world. He is kindly and humane to the underprivileged. Great satisfaction is found in increasing the comfort and well-being of unfortunate or downtrodden people. Still, they have a way of looking at life's problems from the outside, rather than the inside.

So, again it is a very good exercise to look at horoscopes of people who are supposed to have Aquarius on their Ascendants. To name just a few: Bill Moyers, the editor and news commentator is one. Che Gueverra, the revolutionary cohort of Fidel Castro, is another. Leslie Caron, the French-American dancer and actress of the 50's is one. Jimmy Hoffa, the deceased labor leader, has a horoscope that claims to belong in this group. Hamilton Jordan, the banker assistant to President Jimmy Carter, qualifies. Dorothy Hammill, the skating champion, is still another. Lee Iacoca has the facial characteristics, but no published horoscope has been uncovered. One comment applicable to reviewing this group is to be watchful—some do have Aquarius rising; others do not, though reported birthtimes and occupations might suggest that common sign. The first question to ask is, which ones truly have square-shaped heads (and do not be mislead when the Sun sign is Aquarius)? That is a profound, although rough, starting point. However, everyone should be able to agree that only some in this group have the essential physical characteristics and Aquarian personality traits.

Example Horoscopes

Those chosen for illustration are not necessarily admired or denigrated by the whole world. They have been chosen to illustrate the rising sign. In thinking about Aquarius rising from a global viewpoint, one person comes immediately to mind, both because of his physique and his objectives. His photographs and statues have appeared in many places throughout the world. This was mostly in formerly Communist nations, and many of those likenesses are now being removed. But his head is so noticeably square-shaped that in running the *INCARN* program and having choices from four possible rising signs, all could be immediately ignored except those in

Aquarius. This made the task of finding the correct horoscope comparatively easy. The person referred to is Dr. Karl Heinrich Marx—he did have a doctorate degree from the University of Jena in what is now the Eastern sector of Germany. One of his books, which he co-authored with Friederich Engels, *Manifest der Kommunistischen Partei,* which was published in 1848, changed entire nations. His horoscope appears in Figure 33 and Table XXXI.

This biographical sketch of Karl Marx will not be lengthy, but will concentrate more upon dates that can be used by others for further checks. Biographies other than the ones found in a local library might have been more detailed and provided more personal information. What is known is that he was born in Trier (or Tréves), a beautiful old Roman town on the banks of the Mosel River in old Prussia—now West Germany—on May 5, 1818. May fifth is *Cinco de Mayo* in Spanish, and the Sun is in Taurus on that date. The family was Jewish and encountered various degrees of oppression. When Karl was six, in 1824, the whole family was baptized as Protestants. Whether this reduced persecutions or ill treatment is not known. Reports are that Karl's father wanted him to have a good education, even though he had only average grades in the lower schools. He was sent first to the University of Bonn, and later to the University of Berlin, where he studied history and philosophy. Receiving his undergraduate degrees, he studied the same subjects at the University of Jena and had the PhD Degree conferred upon him in 1841 (probably June). He was strongly influenced during these student periods by the philosophies of Georg Wilhelm Friedrich Hegel. After graduation Dr. Karl Marx decided upon journalism. He became editor of the *Rheinische Zeitung* of Cologne in 1842. After a little over a year, this paper was closed by order of authorities in May of 1843. He had just married Jenny von Westphalen in March, two months before. The family moved to Paris, and Karl Marx wrote *Misère de la Philosophie*. Upon returning to Germany, he collaborated with Engels in writing the *Communist Manifesto*. There was another expulsion in July of 1849. This was the pattern of his life until he finally died an early death on March 14, 1883.

Other than these meager facts, it has been written that Karl Marx had few close friends, with the possible exception of Engels. It was also written that he did enjoy a warm home life and being with his children. Most of the time he lived in poverty and suffered persistent illnesses. The main thesis in his writings was that throughout history there had been two classes of people—the haves (oppressors) and the have nots (oppressed). From this typically Aquarian simplistic idea came revolutions.

The birth time for Karl Marx has been listed as 2:00 AM LMT. While that even hour time of its own accord is ill-defined, the horoscope left by Maurice Wemyss does not agree with it. But of far greater importance, Wemyss's horoscope is almost exactly in agreement with the one produced by the *INCARN* algorithm. The difference of a few minutes on the Ascendant could easily be attributed to the relative accuracies of formulas used for calculating horoscopes in the two different periods, one using a computer, the other using manual techniques and logarithms. One might speculate that Wemyss knew and used the incarnation theory. Further tests on other of his horoscopes should prove that point. Meanwhile, the Karl Marx horoscope by him is certainly the most accurate of all published horoscopes for important persons that have been tested during the last half century. None other comes so close. Therefore, there is no disputed horoscope for comparison purposes.

Both the Wemyss figure and the *INCARN* figure show Saturn, and the then undiscovered Pluto, in the first house. Saturn in the house of the physical body attests to his chronic illnesses. Moon, the ruler of the sixth house of health in carrying out work, is contraparallel Pluto. The weaknesses of the body are reconfirmed. Revolutionary Uranus, the other ruler of the Aquarian Ascendant, is elevated and conjunct his Midheaven. It is also conjunct Neptune, the planet of idealism and illusion. Neptune is inconjunct Jupiter and his Midheaven. Mars and Venus are inconjunct Uranus. These are extremely powerful forces at play, and the elevated planets are under siege. Jupiter in the eleventh house says that he may have had more friends than

MAY 05 1818 2:34 AM CET
TRIER GERMANY
49 N 45 56 006 E 24 41
1:58:23 AM TLT 1:32:44 AM GMT
Tropical *Placidus* *True Node*

Naibod Secondary
MAR 14 1883
1:32:44 AM GMT

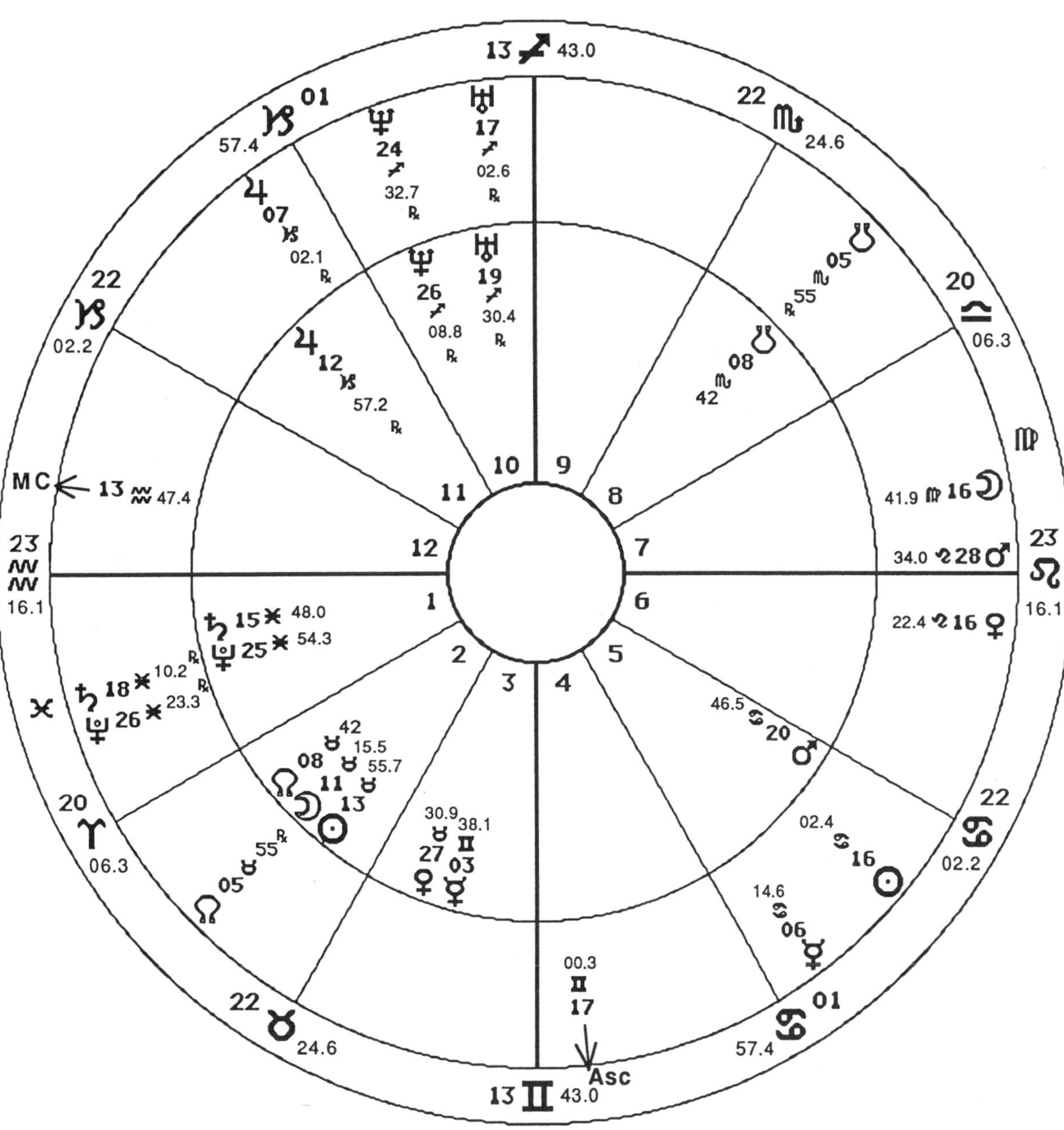

Figure 33. **Horoscope of Karl Marx, co-author of the *Communist Manifesto*, with progressions to the day he died.**

his biographer acknowledges, because of the relatively harmonious aspects in longitude. However, the inconjunct with Neptune also shows that he was deceived by so-called friends and he may have written about them. Mercury, the ruler of his fifth house of children, is conjunct his Sun, and this pair makes fortunate aspects with many other planets in this wheel. Therefore, he did have a warm association with his children and wife. Mars, the other ruler of the fifth house, also makes comparatively favorable aspects, except for an opposition to Jupiter and the contra-parallel with Uranus. This is more in the nature of forced movements while his family, among others, was being forcibly expelled. It also relates directly to his involvements with newspapers and the writing of books. The strength of his ninth house rulers, Mars and Pluto, led to his carrying on this fight for the working man via his own forceful, creative writings (Mars in fifth house parallel and semi-square Mercury). Mercury is in the third house, where personal writings take place. Mercury is conjunct Venus and the pair is sextile Pluto, the other ruler of the ninth house. The literary path is reconfirmed.

Table XXXI. Natal and Progressed Declinations of Karl Marx

Planet	Natal Decln.	03 14 1883 Died
♄	07 S 14.7	06 S 33.5
Asc	13 S 46.7	22 N 49.8
☽	15 N 26.3	08 N 47.0
♇	15 S 56.1	16 S 05.1
☉	16 N 02.2	22 N 30.0
♀	19 N 40.1	17 N 33.6
♆	22 N 06.9	22 N 03.6
MC	22 S 28.3	16 S 42.4
♃	22 S 42.0	23 S 16.9
♅	23 S 06.9	22 S 54.5
☿	23 N 20.3	23 N 47.5
♂	23 N 33.5	13 N 01.8

Let us now talk about the first and seventh house interceptions. This is a very strong indicator of either an occupation utilizing his own physical body, or one concerned with human relations. Whether or not the reader has sympathy for his philosophies, the astrological pattern is present to cause extensive involvement with such matters. In characteristic Aquarian fashion, he wanted to help the second category of peoples in this world, the ones that were oppressed. It cannot be denied that he experienced oppression many times himself.

Numerous dates were given in the biography of Karl Marx, to the nearest month. Several progressions were computed for mid-month dates approximating those events, and they confirmed. However, the only other event besides his birth for which a day was given happened to be the day of his death. Therefore, it was used to illustrate the verification step of close aspects for a known progressed date. On that date his progressed Ascendant was opposite Uranus within 2.3 minutes. Simultaneously the progressed declination of his Ascendant was contraparallel Neptune within 4.7 minutes. The progressed Ascendant, by this time, was making its aspects from the fourth house, which is always involved when death occurs. Slow-moving progressed Pluto, of the first house, was contraparallel his Sun within 2.9 minutes. Preogressed Sun was contraparallel his Midheaven within 1.7 minutes. His death was a newsworthy event, and it caused problems for those following his guidlines. This array of aspects and their accuracies are more than sufficient to show the event.

The square-shaped head for Aquarius rising is so distinctive that nothing else is needed to know the sign is correct for the person having it. In fact, this was the approach used to find suitable horoscopes for this chapter's illustrative purposes. It was not even necessary to look at Pisces rising horoscopes. The procedure was simply to remember which people of prominence had square-shaped heads. That was the procedure for recalling Karl Marx. It was the procedure used for selecting the next two. The first one was a "first lady." Lady Bird (Claudia) Johnson, the wife of President Lyndon Johnson, is classic Aquarius rising. When her photograph was displayed in newspapers or when her image appeared on television, Aquarius simply stood out. Mathematics were not required to arrive at this conclusion. Those horoscopes later examined, showing Pisces on the Ascendant, were immediately recognized for what they were, misleading and erroneous versions.

Yes, Pisces was on the Ascendant of one published horoscope for Lady Bird Johnson that was very briefly examined. But Pisces is just as distinctive in its own way, and for a little Texas talk, no way, pardner. It is just as clear that Lady Bird does not have a Pisces Ascendant as is the fact that she does have an Aquarius Ascendant. The error is by a full house or more in the astrological chart. Before going into proofs, a little personal information is warranted that can be used in the verification process.

Lady Bird was a Taylor. She was the daughter of Thomas Jefferson Taylor, a landowner and merchant. Her mother, Minnie Lee (Patillo) Taylor was from an Alabama family of Scotch and Spanish extraction. She grew up a rather lonely child, because one brother, Thomas, was eleven years older and her step-brother, Antonio, was eight years younger. Her mother died when she was five and she was cared for by Aunt Effie, who came from Alabama to preside at "The Brick House."

Claudia Taylor drove herself to and from Marshall, Texas to attend high school. She was shy and too reticent to make any kind of speech. Although making good grades, she later said that she would rather have caught small pox than to deliver either the valedictorian or salutatorian addresses to her graduating classes. Fate stepped in. She graduated third at the age of fifteen and didn't have to speak in front of the class or catch small pox either. After high school she attended Saint Mary's Episcopal School of Girls in Dallas, a Junior College. After two years there she enrolled at the University of Texas in Austin. She received her BA degree in 1933.

Not long after graduation Claudia Taylor met Lyndon B. Johnson. He was a former school teacher, who at that time had become executive secretary to United States Representative from Texas, Richard M. Kleberg. Kleberg was a part owner of the mammoth King's Ranch. Later, in looking back on the meeting, Claudia said, "I knew I'd met something remarkable, but I didn't know quite what." She married Lyndon Johnson on November 17, 1934, at Saint Mark's Episcopal Church in San Antonio. They honeymooned in Mexico.

In her own right, Lady Bird Johnson did not intend to sit idly by while her husband climbed the political ladder. She became interested in radio and television. Station KTBC came up for sale. She combined $21,000 from her mother's estate and a bank loan of $10,000 to buy it.

Within six months her business instincts turned the station around and it became profitable. She also took a course in speechmaking to overcome her shyness and did a commendable job, when Lyndon became Vice President, entertaining visitors. In fact this was the chief function of a vice president's wife, entertaining foreign political and diplomatic visitors to the United States.

Most people are aware that Lyndon B. Johnson ascended to the presidency when John F. Kennedy was shot. It was said that she was very sympathetic to Jacqueline Kennedy and told her to take her time in moving out. Afterward she found herself in charge of the 132-room White House and its staff of seventy-five. This staff included one person of her own choosing, Mrs Zephyr Wright, who was the long standing family cook. As a comment, Aquarians do have their own tastes about food.

During Lyndon Johnson's presidency, and while occupying the White House, she became immersed in social, political and economic problems. These were her main interests.*U. S. News and World Report* said that Lady Bird Johnson was, "careful, shrewd and a very successful business woman." Within twenty plus years she parlayed her original investment for KTBC into a $6 million fortune. She and her daughters owned 84% of Texas Broadcasting Corporation plus 3000 acres of timberland, 4000 acres of grazing land and the cattle to go on it. Her horoscope of Figure 34 and Table XXXII show some reasons why.

I. It is wise to return to the original structured format, because here there is a contending horoscope, no matter how inappropriate. For starters Mars, Jupiter and Sun are conjunct and parallel one another in the tenth house. They are accompanied by Mercury at the zenith. This planet of communications is conjunct the Midheaven for additional acumen and emphasis upon the spoken word. She may have been too timid to speak in public at first, possibly because of the Mars conjunction. However, she overcame that fear and turned speaking into an asset. Could this be the horoscope of a president's wife and a successful businesswoman? Without one speck of doubt, is the answer.

Another interesting configuration is present to be observed. This is the same intercepted first and seventh houses that Karl Marx had. No planets are present in those houses, but that hardly matters. The rulers are together in the tenth house. In her own way Lady Bird Johnson has a deep concern for the welfare of people. She did more than just have the concern. She formatted the programming of her broadcast station to be more people oriented, and that is one of the key reasons why it expanded. She organized clubs while in Washington to address issues. She held luncheons for women-doers. She worked for improvements. It is interesting that in making comparisons with other president's wives, Eleanor Roosevelt comes up most often among writers and editors, rather than her immediate predecessor. Lady Bird has been an extraordinary person in her own right and a very good example of an ambitious Capricorn Sun with Aquarius rising.

II. If most of the planets were shifted one house position with the twenty-seventh degree of Pisces on the Ascendant, that would be the reported birth time horoscope. This shift does place Jupiter on the Midheaven and Pluto at the Nadir. But, Mars and Mercury in the ninth house would have her doing the broadcasts, not necessarily owning the station. Saturn in the second house would have put the brakes upon her acquisition of wealth. It would have come at a much slower pace, whereas Mars conjunct Jupiter, in Figure 34, caused rapid expansion. Uranus and Venus moved to the eleventh house would have caused her to be much more the comic and closer friends of both technocrats and women. Neptune would have moved to the fourth house where her childhood would have been dreamier and probably more disruptive than it was. The first/seventh house interception would be gone. Too much in the Pisces rising horoscope does not match what we know, and zero mismatches are the limit.

Nothing was said earlier about Uranus and Venus in the twelfth house. Both are in Aquarius. Uranus in this location causes a deep-seated desire to utilize technology in a beneficial manner for aiding society. Her radio station represents the technology. The presence of Venus unquestionably corresponds with her special emphasis upon women-doers. These two twelfth house planets have favorable aspects with her Midheaven and the tenth house group. She has been

DEC 23 1912 | 10:38 AM CST
KARNACK | TEXAS
32 N 39 30 | 094 W 13 06
10:20:55 AM TLT | 4:37:48 PM GMT

Tropical *Placidus* *True Node*

Naibod Secondary
NOV 17 1934
4:37:48 PM GMT

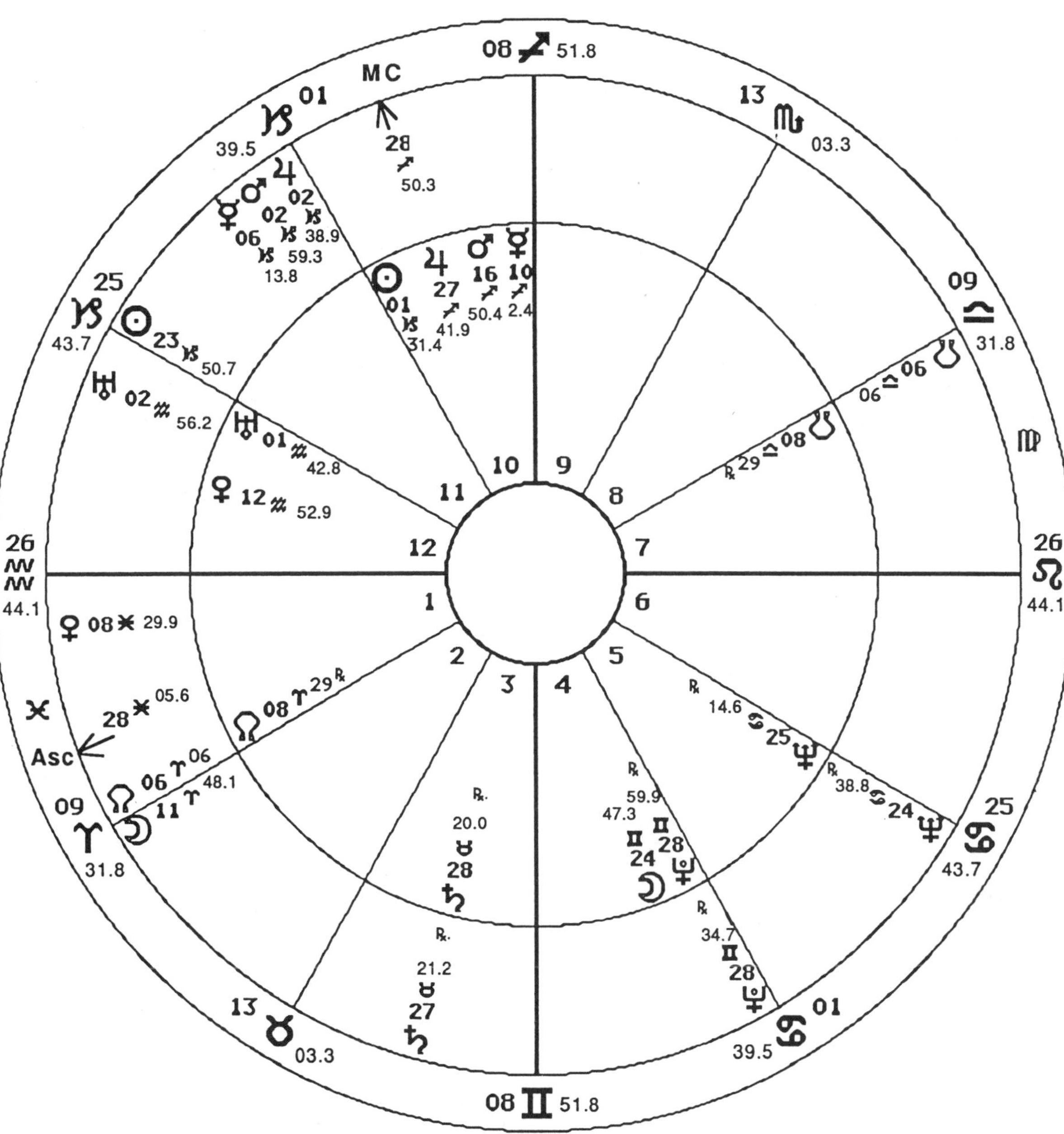

Figure 34. Horoscope of Lady Bird (Claudia) Johnson, first lady and wife of President Lyndon Johnson with progressions to the day she married him.

Table XXXII. Natal and Progressed Declinations of Lady Bird (Claudia) Johnson

Planet	Natal Decln.	11 17 1934 Marriage
Asc	12 S 36.6	00 S 45.6
♇	17 N 15.9	17 N 17.6
♄	17 N 43.1	17 N 35.2
♀	18 S 52.3	09 S 24.9
☿	19 S 26.1	23 S 40.8
♅	20 S 20.4	20 S 03.6
♆	20 N 35.5	20 N 42.1
MC	21 N 47.5	23 S 26.9
♂	23 S 09.7	24 S 00.4
♃	23 S 11.6	23 S 13.1
☉	23 S 26.6	21 S 20.8
☽	28 N 12.7	05 N 09.0

more than successful at accomplishing her goals.

III. There is no better progression than her marriage to Lyndon for showing one of the events with close aspects for the illustrated horoscope. Her progressed Midheaven was parallel her seventh house ruler, Sun, within 0.3 minutes. That had to be an earth shaking, foot stomping, hand clapping event, even for Texas. Progressed Mars was semi-sextile Uranus progressed within 3.1 minutes. This marriage had to receive publicity and it foretold of future accomplishments. Slow moving Jupiter and Pluto were also very close to their natal positions by declination. The Pisces horoscope fails miserably in describing this event. It is looking for a Mercury aspect to describe the marriage, and a Mercury aspect is not very close. Also, a meaningful Midheaven aspect is not to be found. The progressed Midheaven is normally present at an affair of this importance to the public. Also, prior results show that the progressions in declination occur just as often as the ones in longitude, if not more so for important events. This seems to be true even though fewer technical possibilities exist for a declination to form throughout a lifetime.

The next illustrative horoscope for Aquarius rising came about by simply looking at Public Service Television for a few minutes on a recent Sunday evening. That unmistakable square face of Lawrence Welk was leading his band and troop of youthful performers.

While his show contains all of these pretty young faces, it is supposed to appeal to a somewhat older crowd. Whatever the age group that watches this show, it has been on the air a very long time—in fact longer than any other of its type.

Lawrence Welk (see Figure 35 and Table XXXIII) is of German ancestry. He was born into a German colony that settled in North Dakota. Thus, his accent is not affected, it is real. He was the son of Ludwig Welk, a blacksmith in the town of Strassburg. Lawrence was the second from the youngest of eight children. His is the story of growing up in a hard working family, not especially wealthy. He had to quit school in his fourth year to work in the fields. As with most families in these circumstances, everyone had his or her duties, but family members were close. Lawrence Welk's father taught him to play the accordion. When he was thirteen, money was earned playing at weddings, social gatherings and other events where music was appropriate. On his seventeenth birthday his father gave him a $400 accordion.

Table XXXIII. Natal and Progressed Declinations of Lawrence Welk

Planet	Natal Decln.	07 02 1955 1st Show
♂	02 S 15.0	02 N 32.0
☉	04 S 03.7	15 N 11.8
♀	04 N 51.2	24 N 30.9
☽	09 N 56.0	16 N 38.2
♃	10 S 38.4	06 S 29.5
♇	14 N 10.7	14 N 24.6
☿	14 S 43.9	22 N 30.9
Asc	15 S 13.7	18 N 03.1
♄	19 S 13.1	18 S 26.3
MC	21 S 50.1	20 S 46.3
♆	22 N 20.7	22 N 22.5
♅	23 S 29.4	23 S 29.7

Lawrence began to expand his appointments. When radio station WNAX of Yankton, South Dakota opened, he played during the initial broadcasts. He appeared daily with a saxophone player and a piano player. By 1927 the band numbered six players and

MAR 11 1903	5:58 AM CST	Naibod Secondary
STRASBURG	NORTH DAKOTA	JUL 2 1955
46 N 08 04	100 W 09 15	
5:16:54 AM TLT	11:57:31 AM GMT	11:57:31 AM GMT

Tropical *Placidus* *True Node*

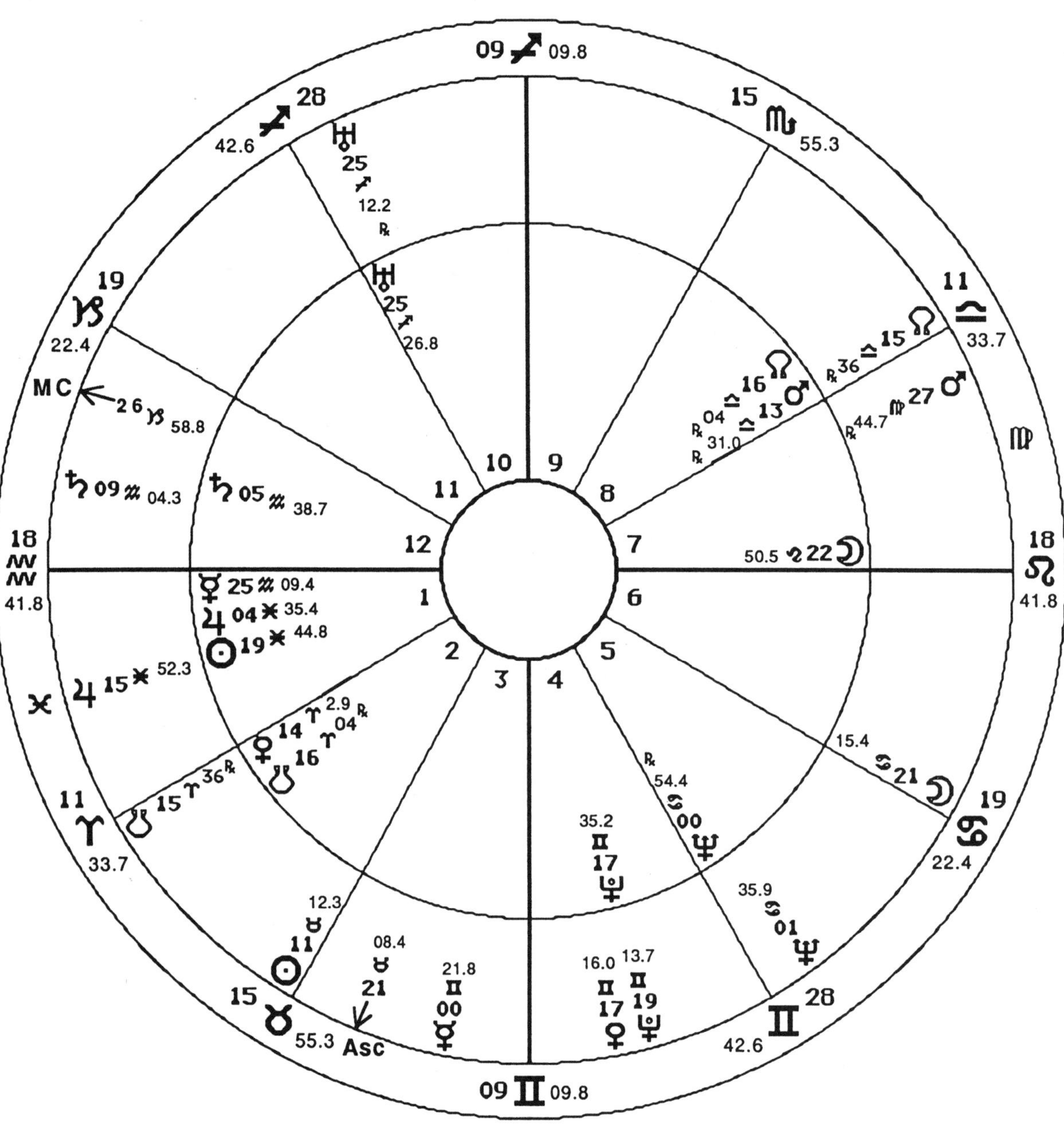

Figure 35. **Horoscope of band leader Lawrence Welk. Progressions are to the day his first show was launched.**

called itself Lawrence Welk's Hotsie Totsie Boys. In 1946 he moved on to the Aragon Ballroom in Ocean Park, California. His reputation and work grew. July 2, 1955, was the day of his debut on ABC with the *Lawrence Welk Show*. On October 8, 1956, the *Lawrence Welk Top Tunes and New Talent Show* was launched. Since then, he has returned to the *Lawrence Welk Show* that appears weekly on Public Service Television and has been there for years.

This is mostly what Lawrence Welk has done in his lifetime. He has organized bands, always having his own name in the title. The size of these bands and the formats have changed over the years, but he manages to retain a popularity with middle class America. In general, he does not appeal to upper classes or to the youth of the nation. This is so, even though he has constantly brought attractive young men and women onto his show, giving them a chance to star. He still plays the accordion as well.

I. Does this horoscope fit a band leader? It appears to, although his reported birth time gives him a 16 Pisces 53 Ascendant. His square face isn't Pisces, and Uranus on the Midheaven of that chart would have made him far more of a revolutionary in the mold of a Karl Marx. Yet both have the intercepted first and seventh houses, as have all three of the Aquarius rising examples. Only this time there is a difference. The horoscope for Lawrence Welk has three planets in the first house and only one in the seventh. The emphasis is very strongly on self. It is his band, his name before the public and his image in most television views. Moon in Leo in the seventh house represents the nostalgia element and his emotion-tinged, but more or less mechanical, presentations of protegees. Even his accent somehow fits, and the somewhat on the gaudy side costuming, which is typical of Moon in Leo. Meanwhile, Venus is earning him money, through the appearances of so many pretty girls, although not without inside clashes over the amounts paid. These positions ring true.

II. Just as with Lady Bird Johnson, the difference between the reported physical birth time horoscope and the soul entry horoscope is roughly one sign difference. There are no intercepted houses in the Pisces rising version. Also, Mars in the seventh house would have caused clashes with females to take on a more personal character. Neptune in the fourth house would have caused his childhood to be far more dreamlike and poetic than it was, and Pluto in the third house would probably not have witnessed him dropping out of school. One after the other, the planets do not fit the houses in that chart.

With the Aquarius rising wheel these planet/house discrepancies do not exist. Pluto in the fourth house trine Mars is consistent with the necessity to leave school and work when still a boy. Neptune in the fifth house embellishes his creative works with the All-American flare. Uranus, the ruler of his first house, is appropriate in the tenth house and sufficient to cause national recognition. Saturn in the twelfth house leans toward an older generation in appeal. Sun is contraparallel Venus, and the subject of exploitation for personal benefit has come up. Mercury contraparallel Pluto confirms the necessity to quit school. The questions about planetary placements in houses are nil.

III. It seems appropriate to use Lawrence Welk's first network show for illustrating a confirming set of progressions. His progressed Ascendant was sextile Mercury within 2.8 minutes. Progressed Sun was contraparallel Ascendant within 1.9 minutes. Evidently concern existed as to whether this German-American who spoke with a heavy accent would make it bigtime. However, progressed Ascendant was coming toward a sextile with his Moon, and progressed Saturn was slowly approaching a sextile with his Midheaven. The ratings kept him going, and they grew. Saturn has a way of making things last.

One fallout of this selection of people with Aquarius on their Ascendants is that each had a first/seventh house interception. The universal welfare characteristic of Aquarius is accentuated with these configurations. It was strongest toward the poor with Karl Marx. The work by Lady Bird Johnson in support of women was above average. The opportunities for new talent provided by the Lawrence Welk show are now legend. In his case, the evidence is that he himself comes first and his young performers second. Yet the similarities are present. The seventh house is the place for teams, groups or bands.

CHAPTER 12. PISCES

Physical Attributes

Pisces on a person's Ascendant has a triangular head, but with convex curves rather than straight lines. It is the counterpart of Virgo, which is definitely triangular. In Pisces the angularity is a little more rounded. In fact, the lower part of the face resembles the faceforward appearance of some fish. Of course, two fish joined by a silver wire constitute the symbol. The fish swim in circles, and often the Pisces rising individual will be aware of too many facts to reach conclusions rapidly. Others might believe they move in circles when confronted by immediate decisions, but that is only one interpretation. Normally they are very alert and sensitive to what is going on around them. They simply prefer to take all items into account. In some ways they see more than other people, and they are constantly aware of what is being received by their sensory organs. Their eyes may be large and bulging, but exceptions do exist. Their skin, usually but not always, has a special watery, liquid or translucent appearance. This is difficult to describe, but it is independent of race. Once this type of soft skin is recognized with the other features, it is just as positive an indication of Pisces rising as the ears are for Capricorn. If one does not see this characteristic present, then the skin will most likely be pale. Pisces is also one of the short signs. The range is typically short to medium. Only a planet like Mercury on the Ascendant would change the height to any great extent. Even with tall Sun signs, Pisces rising tends to be below 5 foot 10 inches in men and proportionately less for women. Furthermore, their hands and feet are small and their limbs match accordingly. Especially in youth, they tend to be shy. Yet their features are generally plastic, their expressions mobile and movements graceful.

Pisces rising can be distinguished from Aquarius by the shape of the head. It is almost the antithesis of square. The physical head shapes of these two signs are really unlike in almost every detail. On the other hand, Pisces rising is often a little more difficult to distinguish from Aries among women. This is because the feminine softening of the ovate Aries head can be fairly close to Pisces in appearance on occasion. However, the main distinguishing features are greater height, more pronounced cheekbones and dimples for Aries. With men the differences are not easily confused. The Pisces chin usually starts with a small, rounded point. In Aries men the chin starts with a big, noticeable bone over which skin is laid. Only when Pisces puts on weight will the features start to converge.

Mental Attributes

Pisces is probably the most tolerant of all the signs when it appears on the Ascendant. This is the mutable water sign, and water is a friendly, comfortable, flowing, acceptable media for most people. They usually get along with others. This is an emotional sign and much is understood—the good, bad, indifferent, right and wrong. Often Pisces will be reticent or timid and accept the idea that other people will do what they want to do. They will go along with the rest of the crowd. For them to know is to forgive. Yet, they themselves can be over-sensitive, and feel more strongly than most about an action before taking it, if, at all. They are not necessarily lazy, but tend to be perspicacious and content to comprehend. When they do respond, the output may be inspirational. They are usually good-natured, courteous, modest, trusting, passionate, affectionate and reserved. Many are fond of music, animals and scenery.

Those with Pisces rising who are less well developed, often appear to be blinded by Neptune, a co-ruler of the sign. Their excesses may take after an unbridled Jupiter. These individuals may then overindulge in alcohol or drugs. Such docile consumption does not always act favorably on development or forward progress. They may accept friends that cause gossip or slander. In other ways ambition may be lacking. An unambitious Pisces may drift in life or become a burden to others. They can be like rudderless boats. Unaccountable adorations or passions can interfere with normal living. While appreciating faithfulness, integrity and loyalty, they may tolerate or simply accept the opposite. Yet they are usually psychic, friendly and sympathetic toward others.

The evolved person with Pisces rising will have much more highly developed ideals and aspirations, although personal aggrandizement is generally not one of them. They often have an understanding of drama, and can put their knowledge into effect. Roleplaying is comparatively easy. They can be highly poetic and originate the indescribable something extra that turns simple acts into fascinating art forms. They learn eventually, that all the world is a stage, and then find themselves among the actors. They know that the whole is greater than the parts and are good at making use of this propensity. That is why many of them gravitate toward universities, theatres, hospitals, churches, government services and institutions that require their sometimes mystical knowledge and inspiration. They can be literary, and they can be moody. At their greatest heights Pisces rising realizes the essential unity of all things and sense-impressions are transcended. Then all records, feelings, signals and assimilated information are blended, and a state of consciousness is achieved full of vitality and essential truth. Pisces is the ruler of the twelfth and last house. It represents a culmination of all previous steps in the journey around the astrological wheel—when the decision is reached to utilize everything consciously or unconsciously remembered.

With this background, deciding upon the rising signs of real people can be a culmination of learned information and abilities. One horoscope shows Caroll Burnett with Pisces rising—but then her year of birth is in question. Anna Pavlova, the great dancer of the early twentieth century, is supposed to be another with Pisces on her Ascendant. No horoscope has been sighted for Pia Zadora, but what about her? Among men there are horoscopes that show David Caradine, Edmund Muskie, Johnny Cash, Bella Lugosi and John Foster Dulles with Pisces rising. That is an interesting assortment of people, but quite different from one another in many ways, wouldn't you say? It is better then that we prove who has Pisces rising.

Example Horoscopes

It was stated earlier that race lacks bearing on the head shape and appearance, including the astrological factors affecting the skin. Just to prove this point, the first example is of an Indian from Bombay. He is the symphony conductor, Zubin Mehta, and a member of the Parsi people, descendants of Zoroastrian Persians. They migrated to the area of Bombay in the eighth century because of religious persecutions. The Parsi race is traditionally prosperous, well-educated and cosmopolitan. They adopted the music of the West. Zubin Mehta's family was no exception. His father founded the Bombay String Quartet and Bombay Symphony Orchestra. In fact, Zubin said that he was brainwashed with classical music from the cradle. By the age of seven he was given violin and piano lessons. By the age of sixteen he conducted a full orchestra during rehearsals.

Despite this immersion in music, Zubin thought at first that he wanted to become a doctor and he liked sports. So he enrolled at Saint Xavier's College. That lasted two years until he was faced with dissecting a lizard. At this requirement he rebelled and shortly after that found himself on his way to Vienna and back to music. He was eighteen and enrolled in the *Akademie für Musik und Darstellende Kunst,* the state musical academy of Austria. There he studied conducting and composition under Hans Swarowsky. He was diligent in his studies. Three years later, at the age of eighteen (1957), he received his diploma.

In 1958 there was an international conductor's competition in Liverpool, England for one hundred contestants. Zubin had never entered a competition before, but he was by now endowed with the Vienna style. He walked off with first prize. This included a one-year contract to conduct the Royal Liverpool Philharmonic Orchestra on a substitute basis. During that period he conducted fourteen concerts and received rave reviews. For two years he substituted for other symphony orchestra conductors throughout the world with critical acclaim. He was asked to conduct the Montreal Symphony Orchestra and made many improvements. When it met his standards this orchestra made a foreign tour. It went to Russia for eight concerts, to Paris for two and to Vienna for one. Zubin was a little apprehensive about returning to the city of his studies. However, after the concert there was a twenty-minute ovation with fourteen curtain calls and two encores.

Zubin Mehta accepted an offer from Mrs. Otis Chandler to become the conductor of the Los Angeles Symphony Orchestra. For over a year he was the conductor of two orchestras, the Montreal and Los Angeles. In characteristic fashion he immediately set about bringing the Los Angeles Symphony Orchestra up to world class standards, including a request (which he obtained) for a $300,000 budget to acquire new stringed instruments, one a *Stradivärius* violin. Ultimately, he gave up his position in Montreal and turned down other offers to concentrate his efforts on the one musical group. Winthrop Sargeant of *New Yorker* wrote, "Mehta...has the capacity to control every sound made by an orchestra, and he does this with the simplest of gestures, every one of which has an immediate and perceptible effect. He has a talent for conveying a mood of serenity or of serene grandeur, to both orchestra and audience, that is rare indeed." Today this short, 5 foot 7 inch man is among the younger generation of leading conductors throughout the world. He is very proud of what he has done, and he even upset New York critics by boldly declaring the Los Angeles Orchestra to be better than the one he was asked to conduct in gotham. Musically, he has a willingness to take risks and to experiment. He is also a practical joker, married to an actress and can be seen on Los Angeles freeways driving his Jaguar sports car.

I. Our question is, does the Pisces rising horoscope of Figure 36 and Table XXXIV represent this world renowned symphony orchestra conductor? His photographs look like Pisces rising. An appropriate old fable is now reappearing on radio and television, to wit: "If it walks like a duck and quacks like a duck, then it is a duck." The one published horoscope observed for Zubin Mehta also had Pisces rising, so it must be a duck. Zubin has a Taurus Sun, and that causes him to be especially stable.

II. This is a bucket chart with Jupiter at the apex. Jupiter is also the handle planet of a T-square and the ruler of both the Ascendant and the Midheaven. To top matters off, Jupiter is closely parallel and conjunct the Midheaven. The other planets of the T-square are Saturn and Neptune, highly appropriate for a symphony conductor whose mission is to get the most from his players. While the aspect from the Moon is rather wide, Jupiter is also in a grand trine with this satellite of the Earth (having dominion over feelings) and with Venus. The art form is established for Venus in the pioneering sign Aries. The Moon is in Leo, who likes a show. Jupiter is so strong it had to result in his being a conductor. The planets in the second house show that Zubin Mehta has been well rewarded for his profession. Mercury in the third makes him a good and persistent student. Pluto in the fifth house causes his creativity to excel. Neptune and Venus are parallel—his conducting is not just music, but serene music.

The earlier leaning toward medicine is easily observed in Saturn, the twelfth house ruler, near his Ascendant and with favorable aspects to Mars and Pluto. Mercury sextile a fifth house Pluto would certainly enjoy a practical joke or two. The other Pluto rising horoscope provided nearly the same interpretations, except it was slightly earlier and brought Mars into the third house. A second house Mars, being a ninth house ruler, looks more appropriate when one considers that performing before audiences is a source of income.

APR 29 1936	11:47 PM IST	Naibod Secondary
BOMBAY	INDIA	DEC 29 1965
18 N 57 53	072 E 50 01	
2:37:18 AM TLT	9:45:58 PM GMT	9:45:58 PM GMT

Tropical *Placidus* *True Node*

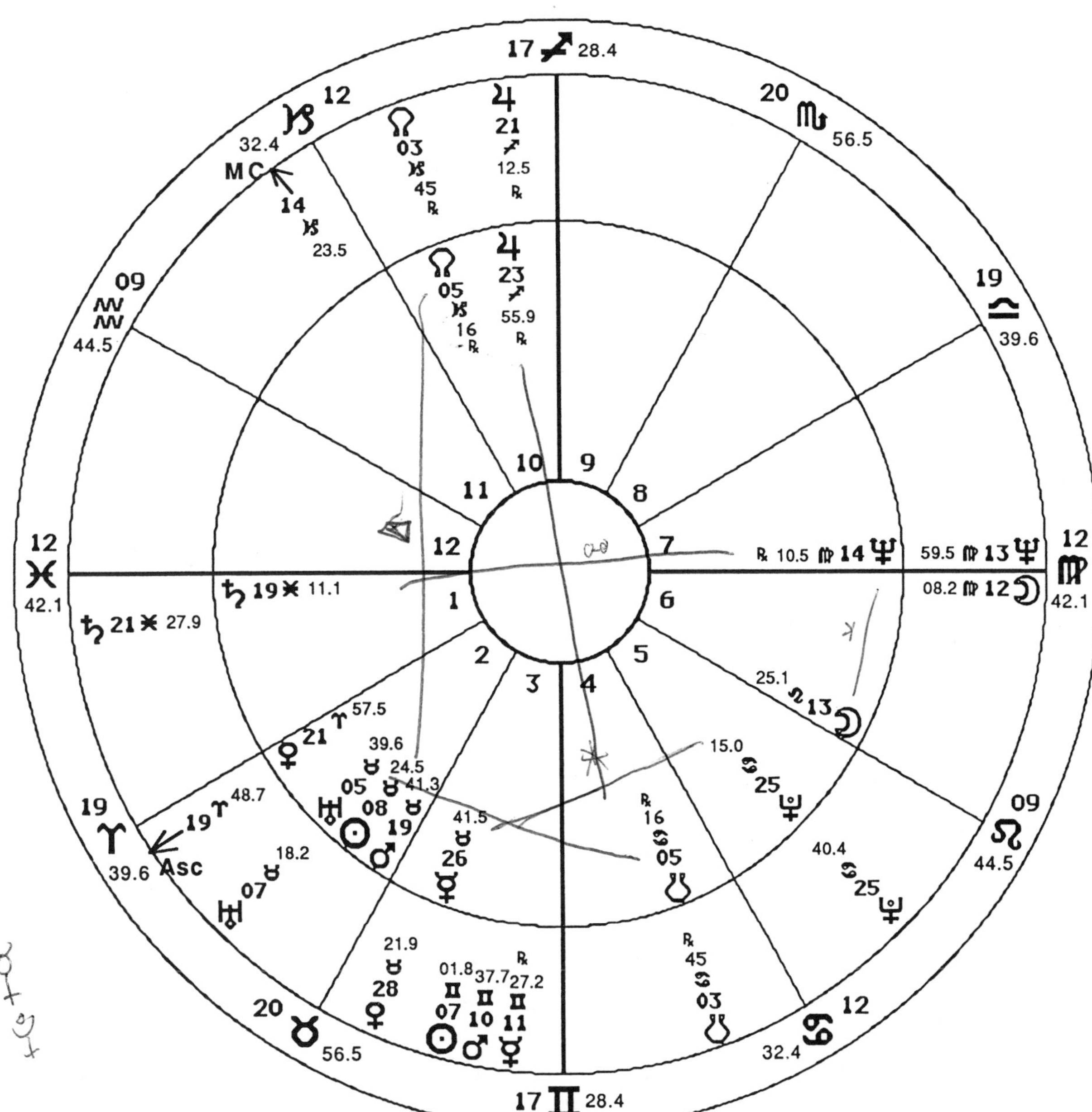

Figure 36. Horoscope of Zubin Mehta, conductor of the Los Angeles Symphony Orchestra. Progressions are to the day he fulfilled a wish and conducted the Metropolitan Opera Orchestra.

III. One of Zubin Mehta's accomplishments was a bit different for a recognized symphony orchestra conductor. He had always wanted an opportunity to conduct the orchestra of an opera. His opportunity came when he was offered the direction of the Metropolitan Opera Orchestra in New York while *Aïda* was performed. This occurred on December 29, 1965. Conducting an orchestra for an opera is challenging and quite different from conducting a symphony. It must include all the musicality of the score plus a sensitivity to each of the singers. Zubin Mehta managed this first time feat with critical acclaim. His progressed Midheaven was parallel that powerful Jupiter within 1.6 minutes. Progressed Sun was parallel Mercury within 4.0 minutes, and progressed Neptune was parallel Venus within 3.0 minutes. Yes indeed those were appropriate aspects, and all were declinations.

Zubin Mheta's head and skin are characteristic of Pisces. His cheeks slope upward in convex curves from a narrow chin. His appearance is fluid. He is short. Even the Vienna foundation of his music is Neptunian in style. Music and the stage are perfect outlets for this sign.

Table XXXIV. Natal and Progressed Declinations of Zubin Mehta

Planet	Natal Decln.	12 29 1965 Met Debut
♄	05 S 58.0	00 S 45.6
Asc	06 S 47.8	07 N 45.1
♆	07 N 10.8	07 N 14.4
♀	07 N 11.4	19 N 06.2
♅	12 N 59.1	13 N 31.5
☽	13 N 46.3	02 N 30.3
☉	14 N 18.7	21 N 29.5
♂	17 N 49.1	23 S 26.9
☿	21 N 33.5	20 N 44.7
♃	22 S 41.9	23 S 13.1
MC	22 S 51.5	22 S 40.3
♇	23 N 15.7	23 N 11.4

It so happens that a Pisces rising female in the next illustration has the same general appearance as Zubin Mehta, especially in the shape of her head and the general appearance of her skin. The main difference is that her skin color is of Italian heritage rather than Parsi. Another small difference is that her eyes are larger. This fits the Pisces rising mold extremely well, and Lizza Minnelli is a very good example of a person with this sign on her Ascendant. She is 5 foot 4 inches tall, which is typical. If she is a bit more forward than the average Pisces rising individual, that has to be caused by her first house Venus and Mercury being in the sign Aries with Aries intercepted there. Venus and Mercury are the planets that match what she does for a living, singing, dancing and acting. Her Sun is also so close that it adds a measure of independence. See Figure 37 and Table XXXV.

Lizza Minnelli is of course the daughter of two celebrities—Vincente Minnelli, the film director, and Judy Garland, the movie star. This gave her a tempestuous life as a child, especially since a divorce followed. She attended schools in California, New York, England, France and Switzerland. Later she said, "The kind of childhood I had can make you or break you. I've had knocks, but I'm not sure it's not better to have them when you're young. At least it teaches you how to handle them when they come later." Her youth was full of pain, forced changes in home life and tears. It was also exciting. At the age of two-and-a-half she had a walk-on role in one of her mother's movies. At the age of seven she danced on stage at the Palace Theatre in New York while her mother sang *Swannee*. She got the leading role in her school play, *The Diary of Anne Frank*. Of course the majority of school plays are successful due to the nature of the audience.

Table XXXV. Natal and Progressed Declinations of Lizza Minnelli

Planet	Natal Decln.	11 08 1964 Palladium
♀	00 S 48.9	08 N 36.4
Asc	01 S 09.1	09 N 38.5
♆	01 S 39.4	01 S 27.1
☉	03 S 24.3	03 N 56.1
☿	05 N 54.6	02 N 20.8
♃	08 S 39.1	07 S 54.1
♄	22 N 15.3	22 N 16.7
♅	22 N 28.5	22 N 32.0
MC	23 S 26.2	22 S 34.8
♇	24 N 02.0	24 N 13.1
☽	24 N 05.5	10 S 54.8
♂	25 N 35.7	24 N 23.8

MAR 12 1946 6:28 AM PST
LOS ANGELES CALIFORNIA
34 N 03 10 118 W 22 35
6:33:03 AM TLT 2:26:33 PM GMT
Tropical *Placidus* *True Node*

Naibod Secondary
NOV 8 1964

2:26:33 PM GMT

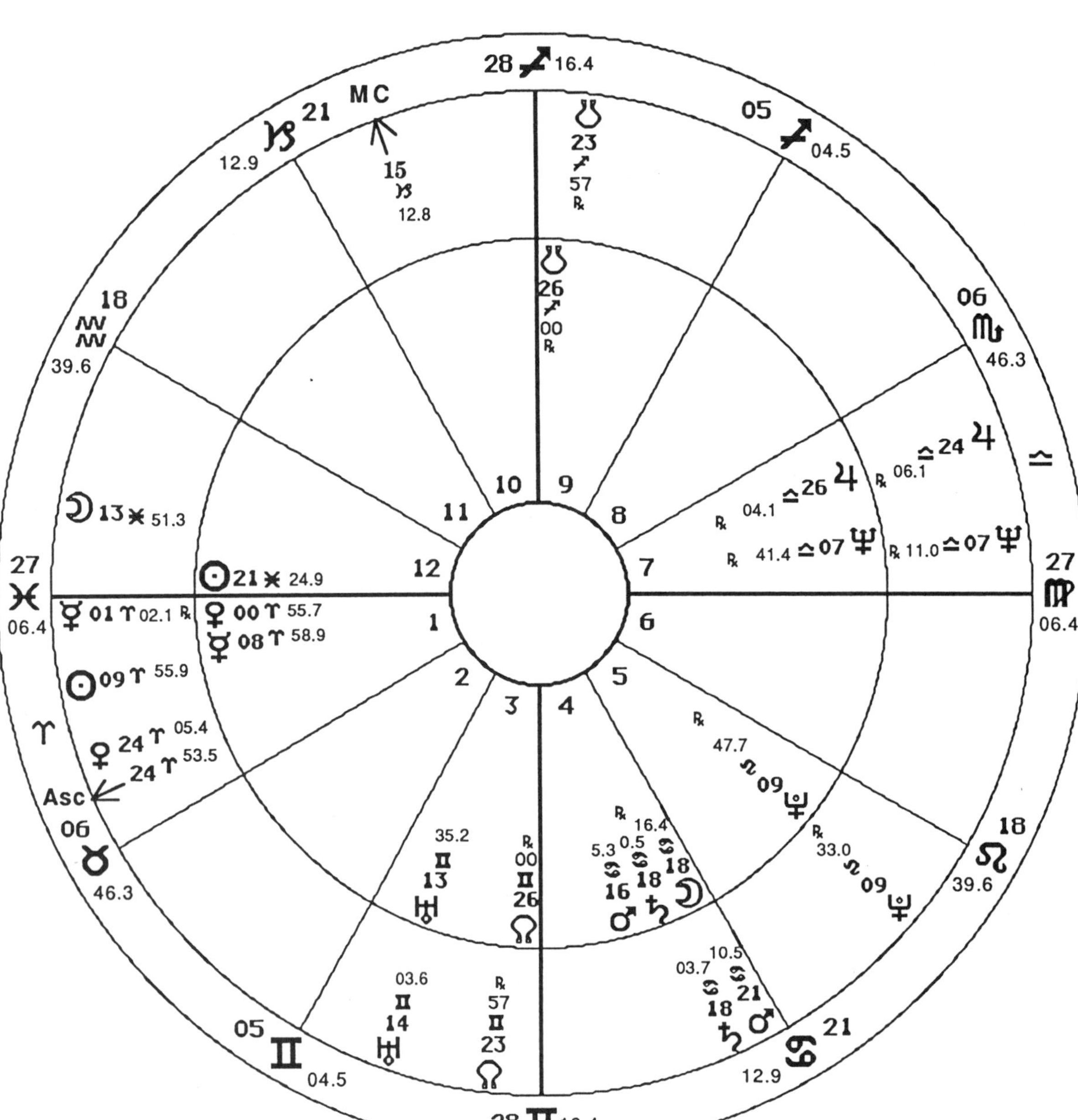

Figure 37. Horoscope of Lizza Minnelli with progressions to the date of the London Palladium Show with her mother Judy Garland.

Frank. Of course the majority of school plays are successful due to the nature of the audience. Her performance, however, was supposed to have been good. After graduation, at the advanced age of sixteen, she found herself alone in New York City with one hundred dollars in her pocket and the consent of both parents, but no savings. That had been her wish. She got by, according to her own analysis, "because of her mother's name and a curiosity factor." She had an auspicious debut on April 2, 1963, in *Best Foot Forward,* which opened at Stage 73 in New York. When that play closed she went on an eight-week tour and soon found other engagements.

She has been called a vibrant performer who can captivate nightclub audiences, sing and romp through musical comedy, or develop a compelling straight dramatic role. Wallace Kerr of the *New York Herald Tribune* wrote, "Lizza Minnelli is certainly appealing, and would be even if she wasn't Judy Garland's daughter....She is easy and confident and accomplished and winning." However, the association does remain between mother and daughter in most people's minds. We should look at her horoscope for more insight.

I. The signatures of a singer, dancer and actress are evident immediately. They are boldly displayed in the first and seventh house interceptions, with four planets present. Those planets are Venus, Mercury, Neptune and Jupiter. Combined, they are about as closely related to singing, dancing and acting as any that could be found. The first three of those planets focus harmoniously upon a fifth house Pluto, which furnishes a large measure of originality. An unusual amount of energy is concentrated in these two houses. The first house planets relate to her consuming need to be her own person. The seventh relates to her being a part of casts and sharing the stage with her mother.

This is a cup type horoscope with Sun at the brim. It is as though she has always found it necessary to concentrate on being herself and creating her own image, as opposed to simply being the child of celebrities. Yet, the cup holds a lot. This twelfth house Sun, which is fairly close to a conjunciton with her Ascendant, forever wants personal recognition for her own accomplishments.

II. A published horoscope exists with the first degree of Taurus on the Ascendant. Taurus—mild, determined, patient Taurus? That cannot be Lizza Minnelli. The Taurus chart shifts every planet clockwise by one house except for the Sun. Gone are the interceptions. The concentration of five planets is shifted, and it now focuses on service. No longer do Venus and Neptune parallel her Ascendant, the planets of song and dance. Instead they would lean toward having art and literature placed in museums for the public to view. The Saturn-Uranus parallel remains, but it would no longer affect her home life and upbringing. Instead, it would affect her education and finances. The Pluto-Moon parallel also would remain. But instead, the locations of those planets would suggest a royal early home life with a broad spectrum of cultural pursuits. The Taurus rising horoscope has little relationship to the Lizza Minnelli we know. The Pisces rising horoscope does.

III. The underlying competition, between mother and daughter, was nowhere more evident than at a show they appeared in together on November 8, 1964, at the London Palladium. Of course they were mother and daughter, and strongly, emotionally attached. However, career-wise, Judy Garland was already loved by an enormous audience. Lizza in many ways desperately aspired to the same kind of attention and affection. This kind of situation calls for opposition and contraparallel aspects. They were present in Lizza Minnelli's progressions for that date. Progressed Venus was opposite progressed Jupiter within 0.7 minutes. Lizza's progressed Midheaven was contraparallel her progressed Uranus within 2.8 minutes, and progressed Venus was contraparallel Jupiter within 2.7 minutes. Only progressed and very slow-moving Pluto was parallel her Moon within 0.6 minutes to provide emotional support. Those aspects told the story. As usual, other progressions for different events were marked by close, appropriate aspects.

So the look of Pisces rising is in the face and skin and short stature. The lower portion of the face comes to a point with outward bending lines, as opposed to the straighter lines of Virgo. The skin is liquid appearing, or it can be pasty or fair. Take for another example, a fellow who is sort of into music, on drums that is. The shyest of the *Beatles,* and the one the girls evidently drool over the most, is Ringo Starr. He was their drummer before they broke up and evidently drool over the most, is Ringo Starr. He was their drummer before they broke up and came, like the rest of them, from the slums of Liverpool. His head could be placed together with Zubin Mehta's and Lizza Minnelli's. You would then see the similarities instantly. Without such an opportunity, photographs are the next best means of studying their likenesses.

Today Ringo has the air of childlike innocence and revenue from the sale of *I love Ringo* buttons. He was born Richard Starkey in Dingle, a suburb of Liverpool. For those who have not been there, Liverpool is the grimy big seaport city of western Britain. It is sprawling, sometimes mean-spirited and full of sharpies. Richard's father, Harry Starkey, was a house painter, and in Liverpool that had its ups and downs. His mother Elsie (Graves) Starkey worked in a fruit store and took jobs as a barmaid to help make ends meet. It seems that Richard was constantly in hospitals as a young boy. Between the ages of six and twelve he suffered from a burst appendix, peritonitis as a result from the burst, a fractured pelvis and pleurisy, to name just a few ailments. Oh yes, it is very foggy and damp in Liverpool. After this sequence of untoward events, Richard got what jobs he could to help bring in a little money. Before he was fourteen he worked as an engineer's apprentice on swimming pool and playground projects. The pay was the equivalent of $15 per week. He later worked as a waiter on a London-to-Wales ship and considered becoming a hair dresser.

When he was still a young boy, Richard fashioned his first drum from an old English tea chest. One Christmas his parents bought him a real set of drums. With those he managed to get on with the *Darktown Skiffles* who played in a Liverpool Club. The pay amounted to a dollar-and-a-half per hour, which was an improvement of sorts over his pay as an engineer's apprentice. As a drummer he didn't have to sing or say very much, but could blend in with the rest of the ensemble in the back. He managed a trip to Hamburg in 1960 with Roy Storme and his *Hurricanes*. Eventually he was given an opportunity to fill in for Pete Best, who was then the *Beatles* drummer. John Lennon told him, "You're in. Shave your beard.....Best keep your sidies."

Brian Epstein, who was the *Beatles* manager, was not too keen on Ringo. "I thought his drumming rather loud and his appearance unimpressive." Yet Epstein was no slouch as a manager. He selected their Edwardian style stovepipe trousers, four-button coats, ankle-high polished boots and moplike, medieval style hairdos. He helped parley the *Beatles* to fame and fortune. The team rose in popularity, and their income soared. It stayed near the top until Yoko Ono came along.

Ringo Starr not only played for the *Beatles*, but he made records that reached the best seller list and he appeared in films such as *A Hard Day's Night* and *Help!*. He made a guest appearance on Ed Sullivan's Show on CBS-TV. On that evening Sullivan's show climbed to its highest rating in history. He was so popular among Americans that once, upon arriving in Miami, he was greeted by a chimpanzee, four bathing beauties, a four-mile long traffic jam and seven thousand adoring teen-age fans, who also shattered twenty-three windows and a plate glass door. Remember, this guy was a reticent back-row drummer who simply played too loud and looked cute. He also talked funny to the American kids, in his Liverpool lingo, and they liked it.

I. Could the Horoscope of Figure 38 and Table XXXVI be the one for this most fortunate fellow? Actually, his published horoscope is fairly close, being only six degrees ahead on the Ascendant. It was cast for five minutes past midnight on July 7, 1940. The one produced by *INCARN* is for the sixth of July, eleven minutes before midnight. Both have intercepted first and seventh houses. He was a team member, and first house Jupiter in Taurus said that he played loud and steady. Similar to Lizza Minnelli's, his horoscope is cup shaped. It holds water and is introspective. Jupiter, the ruler of the first and tenth houses, is the lip planet. There is no doubt that Mercury in Leo conjunct his Moon brought him out of his timid ways, giving him the courage to speak in public when the occasion demanded. This conjunction, with Mars and Pluto just across the border in the fifth house, confirms his occupation as a drummer. Drummers pound, rap and thump, so the Venus influence is less of a necessity. They artfully keep time to the music. Even so, Venus is semisextile the close group of four planets. The signs do confirm.

JUL 06 1940 11:49 PM BST
LIVERPOOL ENGLAND
53 N 24 30 002 W 44 20
10:40:50 PM TLT 10:51:48 PM GMT
Tropical *Placidus* *True Node*

Naibod Secondary
JUN 11 1965
10:51:48 PM GMT

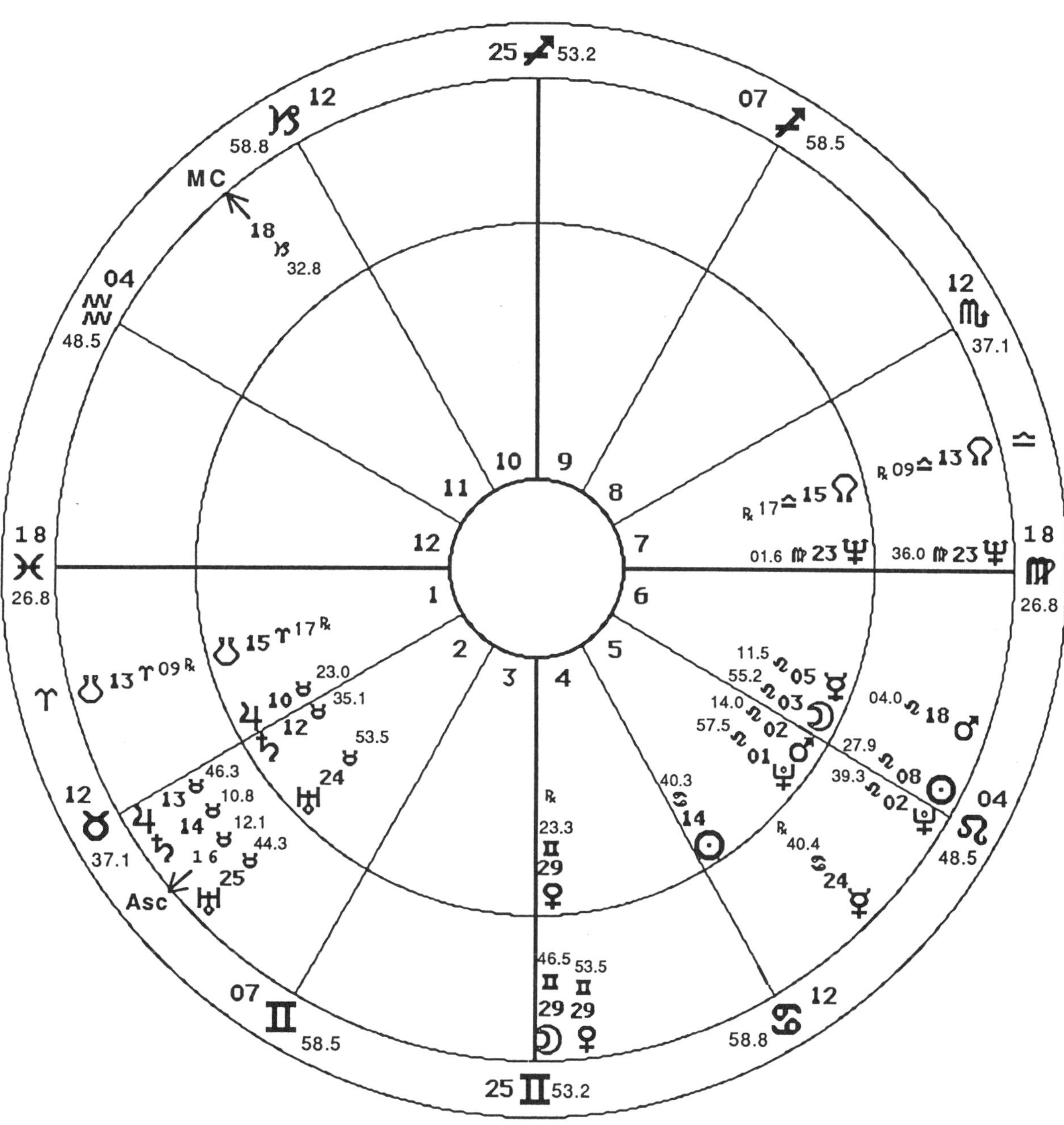

Figure 38. **Horoscope of Ringo Starr, *Beatles* drummer boy. His progressions are for the day he received the Order of the British Empire.**

II. Despite their closeness, several significant differences exist between Ringo Starr's physical birth time horoscope and the one illustrated here. Saturn would be in the first house rather than the second. Sun would be in the fourth house rather than the fifth. Moon would be in the fifth house rather than the sixth, and Neptune would be in the sixth houses rather than the seventh. We need to examine these locations one by one. Saturn is parallel Jupiter. In the second house that represents delayed wealth, coming in very large amounts. With Saturn in the first house the only planet left to indicate wealth is Uranus. It is parallel Venus and shows money from a musical enterprise, but not necessarily in amounts of the same magnitude. Sun in the fifth house adds creative energy to his drumming. In the fourth, Sun would show a cheery home life, rather than one that was a bit more dreary, benefiting mainly from the actions of his mother. Moon in the sixth house adds popularity to Ringo's occupation and, in closest conjunction with Mars, it agrees with his appendicitis and bouts with pleurisy. With Moon in the fifth house his creativity would have been increased, but the boyhood illnesses would more than likely have been confined to the mercurial types. Neptune in the seventh house suggests a surreal relationship with other people. Neptune, in Virgo and the sixth house, would suggest a job of exact details with a dramatic flare, such as writing plays or poetry. You be the judge. These small slips across house borders are profound in establishing correct horoscopes.

Table XXXVI. Natal and Progressed Declinations of Ringo Starr

Planet	Natal Decln.	06 11 1965 Honor
♆	03 N 52.9	03 N 38.7
Asc	04 S 34.3	16 N 41.3
♄	13 N 25.3	13 N 48.8
♃	13 N 50.9	14 N 49.1
☽	14 N 38.0	18 N 31.9
☿	16 N 42.7	17 N 26.2
♅	18 N 43.9	18 N 56.0
♀	18 N 48.7	18 N 00.5
♂	20 N 48.5	16 N 31.1
☉	22 N 38.2	18 N 09.0
MC	23 S 22.9	22 S 09.7
♇	23 N 28.6	23 N 20.3

III. A decision was made to show the set of progressions for an unexpected honor bestowed upon Ringo Starr. This was the day the Queen Mother invited Ringo to a party where he was granted the Order of the British Empire. His comments were, "It was the first time I ever felt British. You know, you never think about royalty. But the Queen Mother, she was a nice lady." The award was apparently some time in coming. The principal indication was progressed Pluto parallel his Midheaven within 2.6 minutes on the day it happened. Progressed Saturn was also parallel Jupiter within 2.1 minutes, progressed Ascendant was parallel Mercury within 1.4 minutes and progressed Moon was approaching a very nice conjunction with Venus. Other progressions for major events confirmed the time of this horoscope. Among them were the date he joined the *Beatles*, the concert at the London Palladium where this group first entered the national limelight and a Command Performance at the Prince of Wales Theater attended by Princess Margaret.

Summary Thoughts

At this point the full circle has been traversed. The style of explanation changed a little between the earlier and later signs with the idea that it might add a little variety to an approach that might otherwise be humdrum. Yet, the signs were given almost equal treatment with three examples for each. The main characteristics of the rising signs were pointed out, and a basis for approaching natal astrology in a structured manner has been established.

Several additional words are in order for selecting correct horoscope times. First, in pursuit of an accurate birth time, ascertaining the correct rising sign puts one in roughly a two-hour band. But already, the interpretations of the horoscope can be better than many of those now in print. So much is riding on the Ascendant sign, including the location of its ruler(s), that without this confirmation the horoscope is already wrong and being misinterpreted. When the first house sign is incorrect, the horoscope is unbelievable to those who really do understand the nature of the signs and unacceptable to thinking readers.

Second, very small changes in time can cause planets to shift into adjoining houses. In the case of Ringo Starr a difference of only sixteen minutes in time caused five planets to move. A good astrologer should be able to recognize which house is correct for each planet, when the matter is brought to their attention and they are thinking about it. This refinement greatly improves upon the two-hour band originally established by the rising sign. Usually this narrows the focus to within a fifteen or twenty minute period. It cannot be emphasized enough. Every placement must fit the person without exceptions of any kind, without doubts and without having to use a vivid imagination to explain away the troublesome positions.

Third, primary day-for-a-year, Naibod progressions do work. Virtually all important events take place in the presence of more than one aspect. If it is known that every major event is going to be accompanied by primary aspects, then the greater the number of events, so confirmed, increases the statistical probability that the horoscope is correct. At this point the vernier scale has been applied. Times must now be correct to within seconds or minutes for this to occur. Be absolute aware that declinations must be used for these validations and they shall not be thrown away. Otherwise, gaps definitely will be encountered.

When a person has applied these three techniques the horoscope should be cast in stone, or in some other permanent form, for longevity and repeated review. Both advanced and beginning astrologers can learn more and more from validated horoscopes. They can also learn to get rid of the excess baggage of false meanings and false techniques caused by earlier timing errors. The interrelationships and nuances of a true horoscope are endless. It portrays an entire life with deep meanings and measurable temporal attributes. When confidence is provided by an accurate horoscope, the realizations are substantially increased.

CHAPTER 13. PLANETS ON THE ASCENDANT

A planet conjunct or parallel the Ascendant provides another means of validating a horoscope and is an excellent verifier of timing. It is like having a vernier scale to make finer adjustments. In fact, the presence of such an aspect can narrow the uncertainty in timing to less than four minutes. Recognizing the effects of each planet is an important adjunct to knowing the characteristics of the signs. Between the two types of aspects, planets in longitude generally move faster than those in declination. Therefore the conjunction in longitude is somewhat better for timing. However, when either is present, an extra dimension has been added to horoscope interpretation. A one degree tolerance for these aspects has been noted and used over time, but this is an empirical, rounded-off figure, and might be further refined. Also, it is possible that the tolerance should be different for longitudes versus declinations. However, comparatively speaking, outstanding improvements can be realized through recognition of these planet-on-Ascendant aspects, both for and against a specific time. When the effects are confirmed, a strong, positive, additional element of assurance is provided that the horoscope is correct. When unconfirmed, a strong negative sense of error should cause rejection. At more than two or three degrees separation, the planet must simply be interpreted as a first or twelfth house location. The nature of the close planetary effects are noted below:

Sun—When Sun conjoins the Ascendant, either by declination or by longitude, the body grows somewhat larger than average for the sign. The ego grows as well. The individual feels compelled to be first in everything. Personal recognition is extremely important to this individual. In society he or she will constantly strive to gain the esteem of others.

Moon—The Moon close to the Ascendant causes considerable motion in life, fostered by a love of change and variety. They invariably have lots of variety. These people get heart, soul and body into their activities. The internal fluids and associated sensitivities are accentuated. Emotions, whose nature depends upon the sign, can run shallow or deep, but will not be mild. Popularity is likely.

Mercury—Mercury is the messenger god. When this planet is on the Ascendant the height increases, the occupation unquestionably involves communications in some form and the hands are active. These natives are constantly on the move and seldom live in one dwelling for long. They will actively write, speak, transmit, point, show, document, or transfer ideas and thoughts.

Venus—Aphrodite confers a special kind of beauty to both men and women when found conjoining the Ascendant. The men are unusually handsome, as in the mold of an Adonis. The women are prettier or artier than average. Whatever sign Venus is in, the greatest attractiveness emerges. Whether it is luminous eyes, silken hair or balanced proportions, one sees a stunning specimen .

Mars—Invariably this planet on the Ascendant causes a proneness to accidents, burns, scalds, punctures, cuts, wounds and abrasions many times in life. The individual likes racing, sports, military affairs, hunting, motorcycles or other masculine pursuits that cause them to be susceptible. Whether male or female, a fighting spirit is present.

Jupiter—If you have seen a Miss or Mister Five-by-Five, then Jupiter is on that person's Ascendant. They eat huge quantities of high calory foods and put on weight between attempts to diet. Jovial by nature and expansive in their ideals, they are pleasant and generous, unless very uncomfortable. The growth in body and mind is outward and noticeable.

Saturn—Without exception, Saturn on an Ascendant causes a shortness of the body compared with others who have the same rising and Sun signs. The personality will be taciturn by nature. They prefer the traditional and are careful, cautious, and constrained, often suffering chronic illnesses. They mature early, have a serious look and favor elders over brash youth.

Uranus—When Uranus is conjunct or parallel the Ascendant, changeable, unorthodox, professional energy is on display. They will be unusual, modern, technical or advanced thinkers. Work will be in computers, radio, television, engineering, physics, chemistry, space or similar areas. Inclined toward inventiveness or revolutionary concepts, they have tastes that are different from the ordinary.

Neptune—Neptune, precisely on the Eastern-most point of a horoscope, invariably causes the person to be dramatic, idealistic, cultured or filled with illusions, whether male or female. Their vision will be far-sighted, dreamlike, or unreal. A special flare will be present in their mannerisms, their hair or their looks. Neptune embellishes, refines and adds frosting on the cake.

Pluto—Find Pluto on the Ascendant and you find an energetic person with extraordinary abilities. They will be extremely resourceful, never say quit, are very adaptable and can come up with solutions when everyone else fails. Pluto was the lord of the underworld, where treasures are stored for future use. These people always have something in reserve.

Of the thirty-six example horoscopes, thirteen, or slightly over one-third, had a planet on the Ascendant by declination or conjunction. These aspects are so strong in their effects upon the person that they are unmistakable, and can be readily distinguished from planets simply being in the first house. No reason is needed to hedge on interpretations because the forces are obvious. The tabulation below should make an interesting review:

TABLE XXXVII. CELEBRITIES WHOSE HOROSCOPES HAVE PLANETS ON THEIR ASCENDANTS.

ASPECT	INDIVIDUAL	COMMENTS
Moon on Ascendant	Shirley Maclain Chris Evert Dame Margot Fontain	All got their bodies into the swing of their occupations
Mercury on Ascendant	David Souter Alexander Solzhenitsyn Isaac Stern Lawrence Welk	Reading, writing, speaking or leading with active hands

Pluto on Ascendant	Norman Schwarzkopf Liv Ullman Neil Simon	Extraordinary resourcefulness and ability to produce
Neptune on Ascendant	Albert Einstein	Idealism and dramatic appearance
Mars on Ascendant	Norman Schwarzkopf	Purple heart (besides being a military officer)

Comments in the above table are virtually self-evident. It is interesting that nine of the aspects to the Ascendant were parallels and four were conjunctions, a ratio of over two to one. The sample size was too small to read much into this summarization although corresponding ratios in other areas might be significant. Contraparallels and oppositions were disallowed. Parallels rarely exceed twenty-five degrees North or South of the equator, except for the Moon, and movements are slower than the same planet's motions in longitude. Slow speed does not increase the probability of a parallel, but the effects may be longer lasting. This is similar to the comparison between the velocities of outer versus inner planets. Another way of looking at probabilities though, is to consider that a parallel within one degree can occur once out of about fifty to fifty-six degrees, the full angular range North and South of the equator. A conjunction in longitude can occur once in three-hundred-sixty degrees. Thus, the probabilities in favor of parallels might be higher than two-to-one, although the effects of velocity on increasing the number of aspects within a period of time needs to be taken into account.

In every case, the planet on the Ascendant caused an intensification and personification of forces corresponding to the nature of the planet, versus the condition that would have existed if that planet had simply been in the first house. For example, Sun in the first house enjoys regal treatment and the trappings of authority. Sun on the Ascendant causes the structure of the body to grow in size along with egocentric traits to match. Moon in the first house can be downright introspective, but on the Ascendant the body is invariably flowing and active. Mercury in the first house produces a liking for literature or other forms of communication, but on the Ascendant this propensity involves the person directly and relocations occur. Venus in the first house is attuned to art, music and attractive clothes. Venus on the Ascendant transforms the body itself into a beautiful person. Whether male or female, Mars in the first house causes a liking for sports, the military, working with metals or masculine pursuits. On the Ascendant Mars causes a personalized combative spirit to exist in defense of honor and truth, plus direct participation in these Martian affairs, and a susceptibility to accidents. Jupiter, further into the first house, does not necessarily produce the craving for rich food and the obesity that Jupiter on the Ascendant does. Rather, the orientation toward expansion and a positive attitude is simply present. Saturn in the first house brings conservatism and a liking for the traditional and time-honored. On the Ascendant, Saturn constraints become physical and mental—in the size of the body and in personality traits. Uranus in the first house causes an affinity for technology, the new and modern. Uranus on the Ascendant concentrates and personifies these affinities—the individual is a technical professional, is revolutionary and shows Uranian behavior. Neptune in the first house loves the refined elements of life and the dramatic. Neptune on the Ascendant acts out this idealism. It is visible in what they do and the way they look. Pluto in the first house may respect efficiency and those who are good scroungers. Pluto on the Ascendant does these things personally and utilizes hidden resources.

The listing above reflects the effects of some of these planets on the Ascendants of the people listed. The traits should be obvious, although perhaps easier to see and comprehend in some than others. If you knew the person well, those traits would be strongly evident.

CHAPTER 14. A MINI-RESEARCH REPORT

Before reviewing the data collected for further insights, it must be stated that there is good news and bad news. First the bad news. Thirty-six horoscopes are a very small statistical sample upon which to base any research project or to arrive at high-confidence conclusions. But the good news, one hundred percent of these thirty-six horoscopes have been validated. While it is hoped that the next thought is untrue, since it comes from inconclusive evidence, the possibility exists that this will be one of the few astrological research projects in modern history to use accurate horoscopes.

Actual time differences between previously published birth times and the times of validated horoscopes

To start with, it might be useful to look at the actual spreads in horoscope times, i.e. between reported birth times and the times of validated horoscopes. Figure 39 shows the sorted data for the thirty-six horoscopes, from most negative to most positive. Two of the horoscopes were computed without benefit of an available birth time. They are listed as having zero errors, although birth certificate times might have been different. The two greatest discrepancies, over four hours,

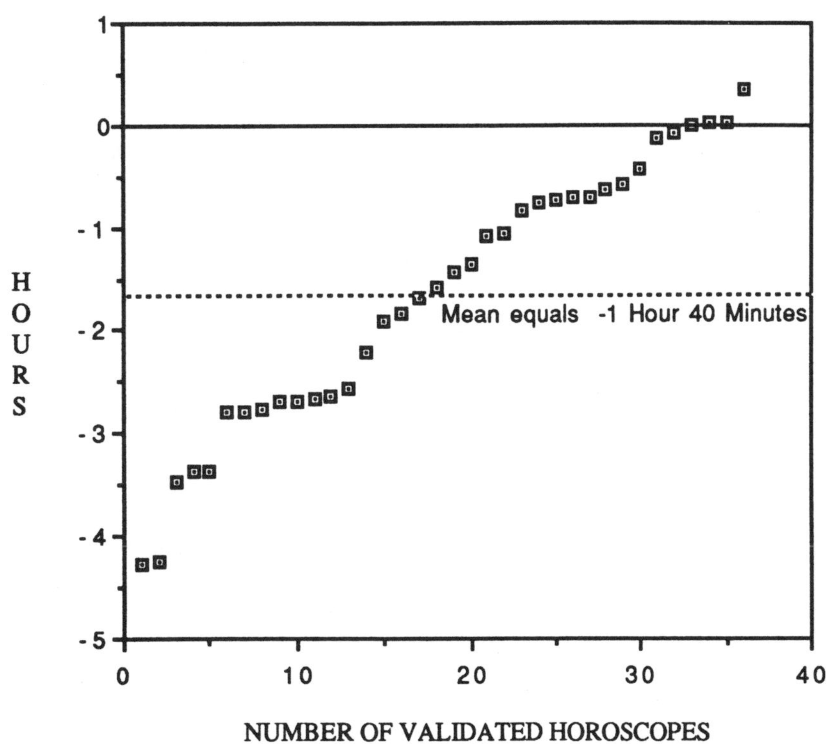

FIGURE 39. TIME DIFFERENCES BETWEEN REPORTED AND VALIDATED TIMES

were for oriental births and the times were given in even hours. It is not certain that a clock or watch was available in those communities, and the two listed birth times have to be considered gross approximations. Four horoscopes with the smallest discrepancies were for European births, and they were originally calculated by European astrologers. The average difference was one-hour forty-minutes negative. That average is somewhat higher than expected from prior experience, but not by very much. If the two, over-four-hour-difference, times are removed, the average reduces to an hour-and-a-half.

More general information can be gleaned from the data. An example is the fact that birth times given to an even hour or half-hour, tended to fall on the left side of the graph, while times given to a minute tended to fall on the right. If one acknowledges that horoscopes for physical birth times do not often match the person, then this illustration should be numerically interesting. To others it may come as a shock, or cause a reaction of incredibility. After having read this far, it is hoped that the former will be the case for the maximum number of readers.

Statistics

Counts were made with respect to several types of data compiled from the computer runs and documentation. Several of these counts and their percentages, with respect to the total number of horoscopes, are revealing (see Table XXXVIII below).

TABLE XXXVIII. STATISTICAL DATA

1. Percentage of Correct Rising Signs from Published Horoscope Birth Data—The unavailable birth times were counted as though correct rising signs had been computed for them beforehand (which is charitable). After making this concession, the proportion correct, to start with, was twelve out of thirty-six, or 33 percent. One third of the published horoscopes, with the correct sign on the Ascendant, is a realistic assessment of how bad the rising sign problem in astrology is today. The estimate of 60 percent for correct badges at an astrological convention is very much in line with these findings. Astrologers really do know their own horoscopes better than other people's, and these figures show that they do, by a plausible margin.

2. Percentage of Correctly Timed Published Horoscopes—Of the thirty-six horoscopes reviewed and verified, exactly one, 2.8 percent, was correctly timed as published. The natal horoscope could actually be delineated thoroughly as it stood without having to make adjustments. Even the declinations were shown, but for two fatal flaws. Neither declination for the all-important Midheaven or Ascendant was included. Allowances must be made, however, for the possibility of someone's oversight, or perhaps for using one of the known astrological computer programs that either doesn't compute these declinations, or doesn't include them in an output display.

3. Distribution of Aspects Meeting the 4-Minute Limit Criteria—Ninety-six aspects were identified for the thirty-six events described. This equates to an average of a little under three aspects per event. Forty-one aspects were in longitude. Fifty-five were in declination. Some events were accompanied by aspects in longitude only or aspects in declination only.

House Systems

The subject of house systems is a fractious one, because there are a lot of contentions, a lot of adherents to one system or the other, and no proofs to date. There are many opinions, but no proofs. An Argument that the Placidus system has too many intercepted houses at the North and South Poles does not represent a proof. Those are just arguments. The truth of the matter is that, people born in those regions would have to be studied versus their intercepted houses and a lack of correlation actually found, for this contention to be valid. Very few babies are born in these polar regions, and for those that have been, no one has performed the necessary studies.

Frankly, the assortment of house systems available in some astrological computer programs is more disturbing than helpful. The question is why any but one should be legitimate. Of course, a user doesn't have to select more than one house system if that is the preference, but the quantity strongly suggests uncertainty and more confusion, or deception, in the astrological world. A typical choice is among Placidus, Koch, Equal, Campanus, Regiomontanus, Topocentric, Porphery and Natural. These choices are mainly available because the programmer found the equations for each one of them. Embedding those equations in the computer program then became a delightful and relatively easy technical task. It also makes a nice marketing frill to show more capabilities. That is true even though questions remain. Are some or most of those systems intellectual frauds? Is there any reason to have a group of valueless and misleading capabilities occupy the computer's memory? Those are the kinds of questions that need to be asked.

Having now leveled the criticism, it must be agreed that there is one good reason to include all of those house systems in the programs that already have them mechanized. That reason is to test and prove validity, or lack of same, if anyone will do so in a reasonable manner. Thinking about this possibility, the validated data was re-examined in connection with intercepted houses. After all, the Midheaven, Ascendant and their opposite poles are identical for most of these house systems. The remaining eight interior houses have different degrees upon their cusps, and some will create interceptions for a given time while others will not. It must be admitted that a bias toward Placidus has resulted from validation procedures and delineations that always appeared to be correct when the interceptions were present. So, those are the ones referred to in the preceding chapters. While there is no intention in this book to compare Placidus with all of these other systems, a short exercise versus the Koch house system was undertaken, without having any idea what the results would be. The results are shown in Table XXXIX, and they are most interesting.

Every interception using Placidus matched an occupation of the celebrity and some had more than one calling in life. Recalculating those same horoscopes with the Koch system of houses provided some agreements near the main axes and disagreements for the more interior houses. Placidus showed twenty-three intercepted houses among the thirty-six people. Koch had two less at twenty-one. Twenty-three out of twenty-three matched the occupations of the test group using Placidus. The Koch count was twelve out of twenty-one. For example, Koch tries to tell us that a fourth/tenth house interception applies to actresses, comedians, writers and a five-star general of the U. S. Army. Placidus said it applied only to the general. Koch shows Dame Margot Fonteyn with a second/eighth house interception. Placidus said that only Alan Greenspan in this group had that specific set of interceptions. Alan Greenspan is the only one whose job is primarily to deal with money. The conclusions might be intuitive, but the statistical approach is to apply a Chi-Square test using the equation

$$X^2 = \sum \frac{(O - E)^2}{E}$$

where O is for the observed data and E is for the expected data. For the Placidus interceptions O equals 23 and E equals 23. Chi square is equal to zero. For the Koch interceptions O equals 12 and E equals 21. Chi square is equal to 3.58. These Chi Square test solutions need to be compared against a significance level. Each interception represents one possibility out of six, for a sig-

TABLE XXXIX. COMPARISON OF HOUSE SYSTEMS VIA INTERCEPTED HOUSES

Intercepted Houses	Evident Effects	Placidus Quantity	Placidus Correct	Koch Quantity	Koch Correct
1-7	The physical body is used in the profession; team work is required or the person represents other people. Also, partnerships.	6	6	4	4
2-8	The occupation relates to finances, investments or economics--either public or private--or to objects saved for the future.	1	1	2	0
3-9	Prior knowledge is used in the occupation, that requires writing, presenting, editing, remembering, studying, traveling, education or practice.	3	3	4	3
4-10	The individual learns self-control in youth to command other people later in life. Occupations are generals, presidents, CEO's, etc.	1	1	7	1
5-11	Creativity is exercised to entertain, give enjoyment, or plan projects. Comedians, entrepreneurs, artists, playwrights and gamblers.	7	7	1	1
6-12	The occupation is in public service to others. One's accomplishments are legacies to mankind. Government employees, doctors, nurses.	5	5	3	3

nificance level of .16667. The tabular value extracted from Chi Square tables is 1.99. Any Chi Square result below this value causes a hypothesis to be accepted. Any result above this value causes a hypothesis to be rejected. Remember that the Placidus value was 0 and the Koch value was 3.58. The hypothesis, that Placidus interceptions are valid to correlate occupations, is proven. The hypothesis, that Koch interceptions are valid to correlate occupations, is rejected.

These statistical results are enough to reaffirm continued use of the Placidus systems of houses, although there is one more major point. Sufficient evidence has been offered to use intercepted Placidus houses as another tool in selecting the correct horoscope. If two horoscopes, with different Ascendants in the same sign, produce two different sets of intercepted houses, then this new confirmation tool can be used as an aid in choosing between them. Simply pick the pair that matches the occupation. Incidentally, precisely this approach was used in choosing Neil Simon's horoscope, and the progressions confirmed this method of horoscope selection.

Closing Remarks and Recommendations

It is hoped that this book has not been written too stridently. While the writing was under way, a conscious effort was made to remove or to refrain from writing a fairly large number of cryptic remarks. The problem is that it is simply exasperating to know why astrology is still called a superstition, when such a large amount of well-meaning published material continues to support that viewpoint. It is difficult to observe countless erroneous horoscopes in print, while knowing that the means are at hand to correct this travesty. The main remedy for this frustration is to try to impart the right knowledge, in a level-headed manner, and hope that it will spread and have beneficial effects.

A return to fundamentals is offered as the best way to start the process of reversal. The first fundamental is that the time of the horoscope must be correct before a realistic delineation can be made. The second fundamental is to apply basic astrology, that has been handed down over the ages, and to stop ignoring doubts, such as a question about the rising sign, and to stop inventing rationale for discrepancies . Know that when one of the basic principles of astrology does not match the individual, something is wrong with the horoscope's timing. The third fundamental is to use all of the basic astrological principles, including declinations and primary progressions, for validation.

Somehow, astrologers must use correct horoscopes in the practice of astrology, else the profusion of wild and unsupported claims will continue. In this vein, a prediction will be made. Only after the majority of astrologers apply a standard for validating natal horoscopes, that is as good or better than the one offered, will the false doctrines, the false systems and the horrendous number of conflicting opinions begin to fall by the wayside. Only then, and when real proofs are given to theories and hypotheses, will astrology find itself more acceptable to clients and to those on the outside looking in. Moreover, unless validated horoscopes are used in research projects, the results cannot be believed.

A conscious effort has been made in this book to provide accurate, observed and carefully checked information for anyone to use in recognizing the rising signs of human beings. This includes the reader. These physical and mental attributes are irrespective of race, creed or color. The validated horoscopes and a small amount of biographical data have been provided for three known celebrities of each rising sign. Quotations and facts about these people were included for correlation purposes and interest. Any person known to most of the world has to be interesting and their images are generally remembered or can be retrieved. While the most readily recognized people tend to be film stars, singers and those who appear frequently in the movies or on television, an attempt was made to provide some balance by including people from other fields. It is believed that at least one or more will be known to the reader. If not, a local library may prove to be helpful.

In summary, the following facts have been identified or reiterated with supporting proofs. It is hoped that the application of this information will be fruitful for all readers.

1. The tropical zodiacal sign on the Ascendant of each human being has a distinct effect upon that person's appearance.
2. The zodiacal sign of the Sun has an underlying effect as well.
3. Comparison of a person's appearance with potential Ascendant signs can be used for preliminary timing and selection of the correct horoscope.
4. Adequate validation of a horoscope is achieved when, the Ascending sign correlates with the appearance, all planets are checked for being in the correct houses

and all tested major events, from cradle to grave, are accompanied by close pertinent aspects. The overall configuration of the horoscope must also fit the individual as known in society.

5. Aspects in both declination and in geocentric longitude are valid.
6. Planets conjunct or parallel the Ascendant have unique additional effects that can be used for verification of a horoscope.
7. Intercepted houses in the Placidus System have important effects upon the nature of a person that coincides with one of their occupations in life.
8. The methods of determining reported birth times vary significantly, and some are given only to the closest observed, or estimated, hour or half hour. While a validated horoscope may possibly coincide with the physical birth time, measured differences normally lie in a band between three or four hours before to fifteen minutes after, the recorded time.

The first edition of *The Rising Sign Problem* was typeset
on a MacIntosh IICX computer, and master copies of the manuscript
were printed on a MacIntosh Laserwriter IINT Printer , both being products of Apple
Computer, Inc. The word processor used was *Write Now*, a product of T/Maker.
Body typeface is Times 12 with Times 18 title headings. *Superpaint*, by Silicon
Beach Software, was used for all graphics. Horoscope calculations were
performed using *INCARN*, a product of Peacock Crest Software,
and all latitudes and longitudes were scaled from the
Times ATLAS of the World

INDEX